PRIVATE SECURITY
AND PUBLIC POLICING

CLARENDON STUDIES IN CRIMINOLOGY
Published under the auspices of the Institute of Criminology,
University of Cambridge, the Mannheim Centre, London School of
Economics, and the Centre for Criminological Research, University
of Oxford

GENERAL EDITORS: DAVID DOWNES and PAUL ROCK
(London School of Economics)

EDITORS: ANTHONY BOTTOMS and TREVOR BENNETT
(University of Cambridge)

ROGER HOOD, RICHARD YOUNG AND LUCIA ZEDNER
(University of Oxford)

Recent titles in this series:

PRIVATE SECURITY AND PUBLIC POLICING

Trevor Jones and Tim Newburn

Policy Studies Institute

CLARENDON PRESS · OXFORD
1998

Oxford University Press, Great Clarendon Street, Oxford OX2 6DP
Oxford New York
Athens Auckland Bangkok Bogota Bombay
Buenos Aires Calcutta Cape Town Dar es Salaam
Delhi Florence Hong Kong Istanbul Karachi
Kuala Lumpur Madras Madrid Melbourne
Mexico City Nairobi Paris Singapore
Taipei Tokyo Toronto Warsaw
and associated companies in
Berlin Ibadan

Oxford is a trade mark of Oxford University Press

Published in the United States
by Oxford University Press Inc., New York

British Library Cataloguing in Publication Data
Data available

Library of Congress Cataloging in Publication Data
Jones, Trevor, 1966– .
Private security and public policing / Trevor Jones and Tim Newburn
p. cm.
Includes bibliographical references and index.
1. Police, Private—Great Britain. 2. Police—Great Britain.
3. Community policing—Great Britain. I. Newburn, Tim. II. Title.
HV8291.G7J66 1998 363.2'0941—dc21 97–45973
ISBN 0–19–826569–7

Typeset by Hope Services (Abingdon) Ltd.
Printed in Great Britain
on acid-free paper by
Biddles Ltd., Guildford and King's Lynn

General Editor's Foreword

The *Clarendon Studies in Criminology* series was inaugurated in 1994 under the auspices of centres of criminology at the Universities of Cambridge and Oxford and the London School of Economics. There was a view that criminology in Britain and elsewhere was flowing with interesting work and that there was scope for a new dedicated series of scholarly books. The intention, declared Roger Hood, its first general editor, was to 'provide a forum for outstanding work in all aspects of criminology, criminal justice, penology, and the wider field of deviant behaviour.' We trust that that intention has been fulfilled. Fourteen titles have already been published, covering policing; prisons and prison administration; gender and crime; the media reporting of crime news, and much else, and others will follow.

Private Security and Public Policing is a valuable addition to the Clarendon series. Jones and Newburn have produced a meticulous, lucid and comprehensive examination of emerging patterns of policing in Britain. They have carefully analysed prevailing assumptions about the dimensions, functions, bonds, boundaries and proportions of private and public policing, and they demonstrate that, although it may be very difficult to make firm assertions about almost any of the issues which can be raised, there is a way forward. They have completed a schematic audit of private and public policing organizations in Britain. And they have tied that analysis into the newly-born criminology of private and public space. Having undertaken a *tour d'horizon* at the national level, Jones and Newburn proceeded to examine how the structure and geography of police organizations may be examined in one area, the London Borough of Wandsworth, knowing as they did so that they were asking some very big questions about the core character and future of policing.

Private Security and Public Policing is thus a book on many planes, empirical, conceptual, historical, geographical, political and sociological, and all of them go to the heart of what policing *is*. It deserves to make an appreciable impact.

David Downes and Paul Rock

Acknowledgements

The research reported in this book was funded by the Economic and Social Research Council (Award no. L210252031). The award was part of the ESRC's Crime and Social Order Programme, and we consider ourselves very fortunate to have been a part of that initiative.

In the course of this research we benefited from the help, support and encouragement of many people. We are very grateful to the Leader, Councillor Edward Lister, and staff of Wandsworth Borough Council for providing access, supporting, and showing considerable interest in the research and the issues it raised. The Commanders and staff of the Battersea and Wandsworth divisions of the Metropolitan Police also gave us much support, as did Alan Parker, the Deputy Chief Constable and Inspector Randolph Otter of the British Transport Police, Alex Thomson of New Covent Garden Market, and Martin Stratten of Wandsworth Parks Police. Les Johnston and Rod Morgan both read and helped significantly improve an initial draft of this book. We gave presentations based on this research to the British Society of Criminology, the Home Office and at Edinburgh, Keele, Oxford, and Reading Universities and at the London School of Economics. We are grateful to all those who participated in these events and helped us clarify our thinking. We are particularly grateful to Robert Reiner who made a crucial intervention at one of these seminars and steered us in a helpful direction. David Smith offered some important insights at the time the original research proposal was being written, and Pam Meadows, the Director of PSI, has supported us throughout the process of getting the job done. We are grateful to Sue Johnson and Peter Hall in PSI's library, and to our colleagues in the Crime, Justice and Youth Studies group for encouragement and friendship.

Contents

List of Figures and Tables

Table of Legislation and Cases

Cases

1

The Sociology of Policing

When people are called upon to explain on what terms and to what ends the police service is furnished they are unable to go beyond the most superficial and misleading commonplace . . . What is true of people generally is true of the police as well. Policemen have not succeeded in formulating a justification of their existence that would recognizably relate to what they actually do.[1]

Over the past two decades, criminologists have become increasingly preoccupied with policing. However, their gaze has been almost exclusively fixed upon that body of state officials which forms what is known as the police service. Indeed, the very term 'police' has come to be associated with members of a 'government constabulary' with a special legal status.[2] This has been reinforced by the assumption that the key feature distinguishing policing from other activities is the capacity to apply the 'legitimate use of force'.[3]

More recently, there has been growing attention paid to the private security industry, and the regulatory activites undertaken by other bodies of officials, outside of the police service. However, the inclusion of the private security sector and these other bodies within 'policing' makes definition problematic. The issue is not resolved by recourse to analytically vague concepts like 'social control',[4] or by attempting to maintain that all order maintenance and rule or law enforcement, including the most informal, is 'policing'.[5] What is required, and what we attempt here, is an empirical investigation of

[1] Bittner, E. (1974) 'Florence Nightingale in pursuit of Willie Sutton: A theory of the police', in H. Jacob, (ed.) *The Potential for Reform of Criminal Justice*, Newbury Park, Cal.: Sage.

[2] Shearing, C. D. and Stenning, P. C. (1987) *Private Policing*, Newbury Park, Cal.: Sage.

[3] Bittner, E. (1980) *The Function of the Police in Modern Society*, Cambridge, Mass: Oelgeschlager, Gunn and Hain.

[4] Bayley, D. (1987) 'Foreword', in Shearing and Stenning (1987).

[5] See, for example, Shapland, J. and Vagg, J. (1987) 'Policing by the public and policing by the police', in Willmott, P. (ed.) *Policing and the Community*, London: PSI.

'policing' in a broad sense, which explores the complexity of order maintenance and rule and law enforcement, with an explicit focus on the relationship between public and private sectors.

Consequently, this book is about *policing* generally. That is, it concerns the activities, functions, and powers of those bodies which it can be agreed are primarily engaged in what we commonly think of as 'policing'. This, of course, includes *the police*; that body of state employees usually referred to as police officers. But importantly, it also includes the activities of a range of other bodies, including non-Home Department police forces, the plethora of regulatory and investigatory agencies and inspectorates attached to national and local government, and, of course, the private security industry.

Karl Popper argued that it is not necessary to provide specific water-tight definitions of terms at the outset of a debate.[6] On this view, it is sufficient that the meaning of key terms is well enough understood for the purposes of discussion, with a clearer appreciation of concepts being the intended outcome rather than precondition of academic dicussion. It is important, however, for us to consider explicitly what is meant by the term 'policing' at the outset, because so much of the writing about policing takes its meaning as given, even though this has, at times, proved to be rather misleading. An important objective for this opening chapter is to develop an explicit working definition of what, for the purposes of the current study, we take to be 'policing'.

In common usage, most people understand the term 'policing' to mean the law enforcement, investigation and peacekeeping activities undertaken by police officers. Indeed, the Concise Oxford Dictionary defines the noun 'police' as the 'civil force of a State, responsible for maintaining public order'. However, it also defines the verb 'to police', which can take several meanings including 'to keep in order; control'. In common usage, the word 'policing' most often refers to broader 'social control' activities, even those of a quite informal nature. 'Policing' activities in this sense are undertaken by parents, teachers, employers, and a whole range of people, as well as by members of police forces. In our view using 'policing' in this way to describe a diffuse range of social control activities has caused confusion in academic discussion. This underlines the need to be clear about what constitutes policing.

[6] Popper, K. R. (1968) *The Scientific Discovery,* New York: Harper and Row.

Several authors have noted an older and much broader meaning of the term 'policing'. Indeed, Egon Bittner, whose work was later criticised for its supposedly narrow definition of policing, noted how the word 'police' had at one time been used to mean the entire edifice of formal, proscriptive regulation, and covered many administrative functions as well as law enforcement ones.[7] Johnston notes that the word is derived from the Greek *polis*, and how, prior to the eighteenth century, it referred to the broad social function of governance of a city or society.[8] More recently, Garland has referred to the work of Patrick Colquhoun, whose 1795 work, the *Treatise on the Police of the Metropolis* outlined his support for what he called a 'system of police'.[9] Although Colquhoun was later to be credited with being an early supporter of a professional police force, as Garland points out, by 'system of police' he actually meant 'a well-ordered system of regulation, inspection and restraint covering the entire social body and involving numerous governing agencies (both "public" and "private") rather than a single specialist "police force".[10] Thus, it is only relatively recently that the word 'police' has come to be associated more or less exclusively with a body of personnel having special legal powers, and entrusted by the State to keep order and enforce the law. However, in some ways the wheel has turned full circle, with the influential writings of Clifford Shearing now returning to this older conception of 'policing' which identifies it with the broader activity of 'governance', which he defines simply as 'the activity or business of governing'.[11] Such a definition seems to us to be overly broad and, as will become clear, we use a considerably narrower definition of policing as the basis for discussion in this book.

A significant part of the sociology of policing has focused upon a relatively broad notion of policing, and has tried to identify and examine the essential features of the specialist body known as 'the police'. A key aim has been to outline either explicitly, or by

[7] Bittner, (1974).

[8] Johnston, L. (1992) *The Rebirth of Private Policing*, London: Routledge.

[9] Colquhoun, P. (1796) *Treatise on the Police in the Metropolis explaining the various Crimes and Misdemeanours which are at present felt as a pressure upon the Community, and suggesting Remedies for their Prevention, by a Magistrate.* Second Edition (originally published, 1795) London: H. Fry for C. Dilly.

[10] Garland, D. (1996) 'The Limits of the Sovereign State', *The British Journal of Criminology* 36(4), Autumn, pp. 445–71.

[11] Shearing, C. (1994) *Reinventing Policing: Policing as Governance*, Paper presented at a conference on 'Privatisation: Retreat or Proliferation of State Control', Bielefeld, Germany, March 24–6.

implication, what it is that distinguishes the functions or the capacities of specialist police forces from other bodies. As will become clear, the bulk of this work has had little to say about 'private' (and other) policing bodies. Nevertheless, it forms an important background to much of what we want to say in this book. This chapter therefore reviews that work which considers what 'policing' is, and examines the research which has looked at how policing agencies operate in practice. First, though, we briefly outline the historical development of the modern professional police service, which has been the focus of the majority of research on 'policing'.

The development of the modern police service

The 'modern' period in British policing began in 1829 with the creation of the 'New Police' as a result of the Metropolitan Police Act 1829. Prior to that policing had been organised in a variety of ways, some of which were 'private' in the way we would generally use the phrase now, and some of which were quintessentially public, such as the institution of frankpledge.[12] As Critchley put it, arising from Saxon times frankpledge 'relied on the principle that all members of a community accepted an obligation for the good behaviour of each other'.[13] The State provided co-ordination and oversight of this structure of private and community policing arrangements, with individuals and collectivities being penalised on those occasions when 'order' was not maintained. As Shearing has argued, 'within this system rule took place "at a distance" with the Crown doing the "steering" and the "rowing" left to communities'.[14]

In eighteenth century England police functions were based within the main units of local government—the parish and the county—and day-to-day policing was the responsibility of constables and of borough and county magistrates. By this stage the office of constable, to which at one time some honour had been attached, was largely devalued, compulsory, and poorly paid when paid at all. The appointment

[12] The terms 'public' and 'private' are far from unproblematic when used to distinguish between policing bodies. In Chapter Two we look in greater detail at how these terms have been, and can be, understood.

[13] Critchley, T.A. (1978) *A History of Police in England and Wales*, London: Constable, p. 34.

[14] Shearing, C. (1996) 'Public and private policing', in Saulsbury, W., Mott, J. and Newburn, T. (eds.) *Themes in Contemporary Policing*, London: Police Foundation/Policy Studies Institute, p. 84.

of 'high constables' varied from one year to life; 'petty constables' were usually appointed for one year only. They were, however, very much community and not state employees and did not, for example, wear uniforms. In contrast to this, one of the key developments in the eighteenth century, of course, was the formation by Henry Fielding of a group of uniformed 'thief-takers' to respond to concerns about rising crime in the capital, though as Rawlings points out, 'the idea of permament, paid, law enforcement officers was not new'.[15] By the 1750s a form of preventive patrol had been established on the main roads leading into London and, by the end of the century, it comprised almost seventy constables. Emsley described the patrols as lasting: '. . . from evening until midnight, or later in case of emergency. The men were armed; each party's captain carried a carbine, a brace of pistols and a cutlass, each patrolman carried a cutlass. The captains received five shillings a night, their men half that.'[16]

Major public disturbances were, however, still dealt with by the military, although increasingly there were concerns raised about using troops for civil 'policing' duties. As we know from a wide variety of sources[17] the whole character of civil society changed in the second half of the eighteenth century and the first few decades of the nineteenth as a result of continuing industrialisation and urbanisation. These increased pressure on the localised nature of policing. Although the policing of the provinces remained haphazard for some time, in London things were further formalised from 1792 with the creation of seven new police offices along the lines of that already established at Bow Street. Continuing concern about disorder, as a result of the Gordon riots and the spectacle of the French Revolution, and about violent crime further increased the pressure on the extant system of policing.[18]

Developments continued to centre on London and were progressively focused around the reformist efforts of the Home Secretary Sir Robert Peel. In the background both the 'bloody code' and the penitentiary system were coming under attack, crime was rising quickly, the gaols were filling up with relatively petty offenders, the prison hulks were the site of widespread disorder and great danger, and

[15] Rawlings, P. (1995) 'The idea of policing: a history', *Policing and Society*, 5, pp. 129–49, p. 138.
[16] Emsley, C. (1983) *Policing and its Context 1750–1870*, London: Macmillan, p. 27.
[17] See, for example, Hobsbawm, E. (1962) *The Age of Revolution 1798–1848*, London: Weidenfeld and Nicholson.
[18] Critchley and James (1971).

there was considerable concern about the perceived rise of disorder among the agricultural classes and the metropolitan poor. At about this time proposals for a coordinated police service for London began to emerge, the term 'police' being quite commonly used by this point. However, it was not until 1829 that Peel succeeded in getting legislation through parliament to establish the Metropolitan Police. Although orthodox histories of the police have presented this development as a logical progression from earlier arrangements, Emsley argued that the new police constables were 'initially at least, probably less efficient than several of the old night watches'.[19]

There has been a long and protracted academic debate between 'orthodox' and 'radical' theorists about the reasons behind the introduction of the Metropolitan Police in the 1820s. Both approaches, however, accord a central role to the control of large perceived increases in crime, and the maintenance of social order. Though the Metropolitan Police was the first, and remains the largest and best known of constabularies, forces were set up in the provinces within a matter of years of the establishment of the new police in London. Whilst being a major influence on the development of forces outside London, the Metropolitan model was experimented with in other areas and was by no means uncritically adopted. Although the central tasks of these forces were similar to those outlined by Rowan and Mayne, the first Commissioners of Police, a wide variety of other duties were soon acquired by local police forces. Many of these— inspectors of nuisances, of weights and measures, inspectors under the Diseases of Animals Acts; the inspection of dairies and shops, contagious diseases, explosives, bridges, even in the case of some borough forces running both fire and ambulance services,[20] together with informal services such as 'knocking up' people for work—were what would most accurately be described as 'service' functions. This expansion of police responsibilities was not enough for some. As Steedman has noted, at one stage there were those (including some county chief constables) who argued that the police should inspect the homes of the poor for cleanliness and space.[21] It was argued that these service-type functions formed an important element in the

[19] Emsley, C. (1991) *The English Police: A political and social history*, Hemel Hempstead: Harvester Wheatsheaf, p. 23.

[20] Critchley, T. A. (1978).

[21] Steedman, C. (1984) *Policing the Victorian Community: The formation of English provincial police forces 1856–80*, London: Routledge and Kegan Paul.

process of legitimisation of the police during the course of the nineteenth century.[22] Nevertheless, in general it was the law enforcement and order maintenance functions that continued to be considered the core activities of police officers. Reiner has argued that one element of police policy which contributed towards their legitimation was the appearance that the police were 'effective'. The criteria by which this effectiveness was judged are illuminating:

By the 1870s then, the police had come to be seen as offering an effective law enforcement service to the middle and upper classes, who complained when its quality seemed to decline. The working class too made use of it, but the less respectable sections of this class were predominantly at the receiving end of law and order campaigns.[23]

From the mid-nineteenth century, then, a professional state police force not only existed but was accorded a degree of legitimacy that would have been unimaginable a century earlier. This was the culmination of a process that began well over a century earlier and in which the work of the Fieldings in the mid-eighteenth century was key. As Rawlings argues: 'In contrast to the eighteenth century paradigm in which individuals and communities were centrally involved in policing, the implication of the Fieldings' work was to restrict, or even to exclude, the people from such involvement by redefining policing as the work of a state bureaucracy.' Indeed, he rightly goes on to argue that the effects of this are visible in present day police work and, further, in the 'broader move away from popular involvement in the criminal justice system to a situation in which control over investigation, trial and punishment is, supposedly, in the hands of professionals and in which intervention is tightly controlled by laws of evidence and procedure'.[24]

More recent developments

Certainly, by the mid-twentieth century the process of expansion of police responsibilities had ceased, and the view of the police as a crime-fighting *force* came back to the fore, partly encouraged by the police themselves.[25] Indeed, when attempts were made to capture the breadth and complexity of police work in official documents, and in

---

[22] Reiner, R. (1992*b*) *The Politics of the Police*, Hemel Hempstead: Harvester.
[23] Reiner (1992*b*) p. 72.   [24] Rawlings (1995) p. 143.
[25] Also by practical changes in the organisation of policing such as the introduction of Unit Beat Policing; see Weatheritt, M. (1986) *Innovations in Policing*, London: Croom Helm.

legislation, *enforcement* rather than *service* was emphasised. Although the purpose of the police is not fulsomely described in English law, Scottish police law is slightly more explicit. The Police (Scotland) Act 1956 describes the duties of the constable as: 'to guard, patrol and watch so as—(i) to prevent the commission of offences against the law (ii) to preserve order, and (iii) to protect life and property'; though it does go on to specify other duties such as executing warrants, giving evidence in court, making reports available to prosecuting authorities and so on. Similarly, in its summary of the main functions of the police, the 1962 Royal Commission on the Police relegated the 'helping' function to eighth and last place in a long list of responsibilities and, in so doing, reflected not only public perceptions of policing functions and priorities, but also the general view of policing put forward by senior officers and the preferred image of policing by the rank and file.[26] Although the service element of the role never entirely disappeared from popular view, recent years have seen increasing emphasis placed by chief constables on those elements of the job that would not generally come under the rubric of law-enforcement or order maintenance.

In the aftermath of the riots in the early 1980s and the Scarman Report which followed, significant changes occurred in the presentation to the public of the nature and limitations of policing. This began with the 'community policing' experiment instituted by John Alderson, the chief constable of Devon and Cornwall, and was followed by a series of programmes in the Metropolitan Police District. The Commissioner at the time, Sir Kenneth Newman, stressed that crime could not be controlled by the police alone, and that significant levels of public co-operation were needed if inroads were to be made. The reorientation of the public face of policing gathered pace under

---

[26] The Operational Policing Review published in 1990, despite emerging from the desire of the police to re-orient itself, and emphasising the 'service' rather than the 'force' element in the role, contained results from a survey of approximately 2,000 police officers which illustrated some of the difficulties that were likely to be faced in promoting such change. It found that officers favoured 'strong, traditional policing', with an emphasis on responding immediately to emergencies, detecting and arresting offenders and investigating crime, and enforcing stricter laws and fines. Community liaison and involvement and a 'more friendly, caring approach' were relegated to a much lower place in the ranking order. The key studies of police rank and file culture are perhaps: Holdaway, S. (1983) *Inside the British Police*, Oxford: Basil Blackwell; Reiner, R. (1978) *The Bluecoated Worker,* Cambridge: Cambridge University Press; Smith, D. J. (1983) *Police and People in London III: A survey of police officers*, London: Policy Studies Institute.

Newman's successor, Sir Peter Imbert, and his 'Plus Programme' in London. The subsequent publication by the Association of Chief Police Officers (ACPO)[27] of a corporate mission statement further underscored a view of policing that increasingly emphasised public service and responsiveness to the 'community'.[28] The Statement of Common Purposes and Values reads:

The purpose of the police service is to uphold the law fairly and firmly; to prevent crime; to pursue and bring to justice those who break the law; to keep the Queen's peace; to protect, help and reassure the community; and to be seen to do this with integrity, common sense and sound judgement.

The working party which produced the Statement of Common Purposes and Values was reconstituted as the 'Quality of Service Sub-Committee of ACPO'. The sub-committee has identified five 'key service areas'[29] which have become the framework for the work of the Home Office, the Association of Chief Police Officers (ACPO), the Audit Commission and Her Majesty's Inspectorate of Constabulary (HMIC) on key indicators of police performance. The five areas are the handling of calls from the public; crime management (including crime reduction, victim support, and crime investigation); traffic management; public reassurance and order maintenance; and community policing. The espousal of such a service-based, consumer-oriented style of policing is now commonplace amongst chief constables.[30] To the extent that the police could realistically ever have been described as primarily a 'law-enforcement' or crime-control agency, the changing 'public face' of policing reflects a significant movement away from such a traditional role. Whether the new 'image' is a more realistic presentation of what the police *actually do* remains open to question, though in limited areas such as crime prevention there is at least increasing police acceptance that 'policing' is not just a matter for the police.

---

[27] Though it emerged from a working party that also included the Police Federation and the Superintendents' Association.

[28] Paul Condon's London Charter announced on 29 Sept. 1993 continued this process.

[29] Weatheritt, M. (1993) 'Measuring police performance: Accounting or accountability?', in Reiner, R. and Spencer, S. (eds.) *Accountable Policing: Effectiveness, Empowerment and Equity*, London: Institute for Public Policy Research.

[30] Reiner, R. (1991) *Chief Constables*, Oxford: Oxford University Press.

The sociology of *the police*

Functional approaches

In what was arguably the first major study of the police in Britain, Michael Banton[31] focused attention on the role of the police officer and his conclusion in many respects set the parameters for future debates. He observed that:

> The policeman on patrol is primarily a 'peace officer' rather than a 'law officer'. Relatively little of his time is spent enforcing the law in the sense of arresting offenders; far more is spent 'keeping the peace' by supervising the beat and responding to requests for assistance.[32]

This observation has permeated much subsequent analysis of police 'work', as did the main research method of detailed participant observation of the front-line workers. This, and many other studies of policing assumed that the term 'police' is clearly understood and unproblematic. Maureen Cain, writing in the 1970s, was critical of the tendency to avoid an explicit definition of the police, and provided a clear functional definition. She stated that the 'police . . . must be defined in terms of their key practice. They are appointed with the task of maintaining the order which those who sustain them define as proper'.[33] However, as Reiner has pointed out, this definition can be criticised on the grounds that it overlooks the variety of tasks which the police are, in practice, called upon to carry out.[34]

Nevertheless, many academic studies of the police function continued in the tradition of analysing what policing *is* in terms of what constabularies *do*. By the mid-1980s the emerging consensus was, despite public views, that the bulk of police time was not actually spent engaged on tasks that were 'crime-related', but how the work that was actually being done should be classified was unclear. For some, the conclusion to be drawn was that police officers 'frequently have to act as untrained and temporary social workers', and that the profession was in fact a 'secret social service'.[35] Several studies,

[31] Banton, M. (1964) *The Policeman in the Community*, London: Tavistock.
[32] Quoted in Reiner, R. (1992*b*) *The Politics of the Police*, op. cit.
[33] Cain, M. (1979) 'Trends in the sociology of police work', *International Journal of the Sociology of Law*, 7, 2, p. 158.
[34] Reiner (1992*c*); 'Police Research in the United Kingdom', in M. Tony and N. Morris (eds.) *Modern Policing: Crime and Justice: A Review of Research*, Chicago: University of Chicago Press.
[35] Punch, M. (1979) 'The secret social service', in Holdaway, S. (ed.) *The British Police*, London: Edward Arnold.

however, showed that this 'service' work was widely regarded in mainstream police occupational culture as 'bullshit'[36] and very much the poor relation of 'real' police work—generally viewed as 'law-enforcement' or 'crime-fighting'.[37] Ericson has argued that the primary activity of the public police is increasingly to act as 'knowledge brokers', with a very high proportion of police time being spent in 'knowledge production'.[38] His analysis highlights how organisations outside the police access police expertise and information sources as part of their own security systems. It is in this provision of information that the public police make their 'unique contribution to the security quilt'. This is an extremely important contribution in that it focuses attention on relationships between state constabularies and other organisations within the security network, a theme which will be developed further in later chapters.

Recent work has signalled something of a retreat from the above-mentioned consensus that the bulk of police time is devoted to dealing with tasks other than crime. For example, the definition of what counts as 'service' functions is ambiguous and, perhaps more importantly, the application of the labels 'crime', 'service', 'public order' takes place *post hoc*. The police, of course, are not in the position of knowing exactly what calls are about in advance. Calls from the public are frequently far from clear.[39] For much of the time, therefore, the police are working and responding as an emergency (or something on a level just below emergency) service. Whether or not a call is to a 'crime' depends not only whether an offence has taken place, whether an offender is present, and so on, but also on whether the attending officer(s) decides—in negotiation with others—that they are going to record the incident as a crime. Some research has also linked the incidence of crime-related activity in policework to matters of police organisation. For example, Reiner notes that recent changes in the organisation of police forces have increased the number of specialists with a law-enforcement function, and devolved the investigation of routine crime matters to uniformed patrol officers.[40]

---

[36] Reiss, A. J. (1971) *The Police and the Public,* New Haven: Yale University Press.
[37] See Holdaway, S. (1983); Manning, P. (1977) *Police Work,* Cambridge, Mass: MIT Press; Smith, D.J. (1983).
[38] Ericson, R. (1994) 'The division of expert knowledge in policing and security', *British Journal of Sociology,* 45, 2, pp. 149–75.
[39] Shapland, J. and Vagg, J. (1988) *Policing by the Public,* London: Routledge; Waddington, P. A. J. (1993) *Calling the Police,* Aldershot: Avebury.
[40] Reiner (1992c).

This may have had the effect of making policework more crime-oriented.

The work of Shapland and Vagg[41] has also suggested that previous work on the police has, in fact, exaggerated the extent to which police work is dominated by 'non-crime' activities. They divided messages received by the police into five categories: 'potential crime' (including 'actual' crime, but also incidents in which there appears to be the potential of a future crime being committed), 'social disorder' (missing persons, environmental nuisance, abandoned cars), 'roads', 'personal services' (messages to be passed on, keeping an eye on property and so on), and 'police-based' activities (seeking information, dealing with complaints). Under this classification, 'personal services' accounted for under ten per cent of calls, whereas 'potential crime' accounted for over half and 'social disorder' for a fifth—a rather different picture from that painted by other work discussed above.

In addition, the authors of local crime surveys have suggested that national figures tend to underestimate the proportion of police/public contacts that are 'crime-related'.[42] For example, the first Islington Crime Survey (ICS) found 51 per cent of contacts concerned crime.[43] Such a discrepancy between this and the findings from national crime surveys is partly accounted for by the areas covered by the respective surveys—the British Crime Survey (BCS) itself records a higher proportion of crime-related contacts in inner-city areas. Nevertheless, Skogan[44] concludes that the evidence from the BCS is that 'most public-initiated encounters reflected the integration of the police into the routines of everyday life'. They were called upon to preserve tranquillity, ease the flow of traffic, serve as a clearing house for reports of a variety of community problems, assist in civil emergencies, and help people find their way. In this way the police represent the 'visible face of the law' and 'the most accessible "interface" for citizens' interactions with the law'.[45]

---

[41] Shapland and Vagg (1988).

[42] Kinsey, R., Lea, J. and Young, J. (1986) *Losing the Fight Against Crime,* Oxford: Blackwell.

[43] Jones, T. *et al.* (1986).   [44] Skogan (1990).

[45] Fielding, N. (1993) 'Policing and the role of the police', in, Dingwall, R. and Shapland, J. (eds.) *Reforming British Policing: Missions and Structures*, Sheffield: University of Sheffield.

Legal capacities

The work of Egon Bittner provides a definition of the police, not in terms of function, but rather in terms of the special legal capacities that police officers bring to their tasks. For Bittner it is the police's position as the sole agency with access to the state's monopoly of the legitimate use of force which makes them distinctive and accounts for the breadth of their role. As he put it:

The police are empowered and required to impose or, as the case may be, coerce a provisional solution upon emergent problems without having to brook or defer to opposition of any kind, and that further, their competence to intervene extends to every kind of emergency, without any exceptions whatever. This and this alone is what the existence of the police uniquely provides, and it is on this basis that they may be required to do the work of thief-catchers and of nurses, depending on the occasion.[46]

In our view, Bittner was not attempting to provide a universal definition of 'policing', but rather he had the more modest objective of defining what is distinctive about the contribution of public constabularies to policing. Bittner's starting point, quoted at the top of this chapter, was that both public descriptions of, and police justifications for the activities of the police, are extremely unrealistic. He went on to argue that the 'potential' duties of police officers are so broad that 'it compels the stronger inference that no human problem exists, or is imaginable, about which it could be said with finality that this certainly could not become the proper business of the police'.[47] It is the fact that the police are available to deal with all manner of emergencies that sets them apart from other bodies concerned with law enforcement.

For Bittner, however, this was only part of the story, for it is the capacity that the police bring with them to deal with such eventualities which makes them so distinctive. In his words: 'The policeman, and the policeman alone is equipped, entitled and required to deal with every exigency in which force may have to be used, to meet it'.[48] Nevertheless, Bittner noted the persistence of the view that the police are a law enforcement agency whose mandate derives from penal codes. This is underpinned by a number of factors. The first is that, despite evidence to the contrary, it is firmly fixed in the public mind that the police are crucial in determining crime levels at any

---

[46] Bittner, (1971), p. 17.   [47] Bittner, E. (1974).   [48] Ibid.

particular time. This view is given force by police training which is predicated on the belief that the police are 'primarily dedicated to law enforcement'.[49]

The usefulness of Bittner's conceptualisation of policing lies, it is argued,[50] not only in its ability to encompass the range of activities that are or may be undertaken by police officers, but also because it captures what is special about the potential that the police officer brings to such activities. Its main value is perhaps that it is not a 'functional' definition: it does not attempt to define policing solely in terms of what the police currently *do*. There are critics of Bittner's position, however, and Johnston argues that in using the possession of the legitimate use of force as the defining characteristic of policing, Bittner defines out all activities carried out by private agencies.[51] It is to Johnston's criticisms that we now turn.

The sociology of *policing*

As we have seen, until relatively recently, sociological studies of policing focused primarily on the activities of police officers. However, the narrowing of the study of 'policing' to that of the 'police' should not be attributed to Bittner. For example, as noted earlier, in his 1974 paper Bittner explicitly noted that the word 'police' had at one time referred to 'the entire domain of internal, proscriptive regulation'.[52] He also made a number of references to public bureaucracies other than the police, whose primary function is law enforcement. Health inspectors, agents concerned with weights and measures, building inspectors, and truant officers were all quoted as examples of enforcement officers, holding special legal powers over and above those held by ordinary citizens. Bittner noted that such bodies are distinguished from public constabularies by the relatively limited and specific nature of their legal mandate. He therefore clearly recognised that there are a number of agencies concerned with maintaining order and legal regulation, but focused upon the police as the central institution within this network. The subsequent development of the sociology of policing has perhaps overstepped this position with its exclusive focus on the activities of public constabu-

---

[49] See also Fielding, N. (1988) *Joining Forces: Police training, socialisation and occupational competence*, London: Routledge.

[50] By, amongst others, Reiner (1992*b*).   [51] Johnston, L. (1992).

[52] Ibid, p. 21.

laries. However, Bittner should not be held responsible for this development. It appears that what he was actually trying, successfully, to do was distinguish the crucial features of the public constabulary as a body within the broader range of policing agencies.

Recent years have seen growing criticism of the tendency to equate 'policing' with 'the police'. There has been a marked shift in focus towards studies which allow for the fact that '[i]n practice, the vast bulk of policing has always been done by organisations and people other than the police'.[53] This, of course, returns to the broader notion of social control implied by the term 'policing', broader even than the earlier meanings of 'police' as the system of formal governmental regulation. For example, Shearing and Stenning's account of the 'policing' of Disneyworld is clearly based upon a definition of policing as informal social control, as well as more formal regulation.[54] They emphasise the control strategies that are embedded in the environmental design, as well as the activities by Disney employees engaged in the maintenance of order. The notion of policing as social control also appears in work by British researchers. For example, Shapland and Vagg emphasise the important contribution of activity by ordinary citizens in maintaining order, over and above any activities of police officers.[55] They describe such activities as 'policing by the public', and include in this surveillance, indirect challenges to suspicious strangers, and low-level punishment activity, such as blocking-in illegally parked cars. The authors distinguish this kind of behaviour from 'direct punishment' or 'vigilante activity' which occurs, for example, in some townships in South Africa or certain parts of Nothern Ireland. In this view, 'policing' is characterised as a variety of processes of social control, even the most spontaneous and informal. Building on what we said at the outset of this chapter, we argue here that the academic usage of the word 'policing' to mean a range of social control activities has caused some definitional confusion.

Henry notes that definitions of 'social control' are often too broad to be meaningful, often being used to describe all social processes involving 'control' however indirectly, ranging from everyday family

---

[53] Rawlings, P. (1995) 'The idea of policing: a history', *Policing and Society*, 5, pp. 129–49.

[54] Shearing, C. and Stenning, P. (1987) 'Say "Cheese"!: The Disney order that is not so Mickey Mouse', in Shearing, C. D. and Stenning, P. C. (eds.) *Private Policing*, Newbury Park, Cal.: Sage.

[55] Shapland and Vagg (1988).

life to government health, education and welfare policies.[56] In similar terms, Cohen has argued that the notion of social control has become a 'Mickey Mouse' concept, in that it is defined so broadly as to mean whatever one wishes it to mean. He adds that 'in sociology textbooks, it appears as a neutral term to cover all social processes to induce conformity, from infant socialisation to public execution'.[57] In moving towards a more specific definition of social control, Cohen distinguishes between 'planned and programmed responses to expected and realised deviance' rather than 'the general institutions of society which induce conformity'. However, Cohen states that he does not wish to confine his interest to the formal legal-correctional apparatus of the police and criminal justice system. He thus defines social control as all 'those organised responses to crime, delinquency and allied forms of deviant and/or socially problematic behaviour which are actually conceived of as such . . .'.[58] Of course, the hazard present in any attempt to define a concept more tightly is that the attempt will be criticised for excluding important aspects. Sure enough, Henry criticises this definition for ignoring the control exerted by 'private justice' systems. However, the fact that Cohen has provided an explicit definition of social control which can be criticised has helped to take the debate forward.

In a similar way, we would argue that the definitions of the police function offered by authors like Banton and Cain were crucial, even given their limitations. Although their foci are perhaps overly narrow, they provide tangible 'benchmarks' which can then be criticised and improved upon. We feel that much of the recent work on 'policing' has either avoided providing an explicit definition at all, or defined it so broadly as to make it meaningless as a concept. There is therefore a danger that 'policing' may, as Cohen feared for the term 'social control', become a 'Mickey Mouse' concept too. Clifford Shearing is one of the few writers in recent years who has attempted to offer an explicit definition of what he takes to be 'policing'. He defines policing as 'security', and argues that it involves the preservation of an established order against internal or external threat.[59] In

---

[56] Henry, S. (1987) 'Private justice and the policing of labor: the dialectics of industrial discipline', in Shearing, C. D. and Stenning, P. C. (eds.) *Private Policing*, California: Sage.   [57] Cohen, S. (1985) *Visions of Social Control*, Cambridge: Polity Press, p. 2.
[58] Ibid, p. 3.
[59] Shearing, C. (1992) 'The Relation between Public and Private Policing', in M. Tonry and N. Morris (eds.) *Modern Policing: Crime and Justice: A Review of the Research*, Chicago: University of Chicago Press, Vol. 15, pp. 399–434.

his terms, policing involves initiating strategies whose aim is to offer guarantees of security to all those who seek them. Shearing's definition of policing as security has the advantage of being able to capture the essence of a wide range of social control activities. However, we would still regard it as too broad for our current purposes. It is not possible, in our view, to distinguish within Shearing's definition between the general activities of government which contribute to the maintenance of the social order, and the more specific activities of bodies which have as a central and defining purpose the undertaking of social control functions.

In this study we therefore wish to focus on something more specific than policing defined as all 'social control', or than policing defined as 'governance' or the provision of guarantees of security. For example, we are not here primarily concerned with the rule-enforcement activities of teachers and parents, or the surveillance activities of neighbourhood watch groups, although these are at times and in some senses described by the term 'policing', and undoubtedly form an important part of the wider system of social control. A number of authors have argued that there exists a variety of processes and institutional forms of social control along a formal–informal continuum. As Smith has suggested, 'order and discipline are for the most part maintained through informal social controls, or through formal controls administered by a wide range of institutions (like employers, schools and banks)'.[60] Important though informal controls are, we do not find it helpful to consider such controls as 'policing'. Morgan and Smith have argued that we need to consider two kinds of boundaries between types of social control.[61] The first is between the formal and informal methods, and the second concerns the balance between the public and private sector organisations concerned with controls at the formal end of the spectrum. Much of the recent debate about policing has concerned the arena of formal social controls, and the potential for shifting the boundaries between public and private bodies concerned with these. It is at this formal end of social controls that we wish to locate our definition of 'policing' for the purposes of this study.

[60] Smith, D. J. (1987) 'The Police and the Idea of Community', in Willmott, P. (ed.) *Policing and the Community,* London: Policy Studies Institute.
[61] Morgan and Smith (1989).

Towards a working definition of 'policing'

The recent work of Johnston and others has been of great importance in illustrating the complexity of 'policing'. Although, as we shall show, Johnston illustrates neatly the weaknesses of existing attempts to define policing, at no point does he explicitly provide an alternative definition with which to replace them. In part, this relates to his central argument that policing is a broad and shifting notion incorporating the actions of a variety of individuals and agencies. Thus, any definition will be inevitably arbitrary and inconsistent in some way. However, there is a danger that without some attempt at an alternative definition, we fall into the position of assuming that all rule enforcement, order maintenance, or social control, however informal and however carried out, is 'policing'.

It is clearly important to develop a framework within which the 'policing' activities of public, private and other policing agencies can be considered, without automatically distinguishing public from non-public bodies. However, it is equally important that this framework should be clear about whether and in what ways the activities of the public police may be viewed as distinct from those of other bodies. We return in the concluding chapter to the questions of if and how the particular role of the public police can be distinguished from other policing bodies and activities. Here we wish to provide the beginnings of a definition of 'policing' which will act as the basis for what is to be included within the discussion in subsequent chapters.

Although we do not presume to suggest that we are able here to provide a watertight definition of policing, we do think it important to outline in general terms what it is that we wish to focus on. As outlined earlier, what we are interested in is something more specific than simply 'social control'. We are interested in the activities of those regulatory, investigatory and enforcement bodies at the formal end of the spectrum, part of whose defining purpose is to apply social controls. We therefore have to ask: which activities fall within what we consider to be 'policing', and how are these to be distinguished from the myriad forms of regulation and social control that permeate almost every aspect of our lives? *Our focus is those organised forms of order maintenance, peacekeeping, rule or law enforcement, crime investigation and prevention and other forms of investigation and associated information-brokering—which may involve a conscious exercise of coercive power—undertaken by individuals or*

*organisations, where such activities are viewed by them and/or others
as a central or key defining part of their purpose.*

'Policing' bodies

There are a number of organisations—outside of public constabularies—who have, as a central or defining purpose, formal 'policing' functions in terms of crime investigation, law enforcement, order
maintenance, or crime prevention. Bittner noted the range of law
enforcement bodies and inspectorates in the USA, with specific legal
mandates in certain areas of public policy. Similarly, in Britain, there
have been several socio-legal studies of the law enforcement activities
of public bodies other than Home Department police forces. For example, Loveland examined the 'policing' activities of local authorities
dealing with suspected benefit fraud,[62] Hutter focused on the 'policing'
of environmental health regulations,[63] and has carried out work more
recently on the role and activities of the Health and Safety Executive.
The importance of such bodies has not been completely overlooked by
policy-makers. In 1977 the Home Office published a major review of
law enforcement by bodies other than Home Department police
forces.[64] Johnston categorises such bodies as 'hybrid' policing agencies
(being neither Home Department police forces nor private security
companies), and we shall consider the operation of such bodies and the
helpfulness of the term 'hybrid' in later chapters.

We would also include under 'policing' the range of activities carried out by the individuals and organisations which make up what is
generally referred to as the private security industry. In North
America, although Shearing and Stenning are undoubtedly the best-
known theorists of private policing, they were able to draw upon
work by some other academics, for example Becker,[65] Spitzer,[66] and
Spitzer and Scull.[67] In the USA, official interest in the phenomenon

---

[62] Loveland, I. (1989) 'Policing welfare: local authority responses to claimant fraud
in the Housing Benefit Scheme', *Journal of Law and Society*, 16, 2, pp. 187–209.

[63] Hutter, B. (1988) *The Reasonable Arm of the Law*, Oxford: Clarendon Press.

[64] Miller, J. P. and Luke, D. E. (1977) *Law Enforcement by Public Officials and
Special Police Forces*, London: Home Office.

[65] Becker, T. (1974) 'The place of private police in society: an area of research for
the social sciences', *Social Problems* 21, 3, pp. 438–53.

[66] Spitzer, S. (1987) 'Security and control in capitalist societies: the fetishism of security and the secret thereof', in Lowman, J., Menzies, R. J. and Palys, T. S. (eds.)
Transcarceration: Essays in the sociology of social control, Aldershot: Gower.

[67] Spitzer, S. and Scull, A. (1977) 'Privatisation and capitalist development: the case
of private police', *Social Problems* 25, 1, pp. 18–29.

of 'private policing' has a long history.[68] Much of this relates to the activities of the private police forces of the railroad and mining companies. The role of company police forces in industrial disputes in the USA during the late nineteenth and early twentieth centuries was considered by Senate and Congressional committees, and became the subject of a number of governmental reports.[69] Perhaps because of this controversial history, there developed in the USA a 'political consciousness that identified and railed against the dangers of private, and especially corporate, policing'.[70] The central theme of many of these reports was that corporate policing challenged the authority of the US state, and corporations were acting inappropriately as private governments. Ultimately, these 'private armies' constituted a threat to the public interest, which only the state was in a position to promote. This led to the widely-held understanding of policing as something which was legitimate in its public manifestation, but sinister and dangerous in its private one. Nevertheless, employment in contract security continued to grow, and this rate of growth peaked during the 1960s. There was growing interest in, and concern about, the phenomenon of private policing, and in the early 1970s the US Department of Justice commissioned the RAND Corporation to conduct a major review of the private security industry in the USA.[71] Private security was conceptualised in this report as the 'junior partner' in policing, a view which will be considered in more detail in later chapters. This was followed in the early 1980s by another major inquiry into private security, the 'Hallcrest report',[72] which worked within the framework developed by RAND. It analysed the development of private security as an industry, and predicted that 'continuing technological innovations and product development, crime and fear of crime, and strained public resources will all contribute to sustained and dynamic growth of this important segment of the econ-

---

[68] Shearing, C. (1992) *The relationship between public and private policing*, in Tonry and Morris (eds.) *Modern Policing: Crime and Justice: A Review of the Research*, Chicago: University of Chicago Press, Vol. 15.
[69] Weiss, R. P. (1987) 'From "slugging detectives" to "labour relations": policing labour at Ford, 1930–1947', in Shearing and Stenning (eds.) (1987).
[70] Shearing (1992), p. 404.
[71] Kakalik, J. S. and Wildhorn, S. (1972) *Private Police in the United States (the Rand Report)* (4 vols.), National Institute of Law Enforcement and Criminal Justice, Washington: US Department of Justice.
[72] Cunningham, W. C. and Taylor, T. (1985) *Private Security and Police in America* (The 'Hallcrest' Report), Portland: Chancellor Press.

omy'.[73] Shearing notes that the Hallcrest report developed the RAND concepts further, and postulated private security more as an 'equal' than a 'junior' partner.[74] The authors argued for enhanced co-operation between public and private policing agencies, which would accelerate the process of privatisation. Concerns raised by academics and others about threats to privacy and standards within the industry were viewed as technical problems, which could be addressed by stronger regulatory controls through both legislation and voluntary self-regulation.

In Britain, scrutiny of the role of private security is a relatively recent development. In the summer of 1971, the Cropwood Conference at the Cambridge Institute of Criminology concerned the private security industry in the UK.[75] The report of the conference noted that it was not so much the rapid growth of private security which made it the subject of debate, but rather the fact that 'its development has necessitated a fairly fundamental change in a basic social institution: namely, that designed to 'police' our society'.[76] In 1978, Hilary Draper's book provided a detailed account of the activities of 'private police' in Britain, and considered the wider implications for the public police and society at large.[77] In 1979 growing concern about the private security industry led to the publication of a Home Office discussion paper,[78] which considered the case for legal regulation of the industry, a debate which has continued until the present time. Thus, although governmental and academic interest in the security industry in the UK is a recent development when compared with the United States, it is certainly not a subject which has suddenly appeared in the 1990s. However, it is true to say that the work of South[79] and especially Johnston,[80] has led to an unprecedented degree of academic interest in the private security industry in this country, and a renewed focus on its role in 'policing' generally.

---

[73] Ibid, p. 163.   [74] Shearing (1992).
[75] McClintock, F. H. and Wiles, P. (1972) (eds.) *The Security Industry in the UK: Papers presented to the Cropwood Round-Table Conference*, July 1971: Cambridge Institute of Criminology: Cambridge.
[76] Ibid, p. 9.
[77] Draper, H. (1978) *Private Police*, Sussex: Harvester Press.
[78] Home Office (1979) *The Private Security Industry: A discussion paper*, London: HMSO.
[79] South, N. (1988) *Policing for Profit*, London: Sage.
[80] Johnston, L. (1991) *The Rebirth of Private Policing*, London: Routledge.

Understanding Policing

Much of the writing on private security[81] parallels the early sociology of the police in that it tends to focus on function and, more broadly, on the position of this industry in the overall policing division of labour. The most influential description of the function of the private security industry has been provided by Shearing and Stenning. First of all, they argue that what distinguishes private security from the public police is that those working for private concerns rarely perform their work because of a legally defined public duty. As a consequence of this, although public and private bodies may on occasion appear to be performing similar functions, the role they occupy may be quite dissimilar.[82] Second, they suggest that the bulk of private security is essentially preventative in character and, rather than being in the business of preventing crime like public policing bodies, private security is about 'loss prevention'. Shearing and Stenning took issue with the dominant theoretical conception of private security which had developed in North America, namely, the 'junior partner' approach. They argued that this was inaccurate in a number of ways. For example, many of those who control private security see the formal criminal justice system as an adjunct to their own private systems, rather than vice versa, and invoke it only as a last resort. The public police do not directly control the operations of private security, and in terms of resources it is they who are the 'junior partner'. These arguments will be considered in more detail later, when we look at the notion of private justice. For current purposes we focus on Shearing and Stenning's account of the main functions of private security. They argued:

. . . the feature uniting the diverse activities undertaken by private security under the heading of prevention is surveillance . . . Surveillance, despite the somewhat sinister connotations of the term and the vivid imagery of the Pinkerton slogan ('the eye that never sleeps'), is in practice a very mundane

---

[81] So far in this text we have used the terms 'private police' and 'private security' interchangeably. We have done so in the full knowledge that there has been a considerable debate about which term is the more accurate (See, for example, South, N. (1988) *Policing for Profit*, ch. 1). At this stage in our argument we do not wish to opt for one over another. Our preferred terminology will become clear later in the volume.

[82] Shearing, C. and Stenning, P. (1981) 'Modern private security: Its growth and implications', in Tonry, M. and Morris, N. (eds.) *Crime and Justice: An Annual Review of Research*, Chicago: University of Chicago Press.

activity made up of a multitude of functions that when viewed in isolation seem too trivial to warrant the label 'surveillance'.[83]

Johnston criticised this position, however, arguing that like much of the sociology of the police, such thinking is essentialist in character. Equally, it is reductionist—reducing the wide variety of activities undertaken by the private security sector to the single one of guarding. Johnston, in outlining the very diverse functions carried out by private security, argues that far from being able to find their essence captured in a concept like 'surveillance', the reality is that 'private security does anything that public police (or other state officials with special powers) do, and rather more besides'.[84] We will look at this claim in more detail later in the book. The important point to draw from Johnston's position for the discussion here is that he rejects all attempts to see the essential distinction between public policing and private security in functional terms. Indeed, he argues forcefully 'that policing can be defined neither in terms of some essential legal capacity, nor in terms of some essential set of functions'. He argues that:

Any understanding of contemporary developments in policing requires recognition of its 'indivisibility': the fact that public and private forms, far from being distinct, are increasingly connected. More and more, policing is undertaken by a complex and diverse network of public, private and hybrid agencies. To refer to policing as a 'network' does not imply that its components are yet coordinated—in that respect 'patchwork' might be a better term—but does suggest that the actions and reactions of one part will impact on the others. For that reason, any rigorous analysis of contemporary policing has to focus upon what one might call its 'diverse totality'.[85]

Given that the primary focus of this book is the 'diverse totality' of policing, and that Johnston's work on private policing formed the starting point for much of our research that is reported here, it is worth considering in some detail his criticisms of much of the extant sociology of policing. The basis of Johnston's critique is that the formalism of using the capacity to use force legitimately 'draws a rigid barrier between those activities carried out by police and comparable activities carried out by private agents'.[86] His point is that although

---

[83] Ibid, p. 213.   [84] Johnston (1992) p. 191.
[85] Johnston, L. (1996) 'Policing diversity: the impact of the public-private complex in policing', in Leishman, F., Loveday, B. and Savage, S. (eds.) *Core Issues in Policing*, Harlow: Longman, p. 54.
[86] Johnston (1992), p. 189.

there clearly can be important differences between activities that have
the legal authority of the state behind them, and those which do not,
the rigid application of such a conceptual boundary all but excludes
the activities of private policing bodies from the gaze of the sociologist. A fully-fledged sociology of policing, he argues, ought to be able
to deal with all policing activities without separating out the public
police from the remainder. Furthermore, viewing the activities of the
public police as totally distinct from those of other bodies leads to a
number of rather paradoxical situations. First, applied strictly, the
use of such a distinction hides the fact that there are occasions when
the police coerce without the state's legal authority. If they are to be
included in considerations of policing, then 'there is no more reason
to exclude acts of coercion carried out by private security guards
lacking the legal authority of the state: and even less so for excluding those cases where private personnel exercise limited coercive
powers, after being granted the authority to do so by the state'.[87] He
is thus drawn to the conclusion that policing is, in fact, a complex
web of powers and activities, some public, some private and some
that do not appear to fit neatly into either of these categories. In more
recent work, Johnston has begun to flesh out the ways in which he
believes the relationships between, and the differences between, policing bodies are best conceptualised.[88]

    In moving beyond a focus on functions and powers, Johnston
argues that there are two further dimensions along which policing
must be understood: the 'sectoral' and the 'spatial' dimensions. The
first of these refers to classic notions of public and private sector; the
second refers to the level—local state, national state—at which police
and crime prevention services are provided. A number of issues, he
argues, have combined to focus attention on changes along the sectoral dimension of policing. First, as crime has risen (and with it the
demands put upon the police) and the government has attempted to
increase efficiency and value for money from all public services, so
the question of whether it is appropriate that public constabularies
should become such an all-embracing service has arisen. Although, as
Johnston and many others point out,[89] public constabularies have

---

[87] Ibid, p. 190.
[88] See Johnston (1993) 'Privatisation and protection: spatial and sectoral ideologies
in British policing and crime prevention', *Modern Law Review*, 56, 6, pp. 771–92; and
Johnston (1996).
[89] See for example: Shearing and Stenning (1983); Spitzer and Scull (1977); South
(1988).

never truly been monopoly suppliers but have occupied a more or less significant role in a complex policing division of labour, the 1980s and 1990s witnessed the significant 'privatisation' of many previously public sector activities. While at first the criminal justice system and the police were relatively unaffected by this, from the mid-1980s successive Conservative governments have increasingly applied the privatisation policy to the criminal justice system. As well as deliberate policies aimed at increasing the role of the private sector, there has been the re-emergence of what Johnston refers to as 'citizen self-policing', including activities such as vigilantism and citizen street patrols.[90] An important focus of Johnston's argument, however, is the increasing attention given to what he calls the 'hybrid' areas of policing. By this he means those policing activities undertaken by bodies which occupy 'an ambiguous position with respect to the public–private sectoral divide. Examples that he gives include such bodies as the Ministry of Defence Police, the British Transport Police and municipal policing bodies. He reviews the powers of different 'hybrid' policing bodies, and examines the extent to which each of them could be considered to be open to public scrutiny and accountability.

Not only has there been movement along the sectoral continuum, he argues, but changes in the spatial balance of policing are also visible. More concretely, he suggests that British policing has been undergoing a century-long process of centralisation, a process that has gathered pace since the 1960s. Three factors have been central to this process. First, legislative centralisation brought about by the Police Act 1964—which established the tripartite structure for police governance and amalgamated forces—and the Local Government Act 1972 which reorganised local government. Secondly, the political and industrial unrest of the 1970s and early 1980s led to the establishment of new levels of national police co-operation and, in the words of one author, to the establishment of a 'de facto national police force'.[91] Thirdly, increasing European influence has further internationalised police co-operation and organisation.[92]

---

[90] Johnston (1993), p. 772.   [91] Reiner (1991).

[92] See, for example, den Boer, M. and Walker, K. (1992) 'European Policing After 1992', *Journal of Common Market Studies*, 31, 1, pp. 3–28; Fijnaut, C. (1991) 'Police cooperation within Western Europe', in Heidensohn, F. and Farrell, M. (eds.) *Crime in Europe*, London: Routledge; Walker, N. (1993) 'The international dimension', in Reiner, R. and Spencer, S. (eds.) *Accountable Policing*, London: IPPR.

Johnston concludes that the spatial and sectoral restructuring that appears to be taking place in British policing is indicative of a broader process of fragmentation of social structures and systems for maintaining order and, following Reiner,[93] suggests that this is best described as 'postmodern policing'. The argument is that policing now reflects the processes of pluralism, disaggregation and fragmentation that are visible in other sections of society. More particularly, he argues that:

> . . . policing is subject to what Reiner calls an organisational 'bifurcation' or, to what one might call in the context of the present article, a 'spatial polarisation': on the one hand, a small number of centralised (and, arguably, coordinated) agencies at national and supra-national levels; on the other hand, a large number of decentralised (and, arguably, fragmented) agencies at the local level. Clearly, given the preceding discussion, it is apparent that bifurcation will consist of a complex of public, private and hybrid agencies intersecting at different spatial levels.[94]

Johnston's work has been crucial in refocusing the debate about policing in Britain. Indeed, as Johnston pointed out in the preface to his 1992 book, there has been very little empirical work in the field— a gap which this book is intended to help begin to fill. There are few if any rigorous studies of the private security industry's actual structure and functions, and how its relationship with the public police service actually works in practice. Most of the available information is largely anecdotal, concerning experiences within a few organisations.[95] It is in this context that the research reported here explores the differences between public and private policing, and the growing interweaving that some commentators assert is taking place between the two sectors.[96] In addition, we attempt to take the discussion about policing on from where Johnston left it.

Concluding comment

What we have sought to do in this chapter is to outline developments in the sociology of policing. We have considered that body of work which has sought to identify the core role or function of public con-

---

[93] Similar arguments are set out by Reiner (1992).
[94] Johnston, L. (1993), p. 790.
[95] See for example Birch, G. (1993) 'The Security Sham', *Police Review*, 19 Feb.
[96] Marx, G. T. (1987) 'The interweaving of public and private police in undercover work', in Shearing and Stenning (eds.) (1987).

stabularies. In doing so we have, echoing many other authors, been critical of the tendency in a lot of earlier work to conflate 'policing' with what 'the police' do. Much of this critical comment has come from authors who have taken as the focus of their work the activities of private policing bodies. In turn, therefore, we have looked at this body of work and the attempts these authors have made to distinguish private from public police organisations. Such work, we argued, like much of the sociology of the police which preceded it, on occasion also suffers from a form of functional reductionism. Crudely put, it fails to take proper account of the very broad range of tasks and functions performed by the private security sector. This then is the backdrop to the work reported here. The extant sociology of policing leaves us with a number of important questions. The first is, how are policing activities other than those carried out by public constabularies to be understood? Is it helpful to continue to distinguish between 'the police' and other policing bodies? If so, on what basis should we make such a distinction? How are the relationships and the boundaries between public, private and 'hybrid' policing bodies to be conceptualised? Finally, following Johnston's plea, is it possible 'to develop some conceptual means for dealing with the multifarious activities we call "policing" without isolating those carried out by the police from those carried out by others'?[97] In chapter two we explore in some detail the use and usefulness of the terms 'public' and 'private' as these are perhaps the key analytical categories used throughout this book.

[97] Johnston, (1992), p. 189.

2
The Public–Private Dichotomy

In Chapter One we considered some of the ways in which the grow-ing focus on bodies other than those traditionally viewed as 'the police' has affected the sociology of policing. One of the central aims in this book is to provide a theoretical framework which can be used to make sense of this complex patchwork of agencies which makes up 'policing'. In part this involves attempting to develop a clearer understanding of the nature and the shape of 'boundaries' between the various forms of 'policing' agency. One, and perhaps *the*, key 'boundary' is that between 'public' and 'private' bodies. Up to this point we have used the terms 'public' and 'private' as if their mean-ings were largely self-evident. The brief discussion contained in chap-ter one will already have made clear that the use of this dichotomy is, in fact, fraught with potential difficulties, so much so that some authors have argued that it is an obstacle rather than an aid to analy-sis. Nevertheless, the public–private distinction is an enduring one, and even those who are clearly aware of its complexities continue to employ its terminology.[1] In this chapter we argue that the fact that the terms 'public' and 'private' are still widely applied to policing suggests that, despite their attendant problems, they are still consid-ered useful distinctions. We suggest, therefore, that the main problem lies, not in the inherent complexity of the dichotomy, but rather in the lack of explicitness about its different uses. In the chapter we explore in detail the multiple meanings below the surface of the con-cepts 'public' and 'private', and outline the ways in which the pub-lic–private dichotomy retains utility in considerations of policing. This will provide the theoretical basis for the more detailed consid-eration of other policing boundaries that we undertake in chapter seven.

---

[1] See, for example, the title of Johnston's (1992) book, *The Rebirth of Private Policing*.

The concepts of 'public' and 'private'

The public–private distinction has been described as one of the 'grand dichotomies' of Western thought.[2] However, as Weintraub argues, the public–private distinction 'comprises not a single paired opposition, but a complex family of them, neither mutually reducible nor wholly unrelated'.[3] The notion of what is 'public' is one which 'covers a variety of subjects that are analytically distinct but at the same time, subtly—often confusingly—overlapping and intertwined'.

There is a wide range of distinct interpretations of the 'public–private' dichotomy, each with roots in a different theoretical discourse and tradition. A number of authors have noted the many different meanings of the distinction. For example, Pitkin lists three dimensions of the public–private dimension: public as accessible to all, open to scrutiny, or visible; public as something which affects all or most of us in its consequences; and the notion of public direction or control which covers the idea of public administration and the collective state.[4] With a particular focus upon criminal justice, Shapland argues that the public–private distinction has been applied to structures and agencies in the criminal justice system, to territory, and to tactics (in terms of 'public' meaning formal means of social control as opposed to 'private' informal means).[5] One of the most helpful analyses is that of Weintraub, who highlights four distinct versions of the dichotomy, but stresses that even this list is far from exhaustive. In one sense, 'dichotomising the dichotomy' will inevitably be a simplification, and closer examination will always reveal even more complex meanings below the surface.[6]

In the current context it is important to note two general points. First, that public and private are related terms, and should always be used in conjunction with one another. In other words, 'any notion of public or private makes sense only as one element in a paired

[2] Bobbio, N. (1989) *Democracy and Dictatorship,* Minneapolis: University of Minnesota Press.

[3] Weintraub, J. (1995) 'Varieties and Vicissitudes of Public Space', in Kasinitz, P. (ed.) *Metropolis: Centre and Symbol of our Times,* Basingstoke: Macmillan.

[4] Pitkin, H. (1984) *Fortune is a Woman,* Berkeley: University of California Press.

[5] Shapland, J. (1989) *Views on crime: public and private problems,* Paper presented at the British Criminology Conference, Bristol Polytechnic, July, 1989.

[6] For a detailed consideration of the various meanings of the public–private divide, see Weintraub (1995). For an even more detailed consideration of the concepts, see Benn, S. and Gaus, G. (eds.) (1983) *Public and Private in Social Life,* London: Croom Helm.

opposition'. Secondly, here our focus is upon the broad comparison between two analytically distinct versions of the public–private divide (although where relevant we will make brief reference to further differences within these broad categories). The first type divides public from private by contrasting the *collective* (or matters pertaining to the collective) and the *individual* (or matters pertaining to individuals). The second theorises the public–private distinction by setting that which is *open or revealed* against that which is *closed or hidden*. This distinction allows us to tease out some of the differences between the ways that the public–private distinction has been used— in particular to focus on public and private 'sectors' and public and private 'space'—as a basis for some of the discussions in subsequent chapters.

Conceptualising the public and private sectors

Perhaps the most frequently used version of the public–private dichotomy relates to what are generally referred to as the public and private sectors. This sectoral dimension is a subset of the first of Weintraub's broad categories outlined above, which contrasts the 'collective' with the 'individual'. The sectoral version of the dichotomy contrasts the 'public' or governmental sector, with the 'private' or market sector. In the former, services are provided for all by the government and funded out of taxation. In the latter, consumers purchase services from firms motivated by profit. As we show below, however, the distinction between public and private sectors is more complex than this, and is a matter of degree rather than fundamental nature. The degree of sectoral 'publicness' (or 'privateness') depends on a number of factors. In our view the key ones are: mode of provision (collective or otherwise); source of funding, the nature of the relationship between providers and users; and the employment status of the personnel who deliver the service.

Most considerations of the distinction between public and private sectors begin with the way it is conceptualised within neo-classical economic theory. This contrasts state administration with 'private enterprise' (the operations of individual firms in the free market), and provides a rationale for a limited state role in the provision of 'public' goods and services. The starting point is an economic model of 'perfect competition', which is underpinned by a view of the social world which consists of a multiplicity of rational, self-regarding, utility-maximising individuals. The most effective method of resource allocation in such a society is via the free market, which naturally moves towards the market equilibrium position in which economic efficiency is maximised. The 'perfectly competitive' market is one in which many buyers and sellers come together to bargain over a standardised good or service. The price mechanism conveys information to sellers about the wants of consumers, and to consumers about the quality and availability of the good. Competition between producers provides choice for the consumer, and encourages efficiency in production. If one producer tries to charge an artificially high price for a good, consumers will simply go elsewhere. In the knowledge of this, producers (as profit maximisers) have every incentive to innovate and maximise productive efficiency. If consumers want more of a certain good then the demand for it will rise, increasing the price and encouraging producers to make more of it. Thus, 'market forces' are continually adjusting to attain the optimal outcome. The concept of 'perfect competition' is another theoretical model, based on a range of assumptions that in practice apply to only a relatively specific kinds of market (for example, perfect information, many buyers, many sellers). The model, therefore, is generally to be treated as an 'ideal type'; something which may be used to analyse and compare economic forms, but does not describe what most markets actually look like.

This atomistic and individualistic view of society identifies liberty with private property, and suggests that the 'private' sphere needs to be ring-fenced to protect the liberty of the individual from invasion by the state.[7] This approach can be linked to liberal political traditions which identify freedom and autonomy with the private sphere, and pose them in opposition to the 'public' sphere of state power. However, the model allows for the possibility of collective interests which can arise in response to a range of 'market failures' including the development of monopoly suppliers, the existence of external costs and benefits which are not reflected in the market price, market rigidities (notably, the lack of information and poor labour mobility) leading to slow adjustment, and also pre-existing income inequalities.

One example of market failure, and the key one for our purposes here, is the existence of 'public goods', for which demand cannot be met via the usual operation of the free market mechanism. Public

---

[7] For a helpful discussion of the various strands of liberal economic thinking in this regard, see Johnston (1992) ch. 2.

goods are characterised by jointness of supply: it is difficult or impossible to exclude individuals or groups from their benefits once they have been purchased. Left to themselves, market forces will not provide public goods or services as there is no incentive for an individual consumer to pay for them (as he or she is unable to exclude other people from the benefits). It is rational for the individual to wait for another individual to purchase such a good, and then reap the benefits without paying anything; what is referred to as the 'free rider' situation.[8] Consider the example of a number of highly competitive companies operating factories in an area next to a river. Transporting raw materials into the factories requires a long (and expensive) trip to the place where the river can be forded easily. It would make sense to build a bridge near to the factories, but no single firm has the incentive to provide the outlay for this, since all its competitors will benefit. Clearly, some collective action would increase the efficiency of all the factories, but the system militates against such a solution. The 'public good' characteristics of the bridge suggest that the firms should come to some agreement to provide the bridge and pay for it collectively.

It is important to note that the key characteristic of a 'public good', in this sense, is that it requires *collective* provision. However, this need not necessarily take the form of direct state provision. In certain circumstances such as the above example, it may be relatively easy for economic agents to recognise the 'enlightened self-interest' of collective provision. However, public goods clearly introduce a tension into the market model, between the self-regarding individualistic assumptions and the fact that collective provision is the most economically efficient outcome. Despite this, there are examples of voluntary 'non-state' systems of collective provision of goods and services which appear to work well, not least in the arena of policing and security.[9] Much attention has recently been focused upon schemes in which residents of particular neighbourhoods collectively pay for private security patrols. However, such developments require certain structural conditions to be met, such as sufficient acceptance of collective interests to prevent the free-rider effect eroding participation in the scheme, as well as a relatively well-defined 'neighbourhood' to be policed by such arrangements (i.e. for an element of

    [8] Olsen, M. (1971) *The Logic of Collective Action*, Cambridge, Mass.: Harvard University Press.
    [9] See Johnston (1993).

'excludability' to remain). On occasion, the tension between individual and collective interests may be such that voluntary forms of collective provision cannot be constructed effectively.

Of course, as in other senses, the 'publicness' of a good is a matter of degree. In the above example, although the good in question had a number of public characteristics, an element of excludability was required for the voluntary collective provision to work effectively. It is arguable that with 'pure' public goods, jointness of supply and non-excludability are such that the most likely solution is for some kind of state intervention to ensure that the good is provided. This would overcome the free-rider effect by introducing the element of compulsion, with collective service provision funded by taxation. The degree to which a good is 'public' or 'private' is determined by structural conditions as well as the intrinsic nature of the good itself. Johnston illustrated this with reference to fire protection, which developed from being sold to individual households as a private good, to being collectively provided as a public good.[10] In this connection, Savas's distinction between 'pure' public and private goods, and what he termed 'toll goods' (goods which although consumed collectively can still be charged for individually in proportion to use) is of relevance.[11] In reality, many goods and services have both public and private characteristics, the relative importance of which may shift in response to wider structural changes. Thus, with the growth of relatively concentrated urban dwelling, selling fire protection as an individual service became less effective, as a fire in one house had immediate implications for all neighbouring dwellings. Thus, the benefits of the good were no longer excludable.

Security and policing are often cited as primary examples of public goods. Indeed, Karl Marx himself wrote that 'security is the supreme social concept of civil society'.[12] Even Adam Smith, the hero of latter-day libertarians, was quite clear about the two fundamental 'public' duties of the state; first, 'the duty of protecting the society from the violence and invasion of other independent societies', and, secondly, 'the duty of protecting, as far as possible, every member of the society from the injustice or oppression of every other member of it'.[13] Thomas Hobbes had earlier described the anarchic 'state

[10] Johnston (1992).
[11] Savas, E. S. (1982) *Privatising the Public Sector*, New Jersey: Chatham House.
[12] Quoted in Spitzer (1987) p. 43.
[13] Smith, A. (1776) *The Wealth of Nations*, Harmondsworth: Penguin.

of nature' which would exist in the absence of some formal system of upholding legal rights and obligations, in which life for most would be 'solitary, poor, nasty, brutish and short'.[14] The need for a system of stability upon which the system of property relations could be built was an important theme of the utilitarians, who later supported the 'preventive' model of the New Police in the early nineteenth century. There is no essential contradiction, therefore, between the notion of a minimalist state, and that of a strong state, which provides the basic framework within which the free market can work.

The degree to which 'public good' arguments apply to policing depends of course on how policing is defined. As we have seen, there is considerable debate about what exactly constitutes 'policing', and the relative balance between law enforcement, crime investigation, order maintenance, and 'social service' functions. The relationship between policing 'inputs' and 'outputs' is tenuous and uncertain, whether the outputs are conceived of as the delivery of services (for example, to victims of crime) or as change in the wider society (for example, reduction of crime rates). In reality, policing consists of a range of services, of which some, to employ Savas's terminology, one might argue are private, some are purely public, and some are toll goods. The multi-faceted nature of policing means that it is extremely difficult to specify output and measure performance.[15]

This gives rise to an important point which is often glossed over by libertarian arguments for more private provision of policing. It concerns what is perhaps the crucial aspect of 'publicness' inherent in policing. This goes beyond 'public good' characteristics of policing which suggest that collective provision is the most economically efficient mode. Rather, it focuses upon the practical and symbolic connections of policing with the defining features of the Weberian concept of the state. These practical connections have been clearly stated by a number of authors. For example, Bayley has argued that the police are *the* key public service in a modern state, because they undertake 'the quintessential function of government, namely, authoritative and forceful regulation'.[16] Similarly, it has been argued that because the police are the most visible representation of social

[14] Hobbes, T. (1651) [1968] *Leviathon*, Harmondsworth: Penguin.

[15] Horton, C. and Smith, D. J. (1988) *Evaluating Police Work*, London: Policy Studies Institute.

[16] Bayley, D. (1983) 'Knowledge of the police', in M. Punch (ed.) *Control in the Police Organisation*, Cambridge, Mass: MIT Press.

authority, they have a unique relationship with the institutions of democracy and their legitimacy.[17] This view is encapsulated by Robert Reiner who has argued that: 'the police are the specialist carriers of the state's bedrock power: the monopoly of the legitimate use of force. How and for what this is used speaks to the very heart of the condition of a political order'.[18]

The symbolic connections of policing with the state and society are, if anything, even more important than the fact of coercive powers. As Loader argues, the central position that the police have occupied in the British psyche has provided them with a quite distinctive 'symbolic power'. In this sense, 'popular attachment to policing is principally affective in character, something which people evince a deep emotional commitment to and which is closely integrated with their sense of self'.[19] In a broader discussion about the different aspects of 'security' in modern societies, Loader notes the strong connection between the provision of security and political authority. He presents the concept of security as a social good, based on the fact that 'public safety is inexorably connected with the quality of our associations with others'.[20] Thus, although 'policing' in its broad sense has historically been delivered by a combination of institutional forms, there are crucial aspects which have come to be identified with the 'public' in terms of the central functions of the state.

Spitzer and Scull's historical analysis of the cycle of privatisation and communitarianisation in social control provides further examples of how, under certain conditions, public goods such as policing can be provided collectively by non-state structures. Their account of the 'privatisation' of social control functions begins with a description of the ancient institution of the hue and cry in pre-thirteenth century England: a collective, informal, unitary and relatively spontaneous reaction to crime. When the office of constable evolved in the thirteenth century, the duties were undertaken as civic or social obligations rather than for pecuniary incentives. Residents of a community took turns in the office. This was a voluntary and informal

[17] Jones, T. (1995) *Policing and Democracy in the Netherlands*, London: PSI.

[18] Reiner, R. (1993) 'Police accountability: principles, patterns and practices', in Reiner, R. and Spencer, S. (eds.) *Accountable Policing: Effectiveness, empowerment and equity*, London: IPPR.

[19] Loader, I. (1997*a*) 'Policing and the social', *British Journal of Sociology*, 48, 1, pp. 1–18.

[20] Loader, I. (1997*b*) 'Thinking normatively about private security', *Journal of Law and Society*, 24, 3, pp. 1–31.

system of social control, partly dependent on the tightly-organised and integrated communities in which they operated. They were clearly distinct from both the profit-orientated systems which sprang up as the nature of the social order changed, and the model of direct state provision of policing which emerged in the nineteenth century.

In Spitzer and Scull's work, the essence of 'publicness' or 'privateness' is not found primarily in the source of funding, but in the nature of *the relationship between those seeking and those supplying services*.[21] However, they identify a number of other features also associated with public provision, of which being supported by taxation is one. In addition, they suggest that public forms of service provision are organised on a bureaucratic basis and directly operated by full-time employees of the state. Their focus, therefore, is upon *how service provision is organised*, and which *personnel* actually deliver the service, as well as on the source of funding. Spitzer and Scull argue that private forms of service provision are predicated on a market or contractual relationship and can be divided into three general levels. First, the offer of a fee or reward by an individual, group, or the state to any individual/organisation to perform specific services. The second level involves an independently negotiated contract between a single party and a single service provider to provide services on an exclusive basis. The third level, characteristic in Spitzer and Scull's notion of 'advanced capitalism' occurs when the state contracts out public service provision, and thus acts as an intermediary between the 'private' provider and public (collectivity of citizens). It is interesting to note that in Spitzer and Scull's terminology, only the direct funding and provision of services by employees of the state can be unambiguously categorised as 'public', and this precludes any institutional form which imitates or is subject to the conditions of the market. This could be taken to mean that the 'public–private' divide is a rather unhelpful one. Alternatively, it can be viewed as a valuable illustration of how 'collective' needs or interests can be met via a range of institutional forms of service provision on a continuum between 'public' and 'private'. At one end of this continuum is centralised state provision, and at the other, perfect competition.

If we turn our attention to the institutions which have 'provided' criminal justice services in the 1980s and 1990s some of the complexity of this sectoral continuum can be illustrated. The 1980s saw

---

[21] Spitzer and Scull (1977).

the introduction of radical reforms into most public services, broadly aimed at introducing 'market disciplines' into public sector management. In general, such reforms included devolved management, the development of performance indicators, the supplanting of political forms of accountability by managerial and financial ones, and the development of 'consumer rhetoric'. For a time, the criminal justice system in general, and the police in particular, were largely immune from this trend. This illustrated an interesting philosophical paradox within Conservative thinking, combining the libertarian desire for a minimal state, with a Burkean emphasis on effective social controls embodied in a strong criminal justice system.[22] However, following the publication of Home Office circular 114 in 1983, market disciplines were increasingly applied to the police service, and other criminal justice agencies. Thus, *inter alia*, some functions such as prisoner escort were contracted out, the Prison Department of the Home Office became an agency, and a small number of prisons were handed over to private companies to staff and operate. By the late 1980s, a complexity of forms had emerged under the rubric of 'public provision' of criminal justice services.[23] By the 1990s a range of quangos, forums, and national and local agencies were involved in the criminal justice system alongside the police, the probation service, and others.

Focusing on policing illustrates this complexity even more starkly. Hoogenboom's work, for example, examines bodies which are not part of state constabularies but which nevertheless undertake 'policing' functions.[24] He found over forty different bodies in the Netherlands with over 20,000 employees with controlling and regulatory powers. In his view, part of the explanation for the growth of such bodies lay in the expansion of the welfare state in Western economies, with the 'welfare complex' beginning to undertake social control functions more usually associated with the 'repressive complex' of the state, for example the activities of benefit fraud investigators. He predicts the development of a 'policing complex' consisting of a combination of the official police, these kinds of regulatory bodies (involved in 'grey policing'), and private security firms.

---

[22] McLaughlin, E. and Muncie, J. (1994) 'Managing the criminal justice system', in Clarke, J., Cochrane, A. and McLaughlin, E. (eds.) *Managing Social Policy*, London: Sage.

[23] Mathews (1989).

[24] Hoogenboom A. B. (1991) 'Grey policing: a theoretical framework', *Policing and Society*, 2, 1, pp. 17–30.

He defines 'grey policing' as 'informal forms of co-operation between different social control agencies for which traditional mechanisms of accountability seem obsolete'.[25] Work such as Hoogenboom's on 'grey policing' has as one of its consequences the problematising of the public/private divide. Indeed, a substantial body of work has focused on the blurring that is developing between public and private sectors. Rosenthal and Hoogenboom argue that 'public' should not be equated with 'governmental', and that 'publicness' refers to the degree to which organisations are affected by what they term 'political authority'.[26] This position builds upon the argument of Bozeman that all organisations, irrespective of legal status, have 'public' characteristics.[27] The notion of a socially useful 'third sector'—between state provision and the market sector—has been associated with a number of authors such as Lipietz.[28] Definitions of this 'third sector' are often rather vague, but in the UK have tended to cover a range of 'not-for-profit' organisations in the charitable and voluntary sectors in which explicit social objectives such as service provision or job creation are pursued outside the traditional public or private sectors.[29] A recent review of the research on the third sector suggests that in Britain, it employs as many as 11 million people and has a turnover of £16 billion.[30] Schmitter has argued that relations between the state and interest groups could be categorised into a number of 'modalities', including official state recognition, government subsidy, devolved responsibility, and informal connections.[31] He argued that an 'osmotic process' is gradually dissolving the public–private divide. Savas also highlighted the wide variety of institutional patterns of ser-

[25] Hoogenboom A. B. (1991) 'Grey policing: a theoretical framework', *Policing and Society*, 2, 1, p. 18.

[26] Rosenthal, U. and Hoogenboom, B. (1988) 'Some fundamental questions on privatisation and commercialisation of crime control, with special reference to developments in the Netherlands', Paper presented to the eighteenth criminological research conference on the privatisation of crime control, Council of Europe, Strasbourg, 21–5 Nov. 1988.

[27] Bozeman, B. (1987) *All Organisations are Public,* San Francisco.

[28] Lipietz, A. (1992) *Towards a New Order: Postfordism, Ecology and Democracy*, Cambridge: Polity Press.

[29] Wilson, S. (1996) *New Challenges for Work and Society: Can the Social Economy Provide An Answer?* Report of a Seminar of the Franco-British Council, 5–6 Dec. 1995. London: Franco-British Council.

[30] Cameron, A. (1997) 'In Search of the Voluntary Sector', *Journal of Social Policy* 26, 1, pp. 79–88.

[31] Schmitter, P. (1974) 'Still the century of corporatism?' *Review of Politics*, 36, pp. 85–131.

vice provision, from direct government provision, through voluntary service and self-help, which again may be interpreted as undermining the notion of a simple 'public–private' sectoral categorisation.[32]

Johnston develops this line of thinking in his illustration of the complex modes of provision of policing which, he argues, cannot be simply demarcated into a public–private sectoral divide. As outlined in chapter one, he postulated the existence of 'hybrid' policing agencies, which in his view do not fit neatly into either category. In outlining the contents of the category, he lists five main types of hybrid policing agency. The first are bodies engaged in functions related to state security, such as MI5. The second, special police forces whose constables are given powers relating to specific Acts of Parliament, and examples include parks police employed by local authorities and the proctors in the University of Oxford. Third, a number of government departments have sections who engage in investigative, regulatory and law-enforcement duties (for example, Inland Revenue tax inspectors). A fourth category covers those people employed by local authorities in investigative and regulatory functions (for example, environmental health officers). Finally, there is a miscellaneous category which covers bodies such as the British Telecom Investigations department. In chapter seven we look in more detail at the organisation and activities of the 'hybrid' policing bodies operating in the London Borough of Wandsworth, and question whether the concept of 'hybrid' policing bodies actually helps our understanding of the sectoral complexity of policing. For current purposes it is sufficient to note that some authors have used evidence of growing fragmentation and complexity in the provision of policing services to question the continued usefulness of a public–private sectoral division.

The existence of a range of 'policing' bodies, and the growing connections between them, certainly has important implications for our thinking about policing. There is no doubt that the 'public service' ethos of state agencies has been affected by the application of market principles and business management methods. In a similar way, the reverse process may be true of profit-oriented private companies who are increasingly undertaking what have hitherto been perceived as 'public services'. For example, private guarding companies have had to address some very different issues in providing 'public'

---

[32] Savas (1982).

services such as prisoner escort, compared to more typical guarding contracts with private property owners. An important question for future research is the degree to which the 'profit-ethos' of such organisations is being challenged and transformed by involvement in such activities. However, the existence of some 'sectoral blurring', however significant, does not mean that the terms 'public' and 'private' are no longer of any use in helping us to understand the changes that are taking place. They still help us to locate different institutional forms on a continuum, and to compare them with each other. 'Publicness' or 'privateness' in the sectoral sense is a matter of degree, as well as nature. Thus, a public sector body which earns some additional income by selling services in the market is still something separate and distinct from a private sector agency which undertakes contracted-out 'public service' work. Of course, if a public sector agency became entirely dependent on making profits for its organisational survival, then we would suggest that its ethos and nature would have become indistinguishable from a private sector firm.

In policing, as with other largely collectively-provided goods and services, there is an increasing degree of fragmentation and diversity appearing. The result is something which appears to defy simple categorisation. Johnston is one of a growing number of authors who point to the difficulties which attend attempts to divide complex social forms into a neat binary opposition. As with all attempts to dichotomise sharply the social universe, the public–private distinction inevitably involves some simplification. As authors such as Johnston and others have convincingly demonstrated, it cannot be used systematically to sort institutions or practices into neat, hermetically-sealed categories. However, the crucial point is that there is a purpose to this simplification. It is a didactic model which corresponds to reality sufficiently to allow different forms and systems to be compared with each other and explained. The public–private divide is a conceptual tool which we can use to compare social phenomena in a way which furthers our understanding of the social world. Consequently, it is our contention that the notion of a sectoral continuum from public to private remains useful. At one end of the continuum, services are directly provided by the state, funded out of taxation, undertaken by employees of the state, and organised on a strictly non-market bureaucratic basis. At the other end of the continuum, individuals purchase services on the free market from a large number of competing firms. In reality, most forms of service provision will fall somewhere between the two, with a combination of state, market and 'third sector' modes of provision. Despite this, there remain important and enduring differences between 'public' and 'private' forms of provision. The concepts 'public' and 'private' provide markers for comparison which, despite their limitations, still help us to make sense of the complexity of forms. In Johnston's work, for example, where the fragile nature of the public–private dichotomy is a central theme, the terms 'public' and 'private' are still employed frequently, suggesting that the usefulness of the divide is implicitly recognised.

Conceptualising public and private space

We have devoted the first half of this chapter to a discussion of some of the complexities that arise in relation to the practical application of the notion of 'public' and 'private' sectors. However, as we flagged up at the outset, this is only one of the paired oppositions covered by the terms public and private. The second version of the public–private dichotomy we want to consider concerns the distinction between that which is 'open' or 'revealed', and that which is 'hidden' or 'restricted'. It is this which informs the distinction between public and private *spaces*. In simple terms, the crucial aspect of a 'public space' is its openness and accessibility to all. By contrast, private spaces are those characterised by restricted access and, moreover, where access is governed by those that 'own' the space. However, as is the case with the sectoral version of the public–private dichotomy, once we start to delve beneath the surface we find that other factors (such as degree of openness, and nature of ownership) begin to defy a simple binary categorisation. In addition to degree of access, we also need to consider the nature of the controls determining accessibility, and in particular how far these are informal social controls, more explicit physical ones, or some mixture of the two. Once again, despite the complexities which are uncovered by a detailed consideration of this spatial dimension, we will argue that the 'public–private' model retains utility, albeit on a different basis from the sectoral version. It remains useful in helping to order our thinking about the nature of urban space.

The nature of space

Most commonly, the term 'space' refers to a physical environment and the way it is configured (for example, the built environment of the city). However, it can also be used to refer to an interactional and experiential space which, although having some physical attributes, is also a product of social convention (for example, the concept of somebody invading your private space). As Reiss argues: 'the definition of space, and others in relation to it, is a social construction of one's reality as one moves about in everyday life'.[33] There are even more abstract notions of space involving metaphorical schemas, such as Hannah Arendt's 'public realm'. This is defined as a distinctive field of action which can emerge where people are deliberating and acting collectively. This notion of public space has no specific location (in geographical terms), and is structured by institutions, political parties and movements rather than by physical boundaries. Finally, there is, of course, now also a 'cyberspace' of technological information exchange, which itself has major implications for policing.[34]

There is a large and growing literature about the development and use of space in the modern city. Some of the most influential writings about the growth of modern cities combine both the experiential and physical aspects of space. The public realm has been presented as a place of 'heterogeneous sociability'.[35] Social life in the modern city, it is argued, is increasingly being polarised between the important public realm (the state, the market, and bureaucratic organisations), and a private realm of intimacy and emotionality. Perhaps the main focus of much of this work has been on the implications of the built milieu and the design and uses of physical space within the urban enviroment. This view of public space has been most associated with the work of Jane Jacobs.[36] Jacobs was concerned with the city as a human construct, and attacked the planning practices that had come to dominate in North American and European cities by the 1960s. She argued that planners had been increasingly influenced by utopian ideals aimed at controlling social life, through providing social and cultural centres within the metropolis. In these models, the street was seen simply as a thoroughfare, independent of social activities, which

---

[33] Reiss, A. J. (1987) 'The legitimacy of intrusion into private space', In Shearing and Stenning (eds.) *Private Policing*, California: Sage.

[34] Data protection legislation attempts to lay down what aspects of these 'spaces' should be open to all, and which should be restricted.

[35] Kasinitz (1995).

[36] Jacobs, J. (1961) *The Death and Life of Great American Cities*, New York: Random House.

were to occur in allocated buildings and places.[37] Jacobs argued that planning theories did not treat the life of the city as an organic whole, but sought to divide it into discrete functions which could be conveniently packaged into 'containers' of architecture and land. Jacobs felt that this was an explicit rejection of public space and the public realm. She argued that a city thrives on an active use of public space, and in particular the 'intricate ballet' of the street.[38] Weintraub described this notion of the public realm as 'a realm of sociability, mediated by conventions that allow diversity and social distance to be maintained despite physical proximity'.[39] It is clear, therefore, that discussions about space take in both physical and social dimensions.

Feminist writers have focused upon another conception of space, which has contrasted the public realm of the state, market and other life, with the more hidden 'domestic' sphere of family. It is notable that this approach categorises unambiguously as 'public', activities and organisations which would come into the 'private' sphere in the economic/sectoral sense (such as the world of commerce). The conceptual starting point in feminist discourse is to define what is to count as the 'private' realm (the family), and the 'public' realm is a residual category outside of this. Three common themes can be identified across feminist perspectives. First, the argument that other traditions under-emphasise the importance of the domestic sphere. Second, the view that the public–private distinction is deeply gendered, and that women have traditionally been confined to the domestic sphere and to subordinate positions within this. Third, the belief that the classification of the domestic sphere as 'private' serves to shield abuse and domination from political scrutiny and legal redress. This perspective of 'private space' has important implications for the way in which the 'family' is policed.[40]

A number of studies of the policing of domestic violence and child abuse show how the women's movement has challenged traditional conceptions of the 'private sphere' in the policing context. The ideology of domesticity, which was particularly prominent during the 1950s and 1960s, saw 'the home' as a place of security for women, and also as an essentially 'private' sphere largely outside the domain

---

[37] Dunlop, R. (1995) *Public Art and the Contemporary Urban Environment*, Unpublished Ph.D. thesis, University of Westminster.
[38] Jacobs (1961).   [39] Weintraub (1995) p. 296.
[40] Donzelot, J. (1979) *The Policing of Families*, London: Hutchinson.

of the state.[41] Violence occurring in this sphere has largely been hidden and frequently described by police officers as either simply 'domestic' and by implication as 'private' and therefore not their business, or alternatively as 'not real police work'.[42] Such approaches have been strongly challenged by the women's movement, which has led to important developments in policing policy.[43] Their campaigns have attempted to relocate certain forms of violence within the 'public' sphere. Thus, developments in policing policy in relation particularly to domestic violence and child abuse, but also more generally to rape and sexual assault, have resulted in a growing incorporation of such areas within the public gaze, with consequent increasing pressure on the police and courts to intervene in ways which ensure women's and children's safety. Thus, space in this sense is defined both 'physically' in terms of the actual home, and 'socially' in terms of a realm of intimacy.

The boundaries between different kinds of space are not always fixed in a physical sense, and may vary according to social circumstances. Take the example of a public beach, where people like to sunbathe or picnic. In an important sense, this is all 'public space' in so far as it is equally accessible to all. However, when a person or group of people sits down in a particular place, for the time they are using an area, it and an amount of space around it, becomes effectively 'privatised' (by social convention). The amount of space which is private will vary according to the conditions. For example, what is considered to be a generally acceptable 'private space' around groups of people will diminish as the beach becomes more crowded. There is a sense of 'personal space' within public places which may be perceived as threatened at different times. A person who stands very close to another in an otherwise empty lift is more likely to be perceived as invading private space than if the lift was crowded.

Not only are there a variety of different forms of space, but it is also important to note that space itself is not irreducible. Thus, within different kinds of urban space there may, and probably will, exist a host of relatively 'public' and relatively 'private' spaces, delin-

[41] Stanko, E. A. (1988) 'Hidden violence against women', in Maguire, M. and Pointing, J. (eds.) *Victims of Crime: A New Deal?*, Milton Keynes: Open University Press.

[42] Hanmer, J., Radford, J. and Stanko, E. A. (eds.) (1989) *Women, Policing and Male Violence*, London: Routledge.

[43] Jones, T., Newburn, T. and Smith, D. J. (1994) *Democracy and Policing*, London: PSI.

eated both by social convention and by physical controls. For example, an office block containing a number of commercial enterprises will be considered to be 'private space'. However, it is of course routinely accessible to the employees of firms which are based in the block, and other designated people such as cleaners, visitors, maintenance workers and so on. Moving into the block involves moving through increasing degrees of 'privateness'. Away from the public street outside, into the reception area which is still largely open and accessible, although the existence of a reception desk, and possibly security guards, may provide important symbols of exclusion to visitors without clear reason for their presence. Passing reception, one moves into a host of corridors, stairs and lifts. The office areas for each firm will be more private again, usually restricted to those members of that particular firm. Within the area used by one firm, there will again be varying degrees of privateness, the corridors and stairs may be relatively 'public', peoples' individual offices will be more private, and the lavatories being more 'private' still.

In an approach which parallel's some recent work on public and private sectors, Hunter's work on urban space includes an intermediate spatial arena between 'public' and 'private'.[44] He categorises three different kinds of 'order': the public, the parochial and the private, each with its particular institutional and spatial domain. Again, such an approach raises questions as to the utility of a stark division between public and private sectors. It concludes that it is necessary to allow for an intermediate sphere of parochial order. The private order focuses around the institution of the family and informal 'primary groups' based on sentiment, social support and esteem. It is restricted to interpersonal friendship networks and the institutions of kinship. The parochial order arises from the interlocking of these networks and local institutions which service the 'sustenance' needs of the local residential community, such as local stores, schools, churches, and community associations. Finally, the public social order is found mainly in the bureaucratic agencies of the state. The 'public order' is ultimately structured by the state which claims a monopoly over the legitimate use of force. Hunter's argument was that although crime and the fear of crime has led to overwhelming demands on the police and criminal justice system, we should look

[44] Hunter, A. (1995) 'Private, parochial and public social orders: The problem of crime and incivility in urban communities', in Kasinitz (ed.) *Metropolis: Centre and Symbol of our Times*, Basingstoke: Macmillan.

to the private and parochial orders for the source of much of this. For example, fear of crime is not related so much to actual crime but rather to 'symbols of incivility'. These are petty assaults against the social order which produce an 'urban unease'.[45] Hunter argued that the state needs to support stronger parochial orders that will engage in social control activities along with the state and the private order. The limitations of the private order in terms of wider social control can be addressed by linking such networks through parochial institutions such as schools, churches and youth clubs. This will allow a mobilisation of the powerful social control of the interpersonal bond.

Much of the literature on public space and the modern city focuses on the perceived decline of the public sphere, whether this be in terms of actual physical spaces such as parks and market squares, or of a more ethereal 'public sphere' in terms of the propensity to participate in collective action. Kasinitz has noted that the structure of 'public life' appears to be eroding in the urban context. Poverty and homelessness has led to the private lives of the destitute spilling into public places, crime and incivility have discouraged people from occupying public spaces and participating in public life.[46] Some political and design measures intended to reduce crime actually prevent a meaningful participation in public life.[47] Writers concerned with developments in policing have also turned their attention to an apparent shrinkage in a form of the public domain, with the increase in mass private property visible in both Europe and the USA.

Urban space and policing: the growth of mass private property

A concern with what is happening to public space is central to the work of Shearing and Stenning.[48] They explain the rise of 'private policing' primarily in terms of changes in the nature of property relations, and in particular the growth of what they called 'mass private property'. They maintain that private security is growing, both in extent and pervasiveness, mainly because the amount of public space found on private property is increasing. In other words, the natural

---

[45] The 'broken windows' thesis of Wilson and Kelling develops a similar theme. See Wilson, J. Q. and Kelling, G. (1982) 'Broken Windows', *Atlantic Monthly*, Mar., 29–38.

[46] See Kasinitz, P. (1995).

[47] Coleman, A. (1985) *Utopia on Trial*, London: Hilary Shipman.

[48] See Shearing and Stenning (1981; 1983; 1987); and Stenning and Shearing (1981).

domain of the public police is shrinking and that of private security is growing, irrespective of any conscious policy of privatisation or financial squeezing. The prime examples of what they mean by 'mass private property' are large shopping malls, privately-owned 'gated' communities and the growth of large enclosed residential blocks, parks and other open spaces, and large recreational and educational complexes. These are large 'public' spaces which, although (sometimes) privately owned, are to differing extents open to access by the public. The gradual erosion of the natural domain of the public police is, they argue, clearly visible in all these realms:

> The row of single or double family dwellings is pulled down and replaced by a massive high rise appartment building, or a multiple condominium townhouse complex. In the process, a single public street, which was previously patrolled by the public police, is developed into a mass of 'private streets' . . . which in all probability will become the domain of private security.[49]

We consider this explanation of the rise of private security in more detail in chapter four. Our concern here is what the notion of mass private property tells us about how the concepts of 'public' and 'private' may be applied to space.

The concept of mass private property combines distinct versions of the public–private division. On the one hand, it is concerned with the spatial dimension of 'public', with its focus upon changes in both *physical* space and in *experiential* space. On the other, it is also focused upon the sectoral definition of *private ownership*. Thus, it is held that people now tend to live in large private blocks, gated communities or privately-owned condominiums, rather than in houses on traditional public street patterns. They spend more time shopping in privately-owned malls rather than on traditional 'public' high streets, and spend leisure time in large private complexes rather than in publicly-owned parks and open spaces. This argument has strong resonance with Mike Davis' dystopian picture of property developments in Los Angeles.[50] Davis argues that developments in North American cities have increasingly undermined what he termed the 'Olmsteadian notion' of public spaces.[51] This proposed public spaces as 'safety

[49] Stenning and Shearing (1980) p. 229.

[50] Davis, M. (1990) *City of Quartz*, London: Vintage.

[51] This was named after the designer of the main parks in New York, Frederick Law Olmstead. Olmstead envisaged parks as pleasant public (accessible and vibrant) spaces which could offset some of the effects of industrialisation. They would provide a safety valve in which the frustrations and difficulties of modern urban life could be released in an environment of heterogeneous sociability.

valves', where people of heterogeneous backgrounds and beliefs could come together in common places and recreations. Instead, 'today's upscale, pseudo-public spaces—sumptuary malls, office centers, culture acropolises and so on—are full of invisible signs warning off the underclass "other"'. This all represents the 'hardening' of the city surfaces against the poor. Reiss argues that citizens are increasingly becoming 'prisoners' of privately-protected places, when public places are viewed as unprotected by the public police.[52] He notes that in the city, a place of anonymity and impersonality, private space is more tightly controlled and defined. All these authors, like Shearing and Stenning, see public space as having both experiential and physical attributes.

Two of what appear to be essential elements of 'mass private property' are concerned with the nature of space. The *physical size* of the space is certainly an important feature, but more particularly, what makes it 'public space' is the fact that there is more or less *routine access by large numbers of people*. However, the key feature with implications for policing is that the property is *privately-owned* by large corporations rather than smaller property developers.

This combination of the spatial and the sectoral forms of the public–private divide is further confused by the addition of the legal dimension. Early liberal theorists agreed that society should accord individuals some space into which the state should not normally intervene. The emergence of the nation state accompanied the development of a notion of 'public peace' which was to reign in public places. 'Private peaces' were allowed in so far as they did not conflict with the public peace. Thus, in public spaces the 'King's Peace' was to be defined and enforced by public authorities with the help of citizens. In contrast, in private spaces the private peace was to be maintained and enforced by private property owners and/or their agents. As noted above, the notion of private property and privacy developed as a protection of individual freedom from the powers of the state. This protection, however, depended on the assumption of a congruence between private property and private space. In fact, as Johnston points out, there was never a perfect congruence between private space and private ownership. He argues that inns, although privately-owned, depended on routine access by people for their survival. People in these 'private spaces' needed to be subject to the public law

[52] Reiss (1987).

if peace was to be maintained. So although public houses were privately-owned, they came under public jurisdiction. Ambiguity about how far the jurisdiction of the public constable extends into the sphere of private property continues to exist. Johnston cites a November 1988 judgment (*McConnel* v. *Chief Constable of Greater Manchester*) which confirmed the conviction of a man for threatening a breach of the (public) peace, although the incident occurred on private property, where no member of the public was affected. This suggested that in certain cases the jurisdiction of the police constable extends into the 'private' (in the sectoral sense) commercial sphere. However, Beck and Willis noted that 'shopping malls retain their status as private property and all activities—including entry—take place with the consent of the owner'.[53] They refer to a recent legal judgment *CIN Properties* v. *Rawlins and Others* (*The Times* 9 February 1995) which appeared to confirm the private status of shopping centres. The decision was that the public at large had no automatic right to enter the public places of a shopping centre. Johnston refers to the possibility of making a shopping centre subject to a 'walkway agreement' made under section 35 of the Highways Act 1980. This would allow designated walkways to be treated as highways and thus subject to public bye-laws. Kasinitz asks the same question about private shopping centres in the USA:

Does one have freedom of speech in a shopping mall? A citizen clearly has a right to demonstrate or petition on a public thoroughfare. He or she does not have the right to do so in a store. But what about in the 'food court' of a shopping mall—a privately-owned space designed to look like a public space? What if that is the only real meeting place in the community? Court rulings on this matter have thus far been ambiguous.[54]

Reiss provides further examples of this complexity.[55] Many publicly-owned areas are crucially 'private spaces', perhaps the best examples being military establishments. In addition, one criticism of late modern urban developments is not simply that more public life is taking place on private property, but that public spaces (in that there is full public right of way to or through them) are being 'privatised' by subtle design and surveillance techniques. For example, during the 1980s,

---

[53] Beck, A., and Willis, A. (1995) *Crime and Security: Managing the Risk to Safe Shopping*, Leicester: Perpetuity Press, p. 71.
[54] Kasinitz (1995) p. 278.
[55] Reiss, A. (1987) 'The legitimacy of intrusion into private space', in Shearing and Stenning (eds.).

police forces in the UK participated in a scheme known as 'Secured by Design' in which housing developers were encouraged to build in crime prevention design features and advertise these as a selling point to potential customers. This urban safety design approach led to the development of 'cul-de-sac estates', with restricted through ways, built in inward-looking circles to encourage maximum natural surveillance, and self-policing. However, this effectively cut off the residents from 'outsiders', and people wandering into the cul-de-sac, despite the fact that there remains public right of way, may feel that they are encroaching on private space. So as well as privately-owned areas being designed to imitate 'public space' we have the phenomenon of publicly-owned space being designed to look like 'private space'. Further examples of private security agents operating in 'public space' have been seen in recent years with demonstrations against major road building projects. The demonstrations against the Newbury by-pass, for example, gave rise to reports of demonstrators and local people being illegally prevented from using public roads and pathways by the contractors' security guards.

The complexity of the public–private division in physical space becomes more complex when we consider the already complex forms which are appearing within the sectoral dimension. The growth of mass private property has illustrated the increasing disjuncture between private ownership and private space. Furthermore, as we noted in the discussion on the sectoral notions of public and private, there is an increasingly complex range of institutional providers. In Britain, in education, health and other aspects of policy, government reforms have encouraged providers of public services increasingly to imitate aspects of commercial enterprise. Thus, although most schools and colleges remain largely funded from taxation, they are increasingly required to operate within cash-limited budgets, meet set performance standards, and to raise their own income. Similar developments are visible with the development of the 'social market' reforms of the National Health Service, leading to the establishment of independent Hospital Trusts and General Practice Fundholders. Many of the examples of 'mass private property' described by Shearing and Stenning have, in Britain at least, not been owned by private corporations. Rather, many educational institutions, leisure complexes, and hospital sites have been owned and run by 'the state'—in some form or other—or other 'non-market' organisations. For this reason, we argue later that 'mass hybrid property' has been of greater relevance in Britain than 'mass private property'.

Thus, it is impossible to divide the variety of spatial forms which exist within any society into neat opposing categories of 'public' and 'private'. There is a complexity of forms appearing. However, as with sectoral versions of the public–private dichotomy, this does not render the terms 'public' and 'private' redundant. Once again, so long as the terms are used correctly and their limitations recognised, they can be an aid to analysis. Thus, we can postulate a model of public and private space, with degrees of 'publicness' or 'privateness' on a continuum. At the 'public' end, we have large, open spaces, owned by the national or local state on behalf of all, accessible to large numbers of people with few restrictions. Those restrictions that do exist more usually relate to informal social controls, rather than physical controls or laws. At the other end of the spectrum we find the individual household, smaller, less accessible, and largely hidden from wider society.

When considering the nature of space there are a number of levels that potentially need to be considered. First, who has (routine) access to the space? In some of the examples of 'mass private property' provided by Shearing and Stenning, the question of open access to all does not arise. For example, in large office complexes, or university campuses, the property is not open to all. The crucial distinction is that they are large places, to which large numbers of people have access, so that it begins to take on some of the characteristics of 'public space'. Secondly, who owns the space: is it privately-owned, state-owned, or owned by some other body which cannot be categorised as either (for example, such as, a voluntary organisation, a charity, or a quasi-public body)? Thirdly, what kinds of controls prevent/allow people access to the space. Are these largely physical controls (gates, bars, etc.), or are they largely informal controls and signals?

Conclusions

It is clear that when thinking about the contemporary division of labour in policing and the boundaries between different policing bodies, we are entering problematic territory when using the terms 'public' and 'private' as a method of describing such distinctions. However, whilst the terms are far from straightforward, we would argue for a number of reasons that they should be retained. The first

reason is that we do not (as yet) have any alternative conceptualisations with which to replace them. In simple terms, although they
clearly have their limitations, they are the best that we have. This
point is implicitly recognised by authors such as Johnston who continue to employ the terms in their work. A more positive reason for
retention of the dichotomy is that it provides a useful model against
which to measure and understand practices and institutions in the
social world. So long as we are explicit about the version of the public–private dichotomy we are using, we feel that the model still helps
us to understand what is happening in relation, for example, to sectors and space. Confusion arises for two reasons. First, because often
it is not recognised explicitly that the dichotomy needs to be viewed
as a didactic model and not as an analytically accurate description.
Secondly, confusion arises because of the analytically different
versions of the model which use the same terminology. As the above
discussion has suggested, different conceptualisations of the
public–private divide are available, and potentially can be applied to
different dimensions of 'policing'. Thus, the public–private construction in relation to sectoral boundaries (state versus market; individual versus collective) overlaps with, but is analytically different from,
the predominant construction used in relation to spatial boundaries
(state versus individual; open versus closed). Both of these may be
used in relation to policing: the first to describe who provides policing services; the second to describe where policing takes place. The
division is, however, even more complicated than this. For not only
are there various constructions of the public–private divide to consider in each dimension, but, as we have seen, there are conceptions
which combine elements from different dimensions. Thus, the notion
of 'mass private property' is concerned with the essentially sectoral
dimension of 'private ownership', but also the spatial dimension of
'public accessibility'. As we have mentioned, an important part of
Johnston's argument is that the terms themselves are inadequate for
considering the variety of sectoral positions occupied by policing
bodies. His solution is to insert a middle-ground category—hybrid
policing bodies—and we consider these in more detail in later chapters. Clearly, an undifferentiated notion of the public–private divide
is insufficiently broad to analyse the variety of forms occupied by
policing bodies.

It is important that increasing attempts to understand the complexities of 'policing' do not lead to such a thorough deconstruction

of the term that the definition becomes so broad that it is almost meaningless. Similarly, it would be unhelpful, prior to a discussion of the 'private security industry' in modern Britain, to make a case for a general rejection of the 'public–private' divide, and its attendant terminology. The fact is that, despite the complexities of the dichotomy, the term 'private security' is understood well enough by sufficient numbers of people to make it meaningful. The public–private division is an enduring one, which suggests that theorists have yet to develop alternative conceptualistations with which to replace them. Thus, the challenge for writers in this field is to bear these complexities in mind, and be as explicit as possible about the underlying conception(s) of the public–private division they are using.

3

Private Security in Britain

In the opening two chapters we considered some of the ways in which public and private policing organisations have been conceptualised, and examined some of the difficulties in applying the public–private dichotomy to policing. In this and the next chapter we take a closer look at what is generally thought of as the 'private sector' in policing, namely the 'private security industry'. More particularly we examine evidence about the size of the industry, the extent to which it has grown in recent decades, and reasons for the 'rebirth' of private policing.

Much recent discussion about private security has focused upon the reported large growth in size and importance which the industry has seen over recent years. However, it is very difficult to find reliable evidence about the size of the industry, and the respective importance of the various sectors within it.[1] This has not prevented a range of estimates of employment, numbers of firms, and total industry turnover being made, some based on the limited evidence available, and others based on little more than informed guesswork. They include trade union surveys based on workplaces where they are recognised,[2] reports by private consultants into parts of the sector,[3] and individual estimates by trade associations.[4]

This uncertainty about the magnitude of the industry stems from a number of causes: the rapidly changing nature of the industry, with high levels of mobility of firms in and out of the market; the relative importance of small and medium sized firms which are difficult to locate; and the naturally less visible nature of some of the activities undertaken. However, perhaps the three main problems which have

---

[1] Jones, T. and Newburn, T. (1995) How Big is the Private Security Sector?', *Policing and Society*, vol.5, pp. 221–232.

[2] MATSA (1983) *Report on the private security industry*, Esher.

[3] Jordan and Sons Ltd. (1987, 1989, 1993) *Britain's Security Industry*, London: Jordan and Sons Ltd.

[4] British Security Industry Association (1987) *The British Security Industry Association*. London: BSIA.

dogged previous attempts to assess the size of the industry have concerned the different definitions of what comes under the rubric 'private security', the lack of official data upon which to base estimates,
and problems caused by functional diversification into and out of the
industry. This led South to conclude that 'the only consistent and reliable statement that is continually made about the size and the scope
of the private security industry today is that it is hard to obtain consistent and reliable information about it'.[5]

Before examining measurement problems in more detail, it is
important to clarify terminology. Some writers on private security,
notably South,[6] have made a distinction between the private security
industry, and the private security *sector*. South saw the *industry* as
comprising those firms providing products and services in guarding,
alarms, and mechanical and electronic security equipment. The
private security sector, by contrast, is more diffuse, including in addition private investigators, security consultants and in-house security.
Here we depart from this terminology, and when referring to the
private security *industry* we will do so in the broadest sense, as something which covers all the above mentioned components. The reason
for this is that we wish to make comparisons between the component
sectors which go to make up 'private security'. Doing so would make
reference to a wider private security sector confusing. In keeping with
the argument of the previous chapter, the term 'private' is being
used here in the sectoral sense: we are concerned with firms that offer
security-related products or services in the market, and who are
dependent upon the making of profit for their survival.

That said, it is important to note that there are some firms which
are particularly resistant to being described as part of the 'private
security industry'. In particular, in our research some private investigation firms and locksmiths reported that they did not see themselves
as part of the private security industry. The reason for this appeared
to be that they linked the term 'private security' specifically with contract guarding—that part of the industry that most usually has negative associations—or more generally with 'shady' operations (and
often of course with both). This, they felt, cast an unhelpful shadow
over their own businesses. Nevertheless, for the present purposes, we
shall continue to use the private security industry as a generic term,
whilst noting the diversity of the operations which it covers. Before

[5] South, N. (1988) *Policing for Profit*, London: Sage, p. 23.   [6] Ibid.

looking in greater detail at issues of measurement and some of the data available on the size of the industry, we begin by looking in general at the nature of private security in the 1990s in Britain.

Private security in the 1990s

Both Johnston[7] and South[8] provide fairly lengthy descriptions of the activities of the various sectors of the private security industry in Britain. In both cases they divide the industry into three broad sectors; staffed services, security equipment, and investigation. We will follow a similar pattern here, outlining the basic structure and functioning of the industry and assessing likely future developments.

Staffed services

In the public mind when the phrase 'private security' is used the image that most commonly springs to mind is the uniformed security guard. Indeed, there is a tendency for some academics to focus their attention on this part of the sector and we will be critical of this tendency in later chapters. Not only does guarding only make up one part of the overall industry, but even what is generally referred to as 'staffed services' encompasses a broad range of tasks and functions. By the early 1990s, the Business Round Table[9] estimated that, of contract security staff, about 70 per cent are static guards, 20 per cent are employed on mobile surveillance and key-holding, 10 per cent in the transport of valuables and about 1 per cent are found in alarm monitoring stations. Many of the in-house security staff will have a number of functions, some of which are clearly security functions, combined with others which are not so obviously security related, such as public relations and reception duties. The Business Round Table report noted that although the contract guarding side of the industry is often thought of as a relatively new phenomenon it has, in fact, a long history.[10]

Security guards are present in shopping precincts, industrial estates, offices, building sites, hospitals, and colleges, with commercial and retail premises forming the largest single segment of the market.[11] A growing market during the 1980s was the provision of

---

[7] Johnston (1992).　　　　　　　　　　[8] South (1988).

[9] Business Round Table (1994) *The Growing Demand for Security: Opportunities for UK Suppliers*, London: Business Round Table Ltd.

[10] For details see South (1988).　　　　　[11] Business Round Table (1994).

guarding services to the government. Johnston noted this development particularly applied to the guarding of defence installations,
with the Ministry of Defence expenditure on private security contracts undergoing a ten-fold rise in the second half of the 1980s.[12] In
addition, the employment of private security within the criminal justice system has been an important feature of government policy in the
UK over recent years.

It is important, however, to recognise that the private security
industry's involvement in some policing functions is far from new. To
take one example, Sections 2 and 3 of the Immigration Act 1971 provide powers for the detention of passengers pending a decision to give
or refuse leave, or pending removal. Illegal immigrants detained prior
to deportation may also be detained, and the Act provides for such
people to be escorted whilst in transit. The private security industry
has long been involved in such tasks. For example, for the past
twenty years or so, private security companies have held the contracts
for domestic management services for Immigration Act detainees.
This contract was held by Securicor until 1989, at which point Group
4 was awarded the new contract after a competitive tendering
process. This contract requires the company to provide custodial services at secondary examination centres at ports throughout Britain,
and at five immigration detention centres. Group 4 is also responsible for all internal escorting services. Recent evidence from the Home
Office to the House of Commons Home Affairs Committee outlined
plans to increase the private sector involvement in escorting services
overseas for Immigration Act detainees.[13] Press coverage has revealed
the establishment of private sector 'riot squads' at immigration detention centres.[14]

An important recent development in Britain has been the awarding of contracts to private companies to run prisons, the first instance
being the Wolds Remand Centre on Humberside. This was later followed by Blakenhurst and Doncaster prisons. At about the same time,
the government began to consider the possibilities for contracting-
out the court escort and custody service, which until that time had
been carried out by police and prison services. The first contract
for prisoner transportation was in the East Midlands and
Humberside and was won by Group 4, commencing in April 1993.

---

[12] Johnston (1992).   [13] House of Commons Home Affairs Committee (1995).
[14] 'Immigrant riot squads plan "flawed"', *Guardian*, 11 May 1995.

The contract made the company responsible for transporting from all places of custody within the contract area all prisoners (with the exception of high security or category A prisoners) required to appear at court, and the transport of all prisoners from courts within the contract area to their places of custody. Despite the highly publicised early problems, with a number of escapes and prisoners being delivered late to court, privately-run prisoner escort generally appears to have become accepted. A recent customer satisfaction survey conducted by the Home Office Research and Planning Unit covered courts, police, prison and lay observers in the area, and a very high proportion (over 80 per cent) were either satisfied or very satisfied with Group 4's overall performance.[15] In June 1994, Securicor won the contract to undertake escort work in the Metropolitan Police District. By the end of 1995, private companies were carrying out prisoner escort work in over half the country. Most recently, private security firms have been involved in the piloting of electronic tagging systems.

Another area of potential growth of the staffed services element of private security concerns parking enforcement. Part II of the Road Traffic Act 1991 transfers responsibility for street parking control in London (away from the 'red routes') from Metropolitan Police traffic wardens to local authorities. London Boroughs have tended to subcontract this service out to private firms. There is the possibility that such arrangements could be extended to the rest of the country, and one source has estimated a potential UK market of £50 million per year in parking enforcement for the private security industry.[16]

Although often not seen as part of the 'contract security industry' another element of staffed security includes door supervisors (bouncers) at public houses and nightclubs. This segment of the security industry has received a particularly poor press, not least in the assessment of the ACPO evidence to the House of Commons Home Affairs Committee.[17] When relatively high levels of offending amongst 'private security personnel' were identified in a particular police area, this was explained in terms of 'bouncers' giving the rest of the industry a bad name. Publicity about 'strong arm' tactics and criminal

[15] Caddle, D. (1995) *A survey of the prisoner escort and custody service provided by Group 4 and by Securicor Custodial Services*, Research and Planning Unit Paper 93, London: Home Office.
[16] Business Round Table (1994).
[17] House of Commons Home Affairs Select Committee (1995).

involvement on the part of door security staff have led to the establishment of registration schemes involving police checks and some
limited training, often linked to licensing regulations.

The policing and security arrangements for large public events
such as football matches and rock concerts is increasingly involving
the private security industry. Now that the public police can charge
for their services, they are in direct competition with security companies. Football crowds inside grounds are now 'policed' primarily
by stewards, although the public police maintain a presence outside
grounds, and take control when there is disorder. Other aspects of
the staffed security industry include body-guarding (sometimes
called 'close protection') and retail security work undertaken by in-
house plainclothes 'store detectives'. These latter functions overlap
somewhat with the investigatory sector which is considered below.
In addition, there is the growing field of security consultancy, and
risk assessment, which undertakes a wide variety of tasks looking
not only at protection from external crime, but at employee theft,
health and safety at work, fire safety, and internal fraud investigation.

Another important sector of the staffed security industry is the
transport of cash and valuables. This is a highly concentrated sector,
due to the high initial capital costs which are involved in setting up
a fleet of secure vehicles and communications networks. Three large
firms dominate the industry: Securicor, Security Express, and Group
4. The sector has shown strong growth in recent years, growth which
is predicted to continue into the future. Although the stock trade of
'traditional' cash-in-transit, cash collection, and wage packeting has
not shown major growth, other activities like coin collection, telephone and credit card storage and delivery, mobile banking, and
overnight delivery have grown substantially. With the closure of
more high street bank branches, and the growth of sub-contracting
of cash-dispenser filling, this sector is likely to continue to grow over
the coming years.

Much media attention has been focused on the activities of guarding companies offering uniformed patrol of residential areas. The
police have become particularly concerned about such developments,
for they are perhaps the most visible encroachment of private security into the traditional domain of the public police. Unfortunately,
there is no solid evidence about the actual extent of growth of this
phenomenon, but press reports have documented the appearance of

such street patrols in many parts of Britain.[18] *The Times* knew of twenty such street patrols in 1994.[19]

Despite some suggestions that staffed security services are perhaps threatened by technological developments, market growth is still predicted by some experts. For example, independent consultants have estimated a 33 per cent growth in the UK market for 'patrol services' between 1991 and 1995 (International Fire and Security Directory, 1993).[20] Similarly, a report for the BSIA (British Security Industry Association) on the 'manned' (*sic*) guarding sector predicted a growth in the market for contract guarding services over the next five years, although not as great as in the late 1980s.[21] Figures from Jordan and Sons also show rapid growth in the security guarding market during the second half of the 1980s, almost doubling in value during that time.[22]

The contract guarding industry is dominated by five firms, with the market leader (at the time of writing) being Group 4, followed closely by Securicor Guarding Ltd. Other leading firms include Reliance, Securiguard and Shorrocks Guards. Rapid growth during the 1980s slowed during the early 1990s, but prospects for further expansion are good with the growth of contracting out of in-house operations.[23] One fast growing sector is 'keyholding', which involves property owners handing over keys and responsibility for first responding to an alarm call to private security companies. Some of the larger companies have been able to offer an integrated service comprising static guarding, mobile patrols, and central stations network-linked through radio communications which can offer a 24-hour response service.

Security equipment

Although security guarding is often equated with the private security industry, by far the largest sector (in terms of total market size) is accounted for by electronic and mechanical security equipment. This is illustrated by consultants' projections for 1995, which estimated that of a total market size of £2.6 billion, only £615 million (or just

---

[18] See, for example, 'Private policing cuts crime on Islington estates', *Independent*, 16 Aug. 1994.
[19] Stewart Tendler, personal communication.
[20] Quoted in Business Round Table (1994).
[21] BSIA (1994) Evidence to the Home Affairs Committee.
[22] Jordan and Sons Ltd. (1993).
[23] BSIA (1994); Jordan and Sons Ltd. (1993); Business Round Table (1994).

over 23 per cent) was taken up by patrol services and valuables in transit (International Fire and Security Directory 1993).[24] Perhaps the best-known and most widely-used form of physical security are locks and bolts. A number of sources have noted significant growth in the British lock market over the 1980s, but with domestic demand increasingly being met by imports.[25] This sector of the industry consists mainly of small firms, although the market is relatively concentrated with the three top lockmakers having an estimated 70 per cent of the UK-supplied market.[26] The British lock industry has been ill-equipped to develop the new-style electronic locks that are entering the market. The 'physical security sector' includes a number of other elements, for example the small and concentrated safes sector, and providers of perimeter security fencing, shutters and grills, and reinforced glass. Some of these sectors have a clear overlap with non-security activities such as door-making, and the supply of fencing and windows.

It is widely accepted that intruder alarms constitute the largest single sector of the security equipment market. By 1991 an estimated 1,489,000 alarms had been installed in the UK, of which about one million are thought to have been professionally installed.[27] However, two years later Jordan and Sons estimated that while only half a million systems with remote signalling were in place by the early 1990s, over two million audible-only installations had been fitted by the same period.[28] The majority of these were in domestic or small business premises. Estimates of market penetration in the domestic and commercial spheres vary, but it is generally considered to be significantly higher in the commercial sphere. The number of alarm installations approved by NACOSS (the National Advisory Council of Security Systems) has risen significantly over the last ten years. The largest proportion of these are audible only alarms, although an increasing proportion involve remote signalling—alarms set to call a monitoring station through the telephone network, or directly to a central alarms control station or even directly to the police.

There is a fast-growing demand for vehicle alarms, and this element of the alarms sector has expanded rapidly in the light of highly publicised steep increases in recorded autocrime. Three kinds of

---

[24] Quoted in Business Round Table (1994).
[25] National Economic Development Office (1988) *Security Equipment: A growth market for British Industry*, London: NEDO.
[26] Business Round Table (1994).   [27] Ibid.   [28] Jordan and Sons Ltd. (1993).

alarm are available, ranging from cheap DIY systems, through higher specification professionally installed alarms, to alarms for commercial vehicles. The vehicle alarms industry is extremely fragmented, with many small local installers and DIY systems on the market. Sources note that 'there is virtually no UK manufacturing' of car alarms, with the majority of the supply to the West European market coming from the Italian town of Varese.[29]

There has been a growing public focus upon the increasing incidence of Closed Circuit Television (CCTV) systems, and most sources suggest that the manufacture and installation of CCTV equipment has been a steadily growing market over the last decade.[30] In 1993, the BSIA estimated that as many as 150,000 CCTV systems had been installed in retail outlets, offices, schools and hospitals. Increasingly, CCTV is being used to carry out surveillance of public places, with a number of town centre CCTV schemes having received wide attention for their alleged success in crime reduction programmes.[31] The government has strongly supported the development of CCTV systems to monitor public spaces, despite concerns about effectiveness and about civil liberties.[32] In November 1995, the then Home Secretary launched a £15 million 'competition' to encourage the expansion of CCTV and over 800 bids were received from town centres, travel and business areas, neighbourhood schemes, community centres, and schools.[33] This followed a similar £5 million project six months previously. In the same month, public concern about CCTV was heightened when a video of some intrusive CCTV footage was commercially marketed. *Caught in the Act* was a compilation of CCTV footage, reportedly put together from a series of clips purchased from private security companies and local authorities. The film was reported to include footage of violent assaults, as well as sexual acts. It was later withdrawn from sale.

Some sources describe other aspects of the electronic security market including Electronic Article Surveillance (EAS) which is more

[29] Business Round Table (1995).

[30] See, for example, Jordan and Sons Ltd. (1992); National Economic Development Office (1988).

[31] Scottish Office Central Research Unit (1995) 'Does closed circuit television prevent crime? An evaluation of the use of CCTV surveillance cameras in Airdrie town centre', *Crime and Criminal Justice Research Findings No.8*, Edinburgh: Scottish Office Central Research Unit.

[32] See evidence given to the House of Commons Home Affairs Select Committee (1995).

[33] Home Office press release, 'CCTV camera cash claims', 2 May 1996.

commonly known as 'retail tagging'. These trigger an alarm at an exit point if the goods are taken away without the tag being removed. The use of such systems developed mainly in the 1980s in the UK. Hard tags continue to be the main forms of such systems in the garment trade, but security labels (like bar codes) now form the majority of EAS installations. Significant market growth is predicted in future years. A particularly interesting development has seen the extension of EAS installations to the criminal justice system. Electronic tagging was introduced on an experimental basis in Nottingham, London and Newcastle in 1989 as a method of enforcing bail conditions, and as an alternative to prison. There is considerable scope for involvement of the private security sector in that the tag triggers an alarm which warns a private monitoring company if the offender has left his or her house and broken the curfew. Securicor Custodial Services was one of the companies involved in the early trials of the system. The early experiments resulted in failure, with a large majority of the people tagged either removing the tags and absconding or simply continuing to commit further offences (in fact, one was later convicted of murder[34]). In 1991 the Criminal Justice Act introduced the possibility that magistrates could lay down a 'curfew order', which would require a convicted person to remain for up to 12 hours a day in a place specified by that person (usually his or her home). The Home Office introduced a second attempt at trials of tagging in the early 1990s, with regional trials in Manchester, Reading and Norfolk. The application in Britain remains somewhat patchy, although some experiments have claimed a good degree of success.[35] Reports in 1996 suggested that the Home Office was planning to increase the use of electronic tagging by using it as part of a system of house detention for minor offenders. By 1997, it was suggested that the then Home Secretary favoured the introduction of tagging nationwide.[36]

There is a growing demand within the security market for what are known as 'integrated security systems'. These are systems which include a number of different elements (for example, CCTV, access control, and intruder alarms), or perhaps combine security features with fire safety, or other design features of buildings like heating,

---

[34] 'Tagging delay as US equipment fails', *Independent*, 1 June 1995.
[35] See, for example, the Norfolk experiments described in 'On the home stretch', *New Statesman and Society*, 9 Feb 1996.
[36] 'Minor crimnals to be electronically tagged', *Financial Times*, 18 Apr. 1996.

ventilation, or lighting equipment. Integrated systems have the common feature of a communications network linking all aspects of the system to a central supervisory computer. Consultants have predicted a doubling of the UK market in such systems between 1991 and 1995, which makes it the fastest growing sector of the security market. Electronic security equipment is a sector characterised by rapid technological change, and this will continue in the immediate future. Examples of new developments include communications and tracking innovations employing systems which can trace stolen vehicles, and, in the alarm verification field, a range of advances being made through audio and visual verification technology.

Investigation services

Private investigators are perhaps the least visible part of the private security industry. Indeed, many private investigators object to being described as part of the security industry which they equate with the contract guarding sector. This was a central theme to the Institute of Professional Investigators' (IPI) submission in response to the final report of the Home Affairs Committee into the private security industry. This lack of visibility has contributed to a general lack of information about the private investigation sector, with a study carried out by Draper in the 1970s still perhaps the best source of information currently available.[37]

Although there are a number of large, multi-establishment detective firms, the industry is widely thought to be dominated by small, often single-person operations, whose activities are difficult to monitor. Reliable figures about the number of private investigation businesses are thus hard to come by, and we have to use estimates produced by those working within the industry. The Institute of Professional Investigators estimated that by the early 1990s there were about 500 private investigative organisations operating in the UK.[38] In terms of employment, the same report estimated that about 6,000 persons were engaged full-time as sole operatives or in small partnerships (a figure which, incidentally, is similar to the estimates made from the PSI survey later in the chapter). However, a further

[37] See Draper, H. (1978) *Private Police*, Sussex: Harvester Press. This gap is being addressed by a study conducted by the Centre for the Study of Public Order at Leceister University, which involves a national survey of 2,000 private investigators.

[38] Institute of Professional Investigators (1992) *Survey of the UK Investigatory Industry and Profession*, Blackburn: Institute of Professional Investigators.

8,000 were estimated to be involved in investigative activity of some description.

Both South[39] and Johnston[40] give broad details of the investigative sector which are often left out of market reports about the private security industry. Most agencies, according to South, are dependent upon solicitor's offices for the bulk of their work, and direct client approach is rare. An important part of the work of many detective firms is process serving, in which private investigators are tasked with passing on writs or summonses into the hands of those required to be party to legal proceedings. There is also an amount of missing persons work, including witness tracing, and some credit investigation and bailiffing work. Draper has highlighted the growing involvement of private investigators in the financial sector.[41] First, in the field of credit investigation, which saw growing demands on the part of traders, finance houses, and businesses for information on the credit-worthiness of potential customers. There is some overlap with the broader credit-reference sector here, which tends to concentrate on credit enquiries relating to individuals. An area linked to credit reporting is debt collection, and Draper noted that many investigation firms offered this service. There have been increasing legal limits placed upon the methods by which debt collectors can extract payment, although anecdotes of strong-arm tactics are still quite common. Some private investigation firms also offer bailiffing services, although this is increasingly the preserve of specialist bailiff firms. There is a distinction in the bailiffing sector between certificated bailiffs and others. Certificated bailiffs are the 'top end' of the market and are attached to the County Courts, who have a list of accredited bailiffs who execute court warrants for the seizure of goods and property. Much of their work involves the recovery of commercial rents. South noted that some detective firms had shifted into debt collection, and the private bailiffing 'market' appears to have grown substantially in recent years.[42]

Private detectives can and do also become involved in criminal investigation work. Draper found that actual criminal investigation work was rare, perhaps amounting to 10 per cent of the total private investigation work undertaken. One of the main reasons for this is that the resources are not available or would not be considered a justified use of public funds. In popular fiction, the 'private eye' is

[39] South (1988).   [40] Johnston (1992).   [41] Draper (1978).
[42] South (1988).

often employed in divorce cases, in particular the collection of evidence of adultery. However, changes in the law have resulted in fewer contested divorces and a significant fall in this kind of work. Some private detective companies offer specialist services such as undercover agents in industry (to investigate industrial espionage, sabotage or employee theft perhaps), commercial fraud teams, and credit rating work for insurance companies. The IPI reported a survey of its own members and found a wide variety of functions being undertaken by private detectives.[43] The report listed eighteen seperate functions including the following: process serving, litigation intelligence, trademark protection, tracing missing persons, asset tracing, matrimonial/maintenance enquiries, adoption enquiries, retail loss enquiries, handwriting investigation, expert witnesses, forensic evidence, provision of investigative training, accident investigation, reparation defences, arson investigation, criminal defence enquiries, industrial counter-espionage, insurance fraud investigation, corporate fraud investigation, unfair trading investigations, and security consultancy.

The investigatory sector is one in which 'old boy networks' and unofficial contacts with the public police are reported to be rife, but again, there is little empirical information available to support this claim. There are, of course, worrying reports about the abuse of personal privacy, in credit rating for example, with detailed personal files being built up on some individuals. There are also reports about illegal access (through contacts in the police) to the Police National Computer, although again, how frequent such events are is impossible to measure. Johnston also raised concerns about some aspects of the investigatory sector, in particular with its alleged links to the political right, and information-gathering functions for employers associations about particular workers.[44] Again, the evidence on such matters is largely anecdotal, and further specific research is required to shed more light upon this often secret and extremely invisible sector. Both the main associations who represent the sector in Britain are strongly in favour of statutory regulation.[45]

The concern about potential abuses of privacy by private investigators is a well-established one. In 1972 the Younger Committee recommended that private detectives become subject to statutory con-

[43] Institute of Professional Investigators (1991).
[44] Johnston (1992).
[45] Institute of Professional Investigators (1995).

trols.[46] Not surprisingly, detailed information about the nature and extent of malpractice is very difficult to find, but sources have suggested that private detectives have broken the law to satisfy clients, through bugging premises, committing criminal damage or even burglary.[47] The fact that the two main industry associations strongly support regulation suggests that malpractice (or at least the perception of malpractice) is considered to be a problem by a significant number of operatives in the industry. Clearly the major developments in electronic surveillance and tapping equipment that have occurred in recent years have significantly expanded the possibilities for the abuse of privacy.[48]

The size and shape of the private security industry

Measurement problems

As noted above, estimations of the size and shape of the private security industry face three main problems.[49] The first is clearly one of definition; those doing the measuring rarely measure the same thing. That is, there is no agreed definition of what falls within the rubric of 'private security'. A number of estimates focus exclusively upon the element of the industry that is often still seen as the essence of private security: the contract guarding sector.[50] However, the growth of this sector has slowed in recent years, with one of the fastest growing sectors being that of alarms and electronic surveillance devices.[51] The surveys produced by Jordan and Sons provide some of the most detailed information available about the larger firms providing security services and equipment. They define the private security industry as firms 'concerned with the protection of physical property, assets and individuals from theft or violence'.[52] Such a definition includes three main sections: the application of physical or mechanical devices, electrical or electronic apparatuses, and staffed

---

[46] Younger, K. (1972) *Report of the Committee on Privacy*, London: HMSO.

[47] George, B. and Button, M. (1994) 'The need for regulation of the private security industry', A submission to the House of Commons Home Affairs Select Committee, Nov. 1994.

[48] Lyon, D. (1994) *The Electronic Eye*, Cambridge: Polity Press.

[49] Jones and Newburn (1995).

[50] See, for example, Home Office (1979) *The Private Security Industry: A discussion paper*, London: HMSO; Williams, D., George, B. and MacLennan, E. (1984) *Guarding Against Low Pay*, Low Pay Unit; and, more recently, British Security Industry Association (1994).

[51] Jordan and Sons Ltd. (1992).   [52] Ibid.

services. However, as is suggested above, the definition excludes in-house security and private investigators.

Even with broad agreement about definition, a second problem is the paucity of *official data* on which to base estimates. In the absence of public regulation or licensing, it is argued that official estimates inevitably exclude important parts of the industry. For instance, Companies House data (upon which many market research reports are based, including those by Jordan and Sons) include only public or private limited companies. There is no information about sole traders, or partnerships with unlimited liability, despite the widely-held view that such organisations form the majority of firms operating in the industry: '. . . to exclude the "one man and his dog operation" unknown to Companies House, the Inland Revenue, the Department of Social Security and even Yellow Pages, would substantially reduce the size of the industry, but ignore some of its most serious problems'.[53] One relatively under-used source of data which we will utilise later is employment evidence from the Labour Force Survey (LFS) and from the Census of Population. It is possible to provide broad estimates of employment in some elements of the private security industry using occupational and industry codes. However, these are at a broad level of generalisation, and not all the components of the industry (including some of the apparently fastest growing elements) can be identified. This lack of data sources is partly related to the invisible nature of certain parts of the industry. Because of certain structural features of the market for contract security guards, there is a reportedly close relationship with the secondary labour market. Thus, it is relatively common for firms to hire workers on an informal, 'cash-in-hand' basis, as well as make use of temporary and part-time staff, and staff for whom security is a second job. All these features of the security market make exact estimations of total employment almost impossible.

The third major difficulty concerns the increasing *diversification of function* of companies in the industry. South noted how large firms such as Securicor were moving into the development of mobile communications systems, and Securicor have also successfully moved into the tranport industry with a large parcel delivery operation. South also noted the increasing incidence of office cleaning and maintenance firms undertaking security functions as well as their core func-

[53] George, B. and Watson, T. (1992) 'Regulation of the Private Security Industry', *Public Money and Management*, 12, 1, p. 55.

tions. There is no denying that this kind of development causes problems for exact measurement, because 'on a continuum of a whole range of commercial services, it is increasingly difficult to say where the private security sector begins or ends'.[54] This problem, of course, applies to measurement in all industries where firms have diversified either outwards or into the industry's core business. Nevertheless, it is particularly difficult to separate out purely security-related estimates for employment and turnover for companies whose operations cover a number of fields outside security.

Given these problems of measurement, it is important that estimates should be based upon a clear definition of what constitutes the 'private security sector'. Additionally, the sources of evidence supporting the estimates, and the limitations thereof, should also be made explicit. These two conditions have rarely been met by estimators of the private security sector to date.

Existing estimates of the security industry

The existing estimates are based on three measures: total employment, number of firms, and annual turnover. It is important to bear in mind the problems of definition outlined above, as many of the available estimates are either unclear in their definition of the private security sector, or only apply to limited parts of it.

Total employment

The measurement difficulties outlined above have not prevented a range of estimates of the private security industry being made. A review of published material illustrates to different degrees the problems faced by estimators. For example, in the early 1970s McClintock and Wiles estimated that 250,000 'uniformed men' were employed in security functions by private companies, but provided neither a definition of what kinds of functions this included, nor the empirical evidence upon which the estimate was based.[55] At the same time, Randall and Hamilton provided a more modest estimate of 40,000 men and women working in the 'private security sector'.[56] The

[54] South (1988) p. 27.
[55] McClintock, F. H and Wiles, P. (eds.) (1972) *The Security Industry in the UK: Papers presented to the Cropwood Round-Table Conference*, July 1971: Cambridge Institute of Criminology: Cambridge.
[56] Randall, P. and Hamilton, P. (1972) 'The security industry in the United Kingdom', in McClintock and Wiles, (1972).

authors suggested that, of this figure, about 25,000 were working in guarding functions and transport of cash and valuables, with the remainder employed in the manufacture, installation, and maintenance of security equipment. The estimates excluded in-house and private investigative personnel. The 1971 Home Office Green Paper suggested that there were 80,000 people employed as security guards of whom 50,000 were in-house personnel. These estimates excluded security equipment manufacture and installation, as well as much of the cash-in-transit sector. Five years later, Bunyan wrote about the 250,000 employees in the private security industry in Britain, but provided neither definition nor supporting evidence.[57] In 1992 George and Watson suggested the same figure of about 250,000 employees working in the private security sector 'on a broad definition'. However, they admitted that there was 'considerable argument' about the size of the industry, and did not draw on any empirical data to support the estimate. In evidence to the House of Commons Home Affairs Committee in 1994, George and Button provided an estimate of employment for the private security sector of over 300,000 individuals, although again the empirical basis was not made clear.[58] This problem applies to a recent estimate by the British Security Industry Association (BSIA), which put total employment in the industries covered by the association (not including private investigation and in-house security) at 126,900.[59] Elsewhere, using Labour Force Survey data from 1992, we estimated that at least 160,000 people were employed in 'security and related' occupations and in the manufacture of alarm equipment.[60]

It is difficult to form solid conclusions from these figures, in that they estimate the size of different definitions of the private security industry, and at different points in time. Although the overall consensus is that employment in the industry has grown, the extent of this growth depends upon which of the earlier base lines we take. All this supports Johnston's warning that we should regard estimates of employment in the security industry with a great deal of caution and as being, at best, broad indicators rather than exact measures.[61]

[57] Bunyan, T. (1977) *The Political Police in Britain*, London: Quartet, p. 230.
[58] George and Button (1994)
[59] British Security Industry Association (1994), Evidence to the House of Commons Home Affairs Select Committee, Oct. 1994.
[60] Jones and Newburn, 1995.
[61] Johnston (1992).

Total numbers of firms

As we argued above, estimates of total numbers of firms operating in the private security industry are also dogged by the twin problems of definition and supporting evidence (or the lack thereof). In 1971, police forces reported to the Home Office about numbers of organisations providing services in their areas for the protection of persons or property, including the installation of security equipment. Forces in England and Wales knew of 741 such organisations at the time. Bunyan's estimate of 7,000 private security firms in Britain lacked definition or evidence.[62] In 1983, a MATSA survey of the security industry was more cautious in stating that 'there may be over a thousand security companies in existence'.[63] More recent data by market research specialists suggested that there were about 700 companies operating in the 'manned services' market in the UK, although again this clearly represents only a section of the private security industry.[64]

It is widely recognised that the various trade associations and professional organisations that exist within the private security industry cover only a fraction of the firms in operation (a fact which is confirmed by the PSI survey below). However, the numbers of organisations covered by the relevant associations provide at least a baselimit for numbers of firms. The British Security Industry Association (BSIA) covers 240 companies in the UK, but excludes the private investigation and in-house sectors. The International Professional Security Association (IPSA) includes over 3,000 individuals (mainly working in in-house security functions) and over 300 companies. The Association of British Investigators (ABI) has over 450 member companies in its April 1994 membership register. The Institute of Professional Investigators estimated that in 1992 there were over 500 organisations offering private investigation services. The Master Locksmiths' Association (MLA) has a membership of 1,100 individual locksmiths, 340 trade members providing a locksmithing service and 60 associate members who are mostly manufacturers. The National Approval Council for Security Systems (NACOSS) has over 500 members. The Security Services Association (SSA) represents about 190 small installers of security systems, but is changing its constitution to become a technical inspectorate.

---

[62] Bunyan (1977) p. 230.   [63] MATSA (1983) p. 4.   [64] BSIA (1994).

Annual turnover and market size

A number of estimates of total annual turnover of the private security industry have been made over the years. Comparisons over time are confused by the effects of inflation, but a brief review of previous estimates is worthwhile. Randall and Hamilton estimated that the industry had an annual turnover of £55 million.[65] A 1979 Home Office Green Paper suggested an annual turnover in 1976 of £135 million.[66] During the 1980s, the marketing consultancy Jordan and Sons published a series of industry surveys, and these suggested total annual sales during the early 1980s in excess of £400 million. The 1989 report suggested that the market size had increased from £476.4 million in 1983 to £807.6 million in 1987, with the main part of this increase occurring after 1985. The most recent survey suggested that by 1990 the total sales in the industry had grown to £1,225.6 million.[67] The restricted definition of the private security industry used by Jordan and Sons, and the reliance on figures from public and private limited liability firms only, suggests that this is an underestimate.

In evidence to the Home Affairs Committee, BSIA estimated industry turnover as £2,827 million, although we should note that this excluded the investigatory and in-house sectors.[68] In their evidence to the Home Affairs Select Committee, George and Button suggested tentatively that the industry may have a total turnover in excess of £4 billion.[69] Both the Home Office and the Department of Trade and Industry accept that the total industry turnover exceeds £2 billion. Deriving some meaning from this host of figures is even more difficult than in the case of employment estimates, given the problems already mentioned about definition and also the added difficulty of inflation confusing estimates of change over time.

Looking at BSIA companies, there has been considerable growth in turnover over recent years. The BSIA estimated that the annual turnover for the entire industry was much larger (over £2.8 billion in 1993). Given that BSIA membership does not include some elements of the private security industry (for example the investigatory sector), it is likely that the total turnover is significantly higher. There appears to be broad agreement that certain sectors of the security industry are undergoing significant growth in terms of total market

[65] Randall and Hamilton (1972).   [66] Shearing and Stenning (1981) p. 207.
[67] Jordan and Sons Ltd. (1993).   [68] BSIA (1994).
[69] George and Button (1994).

size. The consultants McAlpine, Thorpe and Warrior (MTW) made a number of projections for 1991–95, within which the largest relative growth was displayed by integrated systems, central alarms, and access control.[70] The Jordan and Sons surveys provide indications of the growth of the private security market during the 1980s. For example, by 1990 they estimated a total market size of about £1.2 billion, as Table 1 illustrates.

Table 3.1: Market size of the private security industry 1986–90 (£ million)

	1986	1987	1988	1989	1990
Safes and Locks	106.1	125.4	146.1	160.7	148.3
Intruder Alarms, Access Control, CCTV	326.2	373.2	457.8	462.2	488.3
Security Guarding	151.0	195.0	248.0	320.0	370.0
Staffed services—transport	144.0	158.0	184.0	196.0	219.0
Total	727.3	851.6	1035.9	1138.9	1225.6

Source: Jordan and Sons, 1993

The PSI survey

It is clear from the above discussion that there remains a considerable gap in knowledge about the size and shape of the private security industry. The problems of measurement are substantial, but not so significant that they need undermine further attempts to create a more reliable picture. The approach adopted in our research was to undertake a survey of the industry with a view to providing basic estimates of numbers of firms, employment, turnover, services offered and so on. The first and most fundamental problem in designing a survey was to construct a reliable sampling frame. The best available source would appear to be the British Telecom Business Database.

Design of the survey

The Business Database kept by British Telecom is derived from business to business entries in the *Yellow Pages* and allows a rough approximation of the number of firms in the private security industry as a whole to be estimated. The Business Database contains details of 1.6 million company establishments across the UK and has the advantage over other sources (such as the Jordan and Sons

---

[70] Quoted in the International Fire and Security Directory, 1993.

surveys) in that it has good coverage of small and newly-formed companies, as there is a constant updating process.

The information is broken down into *Yellow Pages* classifications. From these broad classifications, it is possible to pick categories operating within the private security sector. Clearly the number of entries will vary according to how broadly the private security sector is defined. The broadest possible definition allowed by the classifications would include the following within the private security sector: bailiffs, burglar alarms and security systems, car alarm and security, closed circuit television (installers and manufacturers), credit investigation services, debt collectors, detective agencies, lock manufacturers and locksmiths, safe and vault equipment, safes (deposits and removers), security services and equipment, and sheriff officers. Clearly some of these categories will overlap, though the Business Database has guaranteed checks against double counting of firms listed under more than one category.

However, the Business Database (like other sources of information) does have some important limitations. It should be noted that the listings are for business establishments, and not single firms. Thus, the total number of entries for the above categories will be an over-estimate of the total number of firms listed in the Database, as different branch offices of larger firms will be included. However, the importance of smaller single-establishment firms within the industry may mean that this is not such a serious problem as first appears. In addition, although the Business Database is probably the most comprehensive available database of its kind, it does not claim to cover every company in existence. Indeed, whilst it does cover 1.6 million business establishments, estimates for the total number of firms in the UK have been as high as 3 million.[71] For example, because it is based upon business telephone lines it fails to include small investigatory and security consultancies (and any other operations for that matter) which are carried out from home addresses. Given these factors it is reasonable to suggest that the total number of entries within the Database is unlikely to be a vast over-estimate of the total number of firms.

The Business Database for 1994 recorded 8,259 business establishments under the above categories in the *Yellow Pages* (or with British Telecom business lines) in the UK. Given the distribution of business

---

[71] Daly, M. and McCann, A. (1992) 'How many small firms?' *Employment Gazette*, Feb. 1992.

establishments between industry sectors, a random sample of business establishments was selected, stratified by general category (sector) within the industry. A breakdown of the sampling frame is given in Table 2.

Table 3.2: The primary function of business establishments in sampling frame

Business type	Establishments
Bailiffs	165
Burglar alarms and Security systems	2183
Car alarm and security	480
CCTV and VTR	132
CCTV installers	222
Credit investigation	164
Debt collectors	436
Detective agencies	746
Lock manufacturers	56
Locksmiths	713
Safe and vault equipment	132
Safe deposits	13
Safe removers	17
Security services and equipment	2732
Sheriff officers	68
Total	8259

Source: British Telecom Business Database 1994

The overall aim was to conduct about 300 interviews, although in the event 304 were successfully completed. The interviews, which were structured, were carried out by telephone with the Managing Director or another senior figure in each of the 304 firms. The questions asked were about the business as a whole rather than the particular establishment in question. There was, as a consequence, the potential problem of double counting multi-establishment businesses when more than one establishment appeared in the sample. Given the anticipated difficulties in gaining co-operation with the survey, it was decided to deal with any 'doubles' at the end stage when we had gathered our completed interviews. In the event, this only resulted in the responses of three establishments being removed from the survey.

In order to manage the sampling process, the Business Database categories were grouped under five more general headings:

(1) *Security services and equipment*—as in the BT Database;
(2) *Electronic security equipment*—CCTV, burglar alarms and security systems, car alarms and security;

(3) *Investigation services*—detective agencies, credit investigation;
(4) *Bailiffing and debt collection*—bailiffs, sheriff officers and debt collectors;
(5) *Mechanical security equipment*—locksmiths, lock makers, safes and vaults.

Analysis of *Yellow Pages* suggested that most companies offering guarding services were found under the first category, security services and equipment. However, by no means all of the companies found in this category offered such services, a fact subsequently shown by the survey. Furthermore, it became apparent that these five categories did not represent functionally discrete parts of the industry. For example, although companies supplying guarding services are almost exclusively found under the first category, many of these companies also supply security equipment, and some provide other services as well. However, the main aim in dividing the industry in this way was to obtain a sample which broadly reflected the sectoral make-up of the population of companies. A random sample, intially of 500 companies, was selected, stratified by the five broad categories outlined above. In the event, 426 establishments were successfully contacted, out of which 307 agreed to be interviewed.

Response rates

The overall response rate was thus about 72 per cent, although response varied between the different sectors, the highest being in the security services and the CCTV and burglar alarms sectors (78 and 76 per cent respectively). The other three sectors showed similar response rates of between 63 and 65 per cent. Although the response rates are relatively high for this type of survey—thus lending credibility to data collected—problems were encountered in the survey. A relatively large number of establishments (82) had moved or gone away, illustrating the degree of turnover in the industry.

Sources of bias

There are two main sources of bias which are likely to give an over-representation to larger companies in the survey. The first is found in the sampling frame itself. Although as outlined earlier the Business Database is one of the best available for such a survey, it does not cover all businesses. In particular, those businesses not using a separate business line will not be included, almost all of which will be small businesses. A second source of bias is found in the survey method itself. It is likely that there is a bias towards larger businesses among the respondents, because those with permanently staffed offices are more likely to have answered the telephone and thus responded to the survey. Unfortunately, the lack of rigourous information about the sector makes weighting the data to compensate for such biases impossible. Nevertheless, we are confident that the final number of successful interviews reflected the broad sectoral make-up of the overall population in the database. The final breakdown of interviews was as follows: Security services and equipment (99 interviews); Electronic security equipment (107 interviews); Investigation services (37 interviews); Bailiffs and debt collection (27 interviews); and, Mechanical security equipment (34 interviews).

Status of company

As we have suggested, one frequently quoted feature of the private security industry is the relatively high incidence of small single proprietorships or partnerships. Table 3.3 shows the breakdown of business establishments by status for the sample as a whole. In the light of this, the finding that almost half (49 per cent) of the establishments in the sample were private or public limited companies was perhaps surprising. This may be partly explained by the nature of the sampling frame, and the fact that larger firms were easier to track down by telephone interviewers. Nevertheless, it may also suggest that we ought not to assume that sole traders are as predominant as some commentators have suggested.

The table shows that the highest proportion of sole traders and partnerships were found in the non-electronic security equipment sector, of which 80 per cent came into these categories. The private investigatory sector was also characterised by a relatively high proportion of unlimited liability firms, with 73 per cent in this group.

Table 3.3: Trading status of private security companies by sector (by percentage)

Status	Private Security Industry	Security services & equipment	Electronic security equipment	Investigation services	Bailiffs and debt collection	Mechanical security equipment
Sole trader	38	25	34	54	48	62
Partnership (unlimited liability)	14	11	15	19	7	18
Private limited company	45	59	49	27	33	18
Public limited company	4	4	3	0	11	3

However, of those firms in the first sector, 'security services and equipment' (which included the guarding firms), almost 60 per cent were private limited companies.

Table 3.4 confirms that the industry is dominated by single establishment operations: of the business establishments contacted, over three quarters were single establishment firms. This finding is even more striking if we re-emphasise the strong probability that the larger companies were over-represented in the survey. The highest proportion of single establishment firms were found in the non-electronic physical security sector, which covered locksmiths and safe-makers. However, all other sectors displayed similarly high proportions of single-establishment operations, with the exception of the bailiffing sample, of which almost a half were multi-establishment firms.

Table 3.4: Proportions of single establishment firms by sector (by percentage)

Type of firm	Private Security Industry	Security services & equipment	Electronic security equipment	Investi- gation services	Bailiffs and debt collection	Mechanical security equipment
Single establishment firms	76	78	74	78	52	88
Part of multi-establishment firms	24	22	26	22	48	12

As one might expect, of those firms with more than one establishment, by far the majority had five or fewer establishments. The highest proportion were two-establishment firms, although there were a few very large companies operating from multiple sites. Five companies reported having 50 or more sites, and one company working in the electronic security equipment market reported that it had 350 establishments.

Numbers of firms operating in the industry

The BT Business Database is, as we have argued, the best currently available basis for estimating numbers of firms in the industry. However, as we also pointed out earlier, one drawback is that it lists business establishments, and not single firms. The 8,259 establishments listed in our sample frame are therefore undoubtedly an overestimate for number of firms operating in the industry. Nevertheless, the data from the survey combined with the information from the BT Business Database allow us to make a more exact estimate of the

number of firms rather than establishments. Thus, from the percent-
ages laid out in Table 3.4 it is possible to calculate the proportion of
establishments which are in fact single firms in each of the industry
sectors. In addition, using the median values for numbers of establishments (for multi-establishment firms), the total number of such
firms can also be estimated.[72] On the basis outlined above, we estimate the total number of firms in our defintion of the industry to be
about 6,900. Again, recent estimates of the total number of businesses
in Britain suggest that the Business Database misses a large proportion of these. Thus, our figure is almost certainly an underestimate.
Nevertheless, to be able to state reliably that the private security
industry in Britain contains *at least* 6,900 firms is a considerable
advance on what was available before.

Size distribution of businesses

An important aim of the survey was to estimate levels of employment
in the industry. As in all the other areas we have covered so far in
this chapter there is relatively little known about the numbers
employed in firms in different parts of the private security industry.
Particularly during debates and discussions about the absence of, and
the possible need for, regulation of the industry, it is often suggested
that small 'one man and his dog' operations are increasingly dominant—especially in the guarding sector. In our national survey, each
establishment contacted was asked to identify the number of people
employed by the company. The size distribution is contained in Table
3.8. As can be seen, just over half of all firms (51 per cent) reported
that they employed five or fewer people. This was particularly noticeable in the investigatory and physical security sectors in which over
two-thirds of firms had five or fewer employees. By contrast less than
one third of firms in the guarding sector fell into this category. At the
other end of the scale just under one third of firms in the bailiffing
sector empoyed 50 or more people, and 15 per cent of firms in this
sector and 13 per cent of guarding firms employed more than 200
people. However, we should bear in mind the two sources of bias

---

[72] We did not use the arithmetic mean because in some sectors, small sample sizes
suggested that the mean would be an extremely unreliable measure of central tendency.
For example, in the locks and safes sector, there were only 4 companies which reported
they had more than 1 establishment. Of these, 3 had 2 establishments, and one had 56.
This one large firm substantially skewed the mean value upwards.

outlined earlier, which would most likely lead to an over-estimate of the size of firms in the industry. This is confirmed by the most recent figures from the Department of Trade and Industry about small- and medium-sized enterprises. These show that the great majority of businesses (about 90 per cent) have less than five employees.[73] A further point is that companies were asked about *total numbers of employed*, not just those directly employed in security-related functions. The figures presented in Table 3.5 therefore need to be treated with caution.

Table 3.5: Numbers employed by companies in different sectors of the private security industry (by percentage)

No. of employees	Private Security Industry	Security services & equipment	Electronic security equipment	Investi- gation services	Bailiffs and debt collection	Mechanical security equipment
0–5	51	32	62	67	39	68
6–10	17	20	15	14	15	21
11–19	10	13	13	8	8	0
20–49	10	16	5	8	8	9
50–99	3	3	3	3	12	0
100–199	2	2	2	0	4	0
200+	6	13	1	0	15	2

Given the large range of reported values for employment, any calculation of total industry employment using the mean of our sample as an estimate of the population mean will be subject to a large standard error. However, it is useful as a broad indicator to estimate total industry employment using our sample as a broad reflection of the parent population. In our survey, the average number of employees per business was 49.16. Table 3.6 sets out what the industry employment would be if this average was an accurate estimate of the population average (we accept that it likely to be a significant overestimate). On this basis, we might speculate that the total employment size of the private security industry could be as large as one third of a million, with the 'security services and equipment' category on its own being approximately the same size as the total employment of the forty-three constabularies in England and Wales (including civilian personnel).

[73] *Small and Medium sized Enterprise (SME): Statistics for the United Kingdom, 1993*, Small Firms Statistics Unit, Department of Trade and Industry, June 1995.

Table 3.6: Estimate of total employment in the private security industry and its component sectors

Industry Sector	Total no. of firms	Total employment
1 Security services and equipment	2,281	182,596
2 Electronic security equipment	2,547	100,326
3 Investigation services	767	6,182
4 Bailiffing and debt collection	440	33,779
5 Mechanical security equipment	864	10,748
Total	6,899	333,631

Age of businesses

It is now widely accepted that the private security industry has experienced rapid growth over recent years, and this growth has been reflected in linked processes: new firms coming into the industry, and an expansion in the operations of existing firms. The survey allows us to examine the first of these processes in some detail. Table 3.7 looks at the age of businesses currently in operation in the industry and contains some interesting data. First, it confirms that a significant proportion of the sample have a relatively short history: 56 per cent of the sample began trading after 1985. There is therefore quite a high concentration of new firms in the industry taken as a whole, though the proportion is perhaps not as high as some reports would lead us to expect. On the other hand the table also shows that over a quarter of the firms in the sample started trading prior to 1979. Although there appears to be considerable turnover in the industry as a whole, there is also some stability.

Table 3.7: Year firms began trading by sector (by percentage)

Year began trading	Private Security Industry	Security services & equipment	Electronic security equipment	Investigation services	Bailiffs and debt collection	Mechanical security equipment
After 1990	28	34	23	24	41	21
1985–1989	28	29	39	11	15	18
1979–1984	18	19	23	5	11	12
Before 1979	26	16	14	60	33	50

There is a good deal of sectoral variation within these general observations about the industry. Perhaps the most striking finding is the high proportion of long-established firms within the investigation and non-electronic security equipment sectors, of which 60 and 50 per cent respectively began trading prior to 1979. The mid- to late-1980s saw a high proportion of new firms enter the electronic security market, with 40 per cent of our sample having begun trading during this period. We should again note the small sample sizes which require the results of the sectoral analyses to be treated with caution.

Main services/products offered

As we argued in the introduction, breaking down the industry into component sectors was done for methodological reasons in relation to the sampling, and for ease of explanation thereafter. We certainly did not intend to suggest by doing so that each sector could or should be considered to be discrete functionally from other parts of the industry. Table 3.8 shows the breakdown of main services or products offered by the firms in the sample and confirms the earlier suggestion that there is considerable overlap between the sectors, in particular between 'security services and equipment' and that which covers electronic security equipment. The other three sectors are relatively specialised. Although most guarding companies would be found under the first category, a high proportion of the firms in this sector offered other services. For example, 42 per cent provided burglar alarms, and 26 per cent undertook investigative or enquiry work. A substantial proportion of these firms, 38 per cent, also provided safe and lock equipment. Of all the companies under 'security services and equipment' less than half (42 per cent) reported that they provided 'staffed services' in the form of security guards. If we apply this figure to our earlier estimate of 2281 firms in the 'security services and equipment sector' (see Table 3.6), this gives us an approximate estimate of 958 firms offering guarding services. This is comparable to the estimate quoted in a recent BSIA study of the 'manned guarding' industry.[74]

Looking at the other sectors, there were few surprises. For example, 80 per cent of the electronic security equipment sector were involved in the provision of burglar alarms, and 75 per cent in CCTV. However, 38 per cent reported that they provided safe and lock equipment. The other three sectors were largely restricted to the expected areas of operation, though one of the private detective firms

[74] BSIA (1994).

Table 3.8: Main services/products offered by sector (by percentage)

Product/service	Private Security Industry	Security services & equipment	Electronic security equipment	Investigation services	Bailiffs and debt collection	Mechanical security equipment
Burglar alarms	45	42	80	3	4	24
Staffed services	23	42	3	32	44	0
Investigative/inquiry	26	26	2	92	63	0
Debt/rent collection	14	3	0	49	85	0
Security consultancy	52	64	51	41	19	56
CCTV	44	44	75	5	0	24
Safes/locks	36	38	37	0	0	97
Access control	20	12	34	0	0	35
Key holding	1	3	0	0	0	3
Entry phones	1	2	2	0	0	0
Security lighting	9	7	16	0	0	6
Door entry systems	3	2	6	0	0	0
Car security	5	3	10	0	0	3
Process serving	7	1	0	38	22	0
Others	26	42	15	32	22	9

reported that it supplied burglar alarm equipment, as did one bailiffing/debt collection firm. Of what we termed the 'non-electronic' security equipment sector covering locks and safe equipment, eight companies, (almost a quarter of the total), in fact also supplied intruder alarms. A similar figure reported that they supplied CCTV.

Most important products/services

Respondents were asked to identify the most important type of product/service to them in terms of sales/turnover. A relatively high proportion of the 'security services and equipment' businesses (sector 1) reported staffed services to be their most important area of operation, reflecting the concentration of guarding firms in this group. However, 18 per cent reported that alarms were their most important products and there was, in fact, a considerable level of diversity within the sector. This was very much in contrast to most of the other sectors of the industry where levels of specialisation were considerably higher. In sector 2 (electronic security equipment), for example, 63 per cent of respondents reported that alarms were their 'core business' and a further 22 per cent named CCTV. As can be seen from Table 3.9, in sector 5 (physical security equipment) 77 per cent of respondents

Table 3.9: Breakdown of most important product/service by sector (by percentage)

Product/service	Private Security Industry	Security services & equipment	Electronic security equipment	Investi- gation services	Bailiffs and debt collection	Mechanical security equipment
Burglar alarms	29	18	63	0	0	6
Staffed services	15	38	0	3	27	0
Investigative/inquiry/ process serving	11	4	0	73	12	0
Debt/rent collection	5	0	0	5	54	0
Security consultancy	2	4	2	3	0	0
CCTV	9	4	22	5	0	3
Safes/locks	13	12	3	0	0	77
Access control	4	3	4	0	0	12
Others	11	20	5	16	4	3

named safes and locks as their main product or service and a further 12 per cent named burglar alarms.

Products/services outside the field of security

South has argued that one problem with defining exactly what constitutes the 'private security industry' is the increasing levels of diversification of companies or, more particularly, the fact that there are an increasing number of firms that provide security services but whose main line of business may lie elsewhere.[75] In view of this, we asked the firms in the survey whether they provided any services or products outside the fields of security. Of the 304 firms interviewed, 87 (28 per cent) reported that they came into this category. Such was the range of services provided that it was extremely difficult to categorise them. The products/services that were most frequently mentioned were 'electrical services' (by 12 respondents), fire or smoke alarms (by 7 respondents) and car radios/stereos and telephone installation (by 3 each). Whilst the survey contains little evidence to support the diversification argument, it is possible that this reflects the nature of the sampling frame used, consisting of firms who had categorised themselves in security functions. Further research in related industrial fields will throw more light on this question.

Geographical area of operation

A commonly-quoted feature of the private security industry is the localised nature of many firms. Table 3.10 suggests that although

[75] South (1988).

Table 3.10: Main area of trading by sector (by percentage)

Area of operation	Private Security Industry	Security services & equipment	Electronic security equipment	Investigation services	Bailiffs and debt collection	Mechanical security equipment
Local town or city	16	19	20	3	4	21
County	23	28	22	19	0	32
Region	31	16	35	43	44	35
National	21	27	15	14	44	12
International	9	9	8	22	7	0

quite a high proportion of firms within certain sectors of the industry operate in a relatively limited geographical area, it is not necessarily the case that the industry is dominated by local firms. Taking the sample as a whole, only 16 per cent reported that their main area of operation was the local town or city (see Table 3.13). About a fifth traded across the country as a whole, and almost one tenth did business in other countries.

There was a considerable amount of variation between sectors in this regard. Broadly speaking, sectors one and two (security services and equipment, and electronic security equipment) and sector five (physical security equipment) were relatively highly localised with 47 per cent, 42 per cent and 53 per cent in each sector respectively reporting that their main area of trading was the local county or below. By contrast, detective agencies tended to operate over a wider geographical area, with 14 per cent reporting that they worked nationwide, and 22 per cent doing business in other countries. A high proportion (44 per cent) of the bailiffing firms reported that they operated nationwide, and a further seven per cent said they did work abroad.

Annual turnover

As we suggested in the introduction to this chapter, although there is much speculation as to the amount of money being made by what is believed to be a rapidly expanding private security industry, the absence of regulation means that relatively little in the way of solid data is available on this question. During the pilot stage of the survey, we found that many firms were either unable, or unwilling, to give exact figures about annual turnover. In view of this, we asked firms to place themselves in broad bands as a way of measuring size

Table 3.11: Estimated sales-turnover of private security firms by sector, 1993

Turnover band (£000s)	Private Security Industry	Security services & equipment	Electronic security equipment	Investigation services	Bailiffs and debt collection	Mechanical security equipment
0–249	59	51	57	75	50	76
250–499	16	17	20	6	14	17
500–999	11	15	10	14	9	0
1,000–2,499	8	9	9	6	5	7
2,500–4,999	1	2	0	0	9	0
5,000–9,999	1	1	1	0	9	0
10,000–24,999	0	1	0	0	0	0
25,000–49,999	1	3	0	0	0	0
50,000 +	2	1	3	0	5	0

of operation. Table 3.11 shows the industry to be dominated by small operations, with an annual turnover (in 1993) of under £250,000. Perhaps surprisingly, there was relatively little sectoral variation in terms of annual turnover, though the bailiffing sample had the greatest concentration of very large firms—almost two-fifths having an annual turnover in excess of £2.5 million.

Types of customer

Respondents were presented with a list of 'customer types' and asked to give the three most important in terms of sales-turnover. The

Table 3.12: Most important customers by sector (percentage of companies reporting them in top three in terms of turnover)

Client	Private Security Industry	Security services & equipment	Electronic security equipment	Investigation services	Bailiffs and debt collection	Mechanical security equipment
Private individuals	38	23	60	14	15	58
Shops	12	13	14	0	8	21
Garages	5	6	6	0	0	6
Estate agents	3	3	1	0	4	15
Building contractors	8	13	10	3	0	0
Factories	10	12	14	0	8	6
Banks etc.	13	8	7	33	8	27
Local councils	10	12	8	0	19	15
Other government	7	6	11	6	12	12
Private companies	8	7	8	20	8	6
Solicitors	10	1	0	61	27	0
Others	24	31	23	6	39	24

results are presented in Table 3.12. Taking the industry as a whole, it appears that private individuals are the single most likely kind of customer to be named in the top three (38 per cent of firms indicating that this was the case). Shops, factories, banks and building societies, local councils and solicitors had similar likelihoods of being identified in the top three (with between 10 and 12 per cent of companies identifying them). There are, however, some interesting variations between different sectors. For example, in the electronic security equipment sector three-fifths of companies named private individuals as being among their top three customers, as did a similar proportion (58 per cent) of the locksmiths and safe makers. One third of the investigation firms named financial institutions to be amongst their top three (33 per cent) which probably reflects the amount of credit investigation work undertaken, and over three-fifths (61 per cent) named solicitors as being among the top three customers. Nearly a fifth (19 per cent) of the bailiff/debt collection firms reported that local councils were among their most important customers (perhaps reflecting the use of such firms to recover council tax debts). Over one quarter named solicitors in this category. Interestingly, a relatively high proportion (27 per cent) of the physical security equipment sector named banks and building societies among their top customers, reflecting the demand for safes and strongrooms from this sector.

Membership of trade/professional associations

It is often argued that only a small proportion of the firms in the private security industry are members of trade or professional associations. This was confirmed in our survey as is illustrated in Table 3.13.

The highest likelihood of membership of a trade or professional association was in the investigatory sector where almost half of the firms were members of the Association of British Investigators. However, even the combined membership of the two main industry associations (BSIA and IPSA) came to less than a tenth of the sample (as four companies reported that they were members of both). Taking the industry overall, the findings suggest that firms are most likely to be registered with NACOSS (although this is not strictly a trade or professional association). Of all the firms in the sample, 9 per cent reported that they were NACOSS-registered. Unsurprisingly, given

Table 3.13: Membership of trade/professional associations by sector (by percentage)

Trade/Professional Association	Private Security Industry	Security services & equipment	Electronic security equipment	Investigation services	Bailiffs and debt collection	Mechanical security equipment
British Security Industry Association	4	7	5	0	0	3
International Professional Security Association	6	16	2	3	0	0
Master Locksmiths Association	6	2	2	0	0	38
Association of British Investigators	6	0	0	46	7	0
Institute of Professional Investigators	3	1	0	16	4	0
Security Services Association	2	2	4	0	0	0
National Approval Council for Security Systems	9	8	14	0	0	9

the nature of NACOSS, this likelihood was highest in the electronic security equipment sector. As with the investigatory sector, the locksmiths appeared to have a relatively high proportion of membership of professional/trade associations, and 38 per cent of the 'physical security' firms interviewed were members of the Master Locksmiths Association. However, these sectoral findings should be treated with caution given the small sample sizes involved.

Methods of recruiting staff

Firms were asked about what methods they used to recruit staff, and the responses are set out in Table 3.14. Taking the industry as a whole, the findings suggest that word of mouth, jobcentres and local press advertisements are the most popular ways of recruiting staff. Almost three-quarters (72 per cent) of firms named 'word of mouth' as a method of recruiting staff, whereas just under half (47 per cent) mentioned jobcentres and two-fifths mentioned the local press. There were some interesting differences between sectors. The investigatory sector showed a strong tendency towards 'word of mouth' recruitment compared to 'other' methods, although a high proportion of the firms indicated that they also used 'other' methods.

Table 3.14: Methods of recruiting private security staff by sector (by percentage)

Type of firm	Private Security Industry	Security services & equipment	Electronic security equipment	Investi-gation services	Bailiffs and debt collection	Mechanical security equipment
Local press	40	55	43	8	41	24
National press	9	14	5	8	11	6
Specialist journal	10	13	6	8	11	15
Jobcentres	47	62	48	16	44	32
Word of mouth	72	76	76	62	74	59
Private agency	10	9	14	5	15	3
Other	22	15	16	41	30	35

Employment of ex-police personnel

It is often argued that the private security industry is a source of employment for people with police or services experience and, furthermore, that this is one of the key areas in which the 'public' and 'private' sectors overlap. Firms were asked if they currently employed any ex-police personnel, and taking the survey as a whole about 17 per cent answered in the positive. Almost a quarter of firms in the 'security services and equipment' sector reported that they were currently employing former police officers. Relatively low proportions (5 and 3 per cent respectively) of the firms engaged in the supply of security equipment (both electronic and mechanical) reported employment of ex-police personnel. However, the highest likelihood of employing ex-police was amongst investigatory and bailiffing firms, of whom about one third (33 per cent) were in this category.

It would be interesting to know to what extent this situation reflects different recruitment strategies on the part of firms in the private security industry. Firms were asked whether they actively seek to recruit police personnel, but the vast majority (78 per cent of the total sample) did not answer. Of the minority that did answer, seven firms reported that they did actively seek to recruit ex-police staff,

Table 3.15: Current employment of ex-police personnel by sector (by percentage)

	Private Security Industry	Security services & equipment	Electronic security equipment	Investi-gation services	Bailiffs and debt collection	Mechanical security equipment
Currently employing ex-police	17	24	5	30	33	3

and sixty firms stated that they did not have such a policy. The firms which were employing ex-police staff were asked why, and a range of answers were given. Legal knowledge and experience, investigative experience, and being used to dealing with the public were three fairly typical responses. Words such as 'disciplined' and 'trustworthy' were also used fairly frequently by respondents when discussing hiring ex-police personnel.

Employment of ex-services personnel

The same question was asked regarding the employment of ex-services personnel, and about a quarter of firms reported that they currently employed such staff. The highest proportions were in the 'security services and equipment' and bailiffing sectors, of whom almost two-fifths (38 and 37 per cent respectively) were employing ex-service staff. Again, the lowest proportions were found in the security equipment sector.

Table 3.16: Employment of ex-service personnel by sector (by percentage)

	Private Security Industry	Security services & equipment	Electronic security equipment	Investigation services	Bailiffs and debt collection	Mechanical security equipment
Percentage currently employing ex-service personne	125	38	15	24	37	9

When firms were asked why they employed ex-services personnel a range of replies were given. It was not possible to group them in a meaningful way. Most responses were quite vague, referring to the fact that ex-service personnel 'know how to wear a uniform', or 'don't mind working on their own'. Some responses were perhaps predictable: ex-services staff were seen as being in 'good physical condition', 'disciplined' or 'very much used to handling situations'.

Similar problems were experienced in obtaining responses to questions about whether firms actively seek to recruit ex-service personnel, with over 70 per cent refusing to answer. However, amongst the firms that did answer, fifteen reported that they did actively seek such personnel, whilst 73 firms reported that they did not. Of course, this kind of information is particularly difficult to obtain via a telephone survey, and requires further in-depth research. During the course of the study, we heard some anecdotes about use of ex-service, and occasionally currently-serving army personnel in security work. For example, a representative of one firm reported that their contacts within the army had enabled them to assemble a large team of off-duty paratroopers to undertake the security work at a rock concert. The head of security with a large NHS Trust informed us that specialist recruitment agencies exist dealing exclusively with ex-service personnel, which are a rich source of employment for many security companies.

Contact with the police service

Some authors have argued that close contacts have developed between the public police service and the private security industry. The opportunities to explore this by means of a short telephone interview were of course extremely limited, but it was possible to ask in general terms about how much contact firms had with the police, and about the general relationship with them.

Table 3.17: Contact between the police and the private security industry, by sector (by percentage)

Contact with police	Private Security Industry	Security services & equipment	Electronic security equipment	Investi- gation services	Bailiffs and debt collection	Mechanical security equipment
A great deal	23	32	25	14	11	12
Some contact	37	36	36	38	26	50
Little contact	30	20	33	35	44	35

There was some variation by sector in the amount of contact with the police individual firms reported. For example, the security services sector (which included most of the guarding firms) and the electronic security equipment sector were the most likely to report that they had a great deal of contact with the police. Almost a third of the former and a quarter of the latter, came into this category. Bailiffs had comparatively little contact with the police, about a fifth reporting that they had no contact at all with them.

Firms were also asked to rate their relationship with the police, and the responses to this question are laid out in Table 3.18. This shows that a very high proportion of the companies in our survey felt that they had good relationships with the police. Nearly 90 per cent of firms described their relationship as 'good' or 'very good', and only one company described the relationship as 'poor'. There was little variation between sectors in this regard.

Table 3.18: Relationship with the police by sector (by percentage)

Relationship with the police	Private Security Industry	Security services & equipment	Electronic security equipment	Investigation services	Bailiffs and debt collection	Mechanical security equipment
Very good	51	59	52	56	35	36
Good	36	30	36	31	48	52
Neither good or poor	12	11	12	13	17	9
Poor	1	0	0	0	0	3

Views on regulation of the industry

There has been growing pressure in recent years, for the government to introduce statutory regulation of the private security industry. At present, no licensing system (or other formal system of government regulation) exists for the private security sector as a whole in Britain (although since 1988, a system of public licensing of private security personnel in Northern Ireland has been in operation[76]). However, there remains no general licensing or regulation of the private security industry and in this respect, Britain contrasts with most other European countries. Austria, Belgium, Denmark, Finland, France, Germany, Greece, Italy, Netherlands, Norway, Portugal, Spain, Sweden, and Switzerland all have some form of legislative control of their private security industry.[77]

Table 3.19 shows that almost two-thirds of firms interviewed (63 per cent) felt that more regulation is needed. However, a sizeable minority (one-fifth) reported that the current level of regulation was

Table 3.19: Views of the private security industry on the question of regulation (by percentage)

	Private Security Industry	Security services & equipment	Electronic security equipment	Investigation services	Bailiffs and debt collection	Mechanical security equipment
Should be more regulation	63	70	54	81	44	65
About the right amount of regulation	20	13	29	8	26	24
Less regulation	4	7	3	3	0	0
Don't know	13	10	14	8	30	12

[76] The Northern Ireland (Emergency Provisions) Act 1987 (Part III 'Regulation of the Provision of Security Services') regulates the employment of private security guards.

[77] de Waard, J. (1993) 'The private security sector in fifteen European countries: size, rules and regulation, *Security Journal*, 4, pp. 58–63.

'about right', and a small minority (4 per cent) thought that there was currently too much regulation of the industry. There was some interesting variation between sectors in views on regulation. Given the argument that further regulation might stifle small businesses, we might expect to find a greater degree of support for more regulation in those sectors characterised by the larger businesses. Given the points made earlier about the over-representation of larger companies in our survey, this might partly explain the high level of support for more regulation. However, within sectors it was not immediately apparent that there was a clear 'size effect' on views about regulation. For example, the highest level of support for more regulation was found in the sector with the smallest size profile, the investigatory sector. However, we should again be cautious about extending this finding to the investigative sector as a whole. As noted earlier, the sample was probably biased towards the more formalised end of the market, and perhaps excluded many of those operations which would be less likely to support public regulation.

A relatively high proportion of the electronic equipment sector felt that there was about the right amount of regulation, which perhaps reflects a more general view that self-regulation in this sector is currently more effective than in other branches of the security industry.[78] The sector with the lowest support for more regulation was the bailiffing sector of which less than half supported more regulation.

Concluding comments

We suggested at the beginning of this chapter that one of the consequences of the absence of regulation of private security is that there is relatively little solid information about the size, structure, and operation of the industry, and little indication that those claiming to talk for the industry as a whole are actually doing anything other than reflecting the views of the most powerful players. On the basis of our analysis both of existing sources of data (the Labour Force Survey, and the BT Business Database) and our national telephone survey, we have been able to provide empirically-based indicators of numbers of people employed in private security in England and Wales together with the number of firms in operation.

[78] House of Commons Home Affairs Select Committee (1995).

We have been careful throughout this discussion to recognise the limitations of our data. Despite these limitations, we believe the picture they present of Britain's private security industry is based on firmer foundations than those previously available. What our data collectively suggests is the existence of a large and relatively vibrant industry employing perhaps as many as one-third of a million people. Although in a general sense the survey confirmed much that was already suggested about the industry, it nevertheless provided significant detail about *inter alia*: the size and status of firms operating in different sectors of the industry; how long these companies had been operating; sources of staff and methods of recruitment; membership of trade/professional associations; and views on regulation of the industry.

One of the key issues raised by the above discussion, and one that is central to the extant literature on private security, is how is the recent growth—assuming that it is possible to show that the industry has been expanding—to be explained? Authors such as Shearing and Stenning, who have probably been more influential in this area than almost any others, are able to produce a considerable amount of data from North America—where there is licensing of private security—to show that there has been an enormous expansion in private security since the 1960s.[79] As we have argued, the information on the industry in Britain tends to be, at best, fairly inaccurate and, at worst, simply a fiction. There are sources of data available, however, which give some indication of trends over time in private security employment, and in the next chapter we consider these and explore competing explanations for the 'rebirth' of private security.

[79] Although in much of their work they are careful to note the breadth of function included under the rubric 'private security', the data they use to illustrate the expansion of the industry tends to focus on guards and investigators. Clearly, one might suppose that including other parts of the industry in the calculations would serve to illustrate the trend they highlight in even starker terms. What it would also do, and this is of some importance for some of the arguments that follow, would be to focus attention on precisely those areas in which the greatest expansion has taken place.

4

The Growth of Private Security

It is generally accepted that private security is a growth industry. Though much academic writing concerns trends in North America, similar developments are held to be occurring in the UK. As far as North America is concerned, Johnston notes that the main burst of expansion probably occurred during the 1960s and 1970s.[1] Shearing and Stenning have also documented large increases in employment in private security, in particular within contract guarding, in Canada and the USA during this period.[2] Comparable data for Britain has been harder to come by, although as we described in the previous chapter a range of estimates of the size of the industry have been made. These suggest that although the private security industry has grown less extensively than in North America, there has also been significant growth in Britain in recent decades. In this chapter we look at measures of the growth of private security over time, and assess different explanations for this growth.

Growth of private security over time

Measurement difficulties outlined earlier have clearly hampered attempts to examine growth in private security over time. In Britain, for example, although the Labour Force Survey (LFS) provides a useful measure of employment in certain parts of the industry, the fact that it was not established until 1973 means that only a short historical picture is available. Estimates produced by the industry itself tend to be extremely partial, being limited to specific sectors of the industry and even then only including the large, mainstream operators. There are, however, other sources which can be used to provide an indication of change over time. One of these is the Census of Population, which makes occupational and industry employment estimates based on a 10 per cent sample of the population. Once

---

[1] Johnston (1996).   [2] Shearing and Stenning (1983).

again, like some of the other data sources we have used, it is important to see the indications provided by the Census data as approximate, especially because there have been a series of changes in the
definitions of occupational categories over the years. Moreover, we
must note that Census data give us a handle on only one sector of
the private security industry, what has been called 'manned guarding'. Although this is clearly a significant drawback when talking
about trends in what is a broad and eclectic industry, it does at least
focus on that part of the industry which preoccupies most writers on
the subject.

Despite these limitations, the Census figures remain the best available estimates for change in employment over time. They suggest that
there has been a sustained growth in employment over the last forty
years of so. As in North America, the biggest expansion appears to
have occurred prior to 1980, with the rate of growth, if anything,
having slowed down in later years (See Figure 4.1).

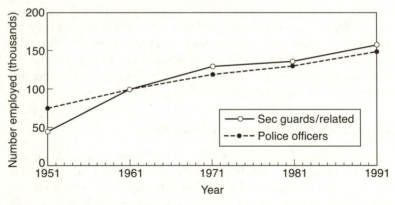

FIG. 4.1 Employment Levels in 'Policing': Great Britain 1951–1991
Source: the Census

The figures indicate that, since 1951, there has indeed been a huge
increase (approximately 240 per cent) in the numbers of people
employed in security and related occupations. The main spurt of
growth appears to have occurred during the 1950s and 1960s. After
1971, the numbers grew by just over a fifth, which over twenty years
is a substantial growth, but perhaps not as dramatic as is sometimes
suggested. However, we should also remember that the figures do not

include employment in what has probably been the major growth area in recent years, namely, the manufacture, installation and maintenance of electronic security equipment. Nonetheless, the available Census data are a helpful source, for much of the current debate is based upon the assumption of a dramatic expansion in employment, particularly in 'manned guarding'. The growth of 'security guards and related' occupations can be contextualised by examining comparable figures which chart the growth in employment of police officers. Figure 4.1 also illustrates the Census estimates for police officers in Great Britain.[3] The rate of growth since 1971 in numbers of police officers is quite similar to that of 'private security personnel' as measured by Census estimates. Taking comparisons back to 1951, the Census estimates suggest that police officer numbers have increased by almost 100 per cent, significantly less than the growth in security occupations (which doubled in size between 1951–61).

Given the already-mentioned difficulties in changes in definition of occupational categories, this is still an illuminating finding. It suggests that employment in security and related occupations probably overtook that of police officers during the 1960s, since when both have shown similar rates of growth over time. It underlines the fact that the expansion of employment in security-type functions is not a new phenomenon, a theme which we develop later in the chapter.

Explaining the growth of private policing

The extant literature distinguishes two general types of explanation for the 'rebirth' of private policing. Each overlaps in some ways with the other, and the distinctions we draw here are not always easy to maintain. The first of the approaches we have called 'fiscal constraint' theory, the second 'structuralist' or 'pluralist' theory. We examine the essential elements of each below, and consider in broad terms how such theories might apply to the growth of private security in Britain.

---

[3] Note that this figure is for police officers only, and does not include civilian employment in the police service, which is not identifiable from Census tables. If we could include figures for civilian employment, the rate of increase in police personnel would be much steeper. Furthermore, the figures are Census estimates rather than official police establishments, and will therefore not be exact. In fact, they slightly over-estimate the official figures, but still provide a good approximation for the current purpose.

Fiscal constraint theories

This is a general term covering a range of theories, and has been used by other authors in the field.[4] In general, the rise of non-public forms of policing are taken to reflect the growing pressures on capitalist states following the breakdown of post-war corporatism. More particularly, efforts by governments to control the rate of growth of public expenditure, liberalisation of markets, privatisation and contracting out, and the range of policies aimed, in Margaret Thatcher's words, at 'rolling back the frontiers of the state', have had major implications for public service provision. In Britain, the police and criminal justice system were in a uniquely favourable position compared to other public services in the early 1980s. However, starting in 1983, similar policies were applied to the police service. The basic argument for 'fiscal constraint' theorists is that policing, like other public services, has seen a growing restriction in funding, and this has led to the private security sector 'filling the gap'. As Reiner succinctly put it: 'British Police PLC is facing competition from a burgeoning private sector, the expansion of which is fuelled by holding back expenditure on public policing'.[5] There are two relatively distinct schools within this overall approach. These we have called the 'liberal democratic' and the 'radical'.

The 'liberal democratic' approach within fiscal constraint theories presents the growth of private security largely as a consequence of restrictions on resources for the state constabularies. First associated with the RAND corporation report on private security in the United States in the 1970s,[6] it has also been characterised as the 'junior partner' approach to the development of private security, an approach which takes the view that the 'policing' functions performed by private agencies are largely complementary and supplementary to the activities of the 'public' police. In the 'junior partner' theory, private security is primarily focused upon the 'preventive' element of policing, and tends not to encroach on the central elements of state policing. Shearing describes how, prior to the RAND study, the official debate about private policing was framed in terms of the need to prevent 'private armies' from challenging the sovereignty of the nation

---

[4] See, for example, Johnston (1996).

[5] Reiner, R. (1995) *Independent,* 12 Oct. 1995.

[6] Kakalik J. S. and Wildhorn S. (1972) *Private Police in the United States* (the Rand Report) (4 vols.) National Institute of Law Enforcement and Criminal Justice, Washington: US Department of Justice.

state. He argues that the RAND report 'transformed the issue of public or private policing from a question of politics and sovereignty to be responded to in absolute terms to a matter of economics and efficiency'.[7] Those who subscribed to the 'junior partner' view of private policing saw it in much less threatening terms, as simply another industry offering a service to the public. These ideas were taken on board by a later government enquiry into the private security industry which resulted in the Hallcrest Report.[8] This recorded the continuing growth of private security in the USA, a pattern of growth so strong that private security might more accurately be thought of as an 'equal partner' rather than a 'junior partner' to the public police.

These theoretical conceptualisations of private policing are considered in more detail later in the book. The current concern is how good an explanation they can provide for the apparent growth of private policing. We shall therefore examine how far recent trends in expenditure on the public police, and the direct privatisation of policing functions, can explain the expansion of private security.

It is clearly impossible to make a case for the absolute restriction of resources for public policing being a central cause behind the rise of private security. Indeed, as figure 4.2 shows, public expenditure on policing has risen substantially in real terms over the last fifteen years at least.

There was a dramatic increase in expenditure on the police in the years immediately following Margaret Thatcher's election victory in 1979, and although this rate of growth slowed somewhat after the early 1980s there was, in total, a 50 per cent increase in real terms between 1979 and 1989. However, during this period there were also substantial rises in crime, whether measured by police statistics or victimisation surveys. Such increases in crime are just one aspect of the increase in the police workload over recent years, calls for assistance, recorded incidents, and the administrative burden on police officers all having grown substantially as well. Thus, whilst real expenditure on public policing has grown, it is probably reasonable to argue that it has been outstripped by the increasing demands upon police resources. Some sources have identified an 'insatiable' demand by the public for more policing, which could never realistically be

---

[7] Shearing C. D. (1992) 'The relation between public and private policing', in Tonry and Morris (eds.) *Modern Policing: crime and justice: a review of research*, Vol. 15, University of Chicago Press, p. 410.

[8] Cunningham and Taylor (1985).

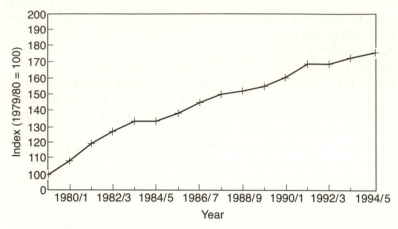

FIG. 4.2 Police Expenditure: England and Wales 1979/80–1994/95
Source: CIPFA Police Statistics adjusted using RPI average earnings index

met by expansion in public expenditure alone.[9] This has led to perceptions of under-funding within the police service, and such a perception forms the central plank of the Police Federation's criticisms of the growth in private security. They have argued that in failing to fund the public police service adequately, the government has introduced privatisation 'by the back door'.

During the late 1980s, the government's privatisation programme was extended to the criminal justice system more widely. As we described in Chapter Three, private sector involvement in detention functions began as far back as 1970, from which point immigration detention centres have been run by private security firms. More recently, of course, we have seen direct involvement of the private security industry in the prison system, both in terms of building and running prisons, and in terms of providing escorts to and from courts/police stations, and undertaking guarding functions within courts. The early 1990s saw widespread speculation that the government was considering a much broader programme of privatisation of policing functions. The Sheehy Inquiry into Police Responsibilities and Rewards (which reported in 1993) reflected the increasingly busi-

[9] Police Foundation/Policy Studies Institute (1996) Independent Committee of Inquiry into the Role and Responsibilities of the Police, *Final Report*, London: Police Foundation/Policy Studies Institute.

ness-like environment which the police occupied.[10] It made over 200 recommendations, including the introduction of fixed-term contracts, performance-related pay, the reduction of starting pay and the linking of pay rates to non-manual private sector earnings. Following a major campaign of opposition led by the police service, a much watered-down version of the report's recommendations were eventually to be adopted by the government.

Although the Sheehy Inquiry was the focus of much of the police service's concern about privatisation, it was perhaps the Home Office 'Review of Police Core and Ancillary Tasks' which initially suggested that a major programme of privatisation could be in the offing. The establishment of the review led to widespread speculation that the Treasury was pressing for a large-scale hiving off of tasks currently undertaken by constabularies to the private sector.[11] The terms of reference of the review were: 'To examine the services provided by the police, to make recommendations about the most cost-effective way of delivering core police services and to assess the scope for relinquishing ancillary tasks.' In the event, the tasks which the Review identified as suitable for privatisation proved to be relatively uncontroversial things such as parking enforcement and escorting wide loads. Although privatisation proposals were not as drastic as had been expected by some commentators, they still provided significant opportunities for the staffed services sector of the private security industry. For example, as we outlined in Chapter Three, private security firms are ideally placed to bid for contracts to enforce local parking regulations, and will increasingly undertake the escorting of heavy loads on motorways and trunk roads (though full-scale privatisation of the traffic policing function has been mooted[12]).

It is clear, then, that the day-to-day practice and the public face of policing in Britain has changed significantly in the past twenty years. Official crime rates have continued to escalate, public faith in the police has fallen,[13] and both of these processes have coincided over the past decade or so with a reformist government determined to

[10] See, Jones, T. and Newburn, T. (1997) *Policing After the Act*, London: Policy Studies Institute.

[11] Home Office (1995) *Review of Core and Ancillary Tasks*, London: HMSO.

[12] See Joslin, P. (1994) 'Traffic and crime go together', *Police*, Feb. 1994; 'Privatisation of motorway policing under review', *Independent*, 10 Mar. 1994.

[13] Skogan, W. (1990) *The Police and Public in England and Wales: A British Crime Survey Report*, Home Office Research Study No. 117, London: HMSO.

overhaul public services, particularly by applying private sector management strategies, and increasing competition through privatisation. However, it is our view that although clearly an important contributory factor, these developments cannot by themselves explain the 'rebirth' of private and other forms of policing. As we have seen, in real terms, expenditure on the (public) police has expanded rapidly in recent years, and the numbers of police officers have similarly grown. Despite the mediating presence of rapidly increasing demands, the contemporaneous growth of the public and the private sector illustrates the difficulty of explaining the rebirth of private policing as a reflection of the state's fiscal crisis. Similarly, although there have been important developments in terms of privatisation of certain police functions, on the whole, the more radical developments feared by some commentators and proposed by others, failed to emerge. We must therefore look to other theories for fundamental explanations of the growth of private policing.

'Radical' versions of fiscal constraint theories see the growth of private security as a natural and inevitable development of capitalist logic. The capitalist state, it is argued, undergoes a series of crises which threaten its legitimacy. The state seeks to legitimise its activities in a number of ways, one of which is to try to enlist the private sector's aid in the fight against crime. Thus, the kinds of 'policing' forms which evolve are the result of the type of capitalism prevailing at a given moment in history. Spitzer and Scull's extensive account of the rise of public forms of crime control, and the subsequent privatisation of these forms is one example of this kind of argument.[14] In their view, the collapse of the tight-knit, homogenous communities of feudal England rendered inadequate the previous informal, voluntary systems of social control. The growth of capitalism and, in particular, the development of an industrial working class, placed public order as a crucial priority for the emerging system: 'a stable public order was a precondition of rational calculation on the part of industrial capitalists'.[15] However, this problem was not amenable to private solutions due to what we described in Chapter Two as the 'free-rider effect'. Spitzer and Scull noted that 'while capitalists as a class required a hitherto unprecedented degree of social order, it was

[14] Spitzer, S. and Scull, A. (1977) 'Privatisation and capitalist development: the case of private police', *Social Problems* 25, 1, pp. 18–29.
[15] Ibid, p. 27.

in the interests of no one of them, as an individual, to provide or contribute to its provision'.[16] Thus, the management of crime became rationalised and transformed into a central responsibility of the state (see Chapter One).

Developments in the second half of the twentieth century, it is argued, have taken capitalism to the stage where publicly-provided forms of social control are themselves becoming less capable of providing the order which the system requires. The protection of profit has become a much more complicated process than it was under nineteenth century industrial capitalism, when the primary concern was with controlling the labour supply. The development of large multinational corporations, and the rapid pace of technological change have made this equation much more complicated. Corporations are increasingly looking to achieve restitution, for flexibility, and for efficiency in responding quickly to changes in consumer demand. All these are arguably more effectively provided by private than public policing.

A related argument here concerns the transformation of 'security' into a commodity within late capitalist societies. Gorz notes the paradox that capitalism actually required uncertainty, and therefore a degree of insecurity, for its development, although individual agents within the system work to reduce uncertainty to operate and profit.[17] Spitzer has argued that security has been 'commodified', created symbolically, through the development of images and expectations.[18] However, Spitzer argues that the pursuit of security via the market is doomed to failure, because 'the more we enter into relationships to obtain the security product, the more insecure we feel; the more we depend upon the commodity rather than each other to keep us safe, the less safe and confident we feel; the more we divide the world into those who enhance our security and those who threaten it, the less we are able to provide it for ourselves'.[19] Loader also usefully develops this point about the self-generating demand for more security. He notes that all bodies concerned with the provision of security have a 'vested interest in fear', and observes that private security firms 'have

[16] Ibid, p. 28.

[17] Gorz, A. (1989) *Critique of Economic Reason*, London: Verso.

[18] Spitzer, S. (1987) 'Security and control in capitalist societies: the fetishism of security and the security thereof', in Lowman *et al. Transcarceration: Essays in the Sociology of Social Control*, Aldershot: Gower.

[19] Ibid, p. 50.

first to generate a demand for their products by stimulating and channelling people's anxieties and desires in particular ways'.[20]

One theme in radical analyses interprets the growth in private security as a sinister widening of the net of state control.[21] Thus, the growth of private security does not so much signal the end of public coercion, but rather helps to establish a two-tiered, interdependent system of social control, which may ultimately be more pervasive (although less *visibly* connected with the state). Although, on the surface, the state police are 'one player amongst many in the system of policing',[22] in reality what is emerging is a coherent policing system, which poses much greater threats to the civil liberties of the individual than the state police alone ever could.[23] On this view, more and more of daily life is coming under the control of an oppressive capitalist state. Although privatisation may appear on the surface as the state giving up powers and responsibilities, this disguises what is in reality an increase in the state's powers of coercion, in that it has at its disposal a formidable 'reserve arsenal' of social control. There is some disagreement amongst radical commentators here, with the legal pluralists noting that private systems of justice may come to challenge the formal state systems of laws and regulations. However, the radical interpretation would be that private security is simply a more subtle manifestation of the coercive powers of the leviathan state, and the evidence of state–corporate alliances suggests the development of selective policing biased in favour of wealth and power.[24]

Structuralist or 'pluralist' theory

Writers in this school depart from those in the fiscal constraint camp in a number of ways. Unlike Spitzer and Scull, for example, they do not view the growth of private policing bodies as illustrative of the ever-widening gaze of a leviathan state. Although the gaze may still be widening, it is not the gaze of the nation-state (which they argue is declining in importance) but is rather the 'unremitting watch' of private corporations. Unlike both the liberal democratic and radical versions of the fiscal crisis theory, authors in the structuralist or plu-

[20] Loader, I. (1997) 'Private security and the demand for protection in contemporary Britain', *Policing and Society*, 7, pp. 143–62.

[21] Cohen, S. (1979) 'The punitive city: Notes on the dispersal of social control', *Contemporary Crises*, 3, 4, pp. 339–64.

[22] Brogden, M. and Shearing, C. (1993) *Policing for a New South Africa*, London: Routledge.

[23] Flavel (1973).   [24] Shearing (1992).

ralist camp view the process as one which involves the increasing importance of 'private justice' and the resolution of conflict in the private sphere without recourse to the official judicial system.[25] Indeed, this is an approach which, in some senses, has more in common with Foucault's vision of a disciplinary society[26] or Marx's notion of a 'maximum security society'[27] than to Cohen's vision of the future of social control.

There are then a number of authors who have suggested that the growth of private security cannot be explained solely in terms of restrictions of public expenditure on the police, or the deliberate contracting-out of functions to the private sector. As discussed in Chapter Two, Shearing and Stenning have argued convincingly that the growth of private security in North America was crucially related to the natural emergence of what they called 'mass private property'.[28] This refers to large, geographically-connected holdings of corporately-owned property to which access is, often routinely, open to large numbers of people, such as shopping centres, retail parks, large educational campuses, leisure parks, and large-scale privately owned residential complexes. Actual figures indicating the extent of growth of these kinds of space are difficult to come by. However, there is a widespread impression that the growth of mass private property has been substantial. Such developments have meant that during the second half of the twentieth century, more and more of public life is taking place on private property. Independently of the fiscal crisis of the capitalist state, the 'natural domain' of the public police is shrinking and that of private security is expanding. People are now more likely to be living, working, shopping, and spending leisure time in places which are protected by private security rather than the public police: 'The modern development of mass private property controlled by vast corporate conglomerates, and so frequently consisting of essentially "public places", is the critical change that has paved the way for the modern growth and influence of private security'.[29]

Shearing and Stenning have thus argued that a 'new feudalism' is emerging, in which private corporations have the legal space and economic incentives to do their own policing. In this view, mass private

[25] Reichman, N. (1987) 'The widening webs of surveillance: Private police unravelling deceptive claims', in Shearing and Stenning (eds.) (1987).

[26] Foucault, M. (1977) *Discipline and Punish*, Harmondsworth: Penguin.

[27] Marx, G. T. (1988) *Undercover: Police surveillance in America*, Berkeley: University of California Press.

[28] Shearing and Stenning (1981).   [29] Ibid, p. 240.

property has given large corporations a sphere of independence and authority which can rival that of the state. What we are witnessing, they argue, is not so much the emergence of an oppressive state–corporate alliance, but a fracturing of sovereignty, and a decline in the pervasiveness of state power. What is emerging instead is a complex network of micro-systems of power, within which ultimate power is not wielded by a single subject, there is no central source of command, and no practical centre of political life. In the future, governance is less likely to be monopolised by nation-states, and more likely to be in the hands of either local communities or, more likely, corporate interests.

The view of private security that underpins this theory is conceptually different is several important ways from the 'junior partner' theory outlined above. Hoogenboom has referred to it as an 'economic theory' which analyses private security in the context of systems of 'private justice', which are not only more pervasive but are qualitatively distinct from the formal criminal justice system.[30] On this view, the goals of private security are analytically different from those of the public police. The ultimate goal of private security is to prevent loss, rather than crime. Of course, it will seek to prevent criminal behaviour which poses a threat to the economic interests of its employers, but this does not change the overall balance of the priorities. We return to these arguments and, more particularly, the evidence on these questions from our local study in Chapter Six. Here, we need to assess the evidence about the rise of 'mass private property' in Britain, and its implications for policing.

Mass private property in Britain

As noted above, empirical evidence about the growth of mass private property is limited. The figures which Shearing and Stenning quote in support of their thesis are restricted to relatively few comments about property developers in one Canadian Province. And yet, the argument has clear resonance with the work of many North American geographers and their analyses of modern cities in North America. It is difficult to gather reliable figures about the range of types of 'mass private property' in the British context.

Developments in the retail sector in Britain do strike a chord with the North American experience. In particular, a number of sources

---

[30] Hoogenboom A. B. (1991) 'Grey policing: a theoretical framework', *Policing and Society*, 2, 1, pp. 17–30.

have drawn attention to the decline of the traditional 'high street' shops, and the development of what has been termed the 'americanisation' of British shopping.[31] These themes were explored in some detail by Beck and Willis who provided an detailed account of the evidence of the growth of 'mass private property' in the retail sector.[32] Over the past twenty years or so there has been a process of concentration in the retail sector, and in particular the growth of supermarkets or superstores, out-of-town retail parks, and large shopping complexes. These trends were particularly noticeable during the 1980s. For example, the number of small retail outlets fell from 188,000 to 85,000 in the twenty years to 1991.[33] In 1983 there were 1,270 superstores in Britain taking up 8.6 per cent of all retail space. By 1992 this had grown to 3,500 such stores accounting for 19 per cent of retail space. Poole noted that the first shopping centres opened in Britain during the 1960s, and by the early 1970s there were around 200.[34] By about 1994 this had multiplied around five times to nearly 1,000 such complexes. Beck and Willis noted that a declining proportion of such shopping centres were located in town centres (falling from over 75 per cent in 1982 to 59 per cent in 1994). Out-of-town retail parks have burgeoned during the 1980s; they first appeared in Britain in 1982 and within ten years this number had grown to 260. There are currently five 'giant' shopping centres, including Brent Cross, the Gateshead Metro Centre, Meadowhall in Sheffield, Lakeside in Essex, and Merry Hill in the West Midlands. However, despite the major attention given to the development of such large centres, it is important to note that they are far from typical. Indeed, a recent report from the British Council of Shopping Centres noted that 'despite the attention devoted to their characteristics and impact, the breakdown of shopping centres by size reveals that the very largest centres . . . are a relatively small proportion of total centre numbers and floorspace'.[35]

These developments—bearing in mind the reservations expressed above—have nevertheless had clear implications for traditional town centres and high streets. Beck and Willis referred to the 'dough-nut' syndrome in which consumers are attracted away from town centre

---

[31] Poole, R. (1991) *Safe shopping: The identification of opportunities for crime and disorder in covered shopping centres*, Birmingham: West Midlands Constabulary.

[32] Beck, A. and Willis, A. (1995) *Crime and Security: Managing the risk to safe shopping*, Leicester: Perpetuity Press.

[33] Ibid.   [34] Poole (1991).   [35] British Council of Shopping Centres (1993).

shops to large out-of-town shopping complexes such as shopping malls and retail parks, leading to debates about the 'death of the high street'. In terms of implications for policing, the same authors found that 'in shopping centres a significant degree of privatisation of policing has already taken place'.

Before attempting to draw direct parallels with the North American experience we should take note of recent evidence of a slowdown in this trend, and a fightback by traditional town centres. There have been belated developments to try to protect the high street in Britain, in terms of active refurbishment of town centres, increasingly supported by government policy. In 1994 the Department of the Environment announced new guidelines intended to restrict out-of-town developments, a development partly related to the government's desire to discourage the use of the motor car. Restrictions were tightened still further later in the year in response to the House of Commons Select Committee on the Environment. Some effects of this more restrictive policy were already becoming apparent by the mid-1990s. For example, only four out of the fifty giant shopping complexes planned during the 1980s actually went ahead, and there was a sharp decline in the number of successful planning applications to develop supermarkets during the early 1990s.

In general then, there have been clear developments of 'mass private property' in the retail sector, particularly during the 1980s, although such trends have slowed during the 1990s. The growth in shopping centres that has already taken place clearly increases the degree to which the shopping public are under the protection of 'private police' rather than public constabularies. However, there is evidence of slowdown, and it is possible that new planning restrictions have made further significant developments in this direction unlikely.

Other developments in the retail sector perhaps suggest that our future focus should be less upon the replacement of public police officers by security guards, but rather upon new technology, electronic surveillance, information exchange, and data protection. For example, there is one trend in shopping which may eventually come to threaten not simply the traditional high street, but also the shopping malls and retail parks. This is the development of the home shopping market, which consists of four segments: mail order, direct selling, direct marketing, and electronic shopping. If this really is the future of shopping behaviour, it will be a more fundamental 'privatisation' than that which has emerged with the growth of shopping malls. These kinds of service allow people to carry out their shopping without even leaving the 'private spaces' of the home or office. Market reports have estimated that in 1994 home shopping accounted for over 4 per cent of the total retail market in the UK, a slight increase in market share from 1988. At present, general mail order has the biggest share of the home shopping market, although other forms have been gaining ground over recent years. The newest development is the electronic shopping market, which, although not as advanced as its counterpart in the USA, is showing some signs of growth in Britain. There is now a satellite TV 'shopping channel', and in November 1995 the press reported that Barclays Bank had launched 'BarclaySquare', a shopping service through which users can order goods from various retailers via the Internet. An increasing number of retailers are looking to participate in online shopping, raising images of the electronic 'virtual mall' of the future.

Another aspect of the mass private property thesis concerns the development of 'privately-policed' work complexes. Any visitor to the centres of most large cities in Europe or North America would note a concentration of large office blocks and work complexes. However, in Britain at least, the evidence suggests that the long-term trend is towards smaller rather than larger workplaces. The first half of the twentieth century saw a gradual increase in the average size of workplace. However, during the last twenty years or so there has been a noticeable decline in the proportion of total employment in larger establishments. One of the many reasons given for the decline in trade union membership in Britain over the last twenty years is the disappearance of the kind of workplaces where they had previously flourished, in particular large manufacturing establishments. The British Census of Employment shows that there has been a clear trend away from larger workplaces. Although the data cover only establishments with more than 25 employees, there is evidence that the growth in workplaces below this size is even greater. Thus, for example, between 1977–1987 there was a 12 per cent increase in the number of workplaces with 25–49 employees, and a 37 per cent decrease in those with more than 2,000 employees.

Recent evidence about the growth of small firms also suggest that the mass private property thesis has limited applications to British workplaces. Figures from the Department of Trade and Industry show that small firms (employing less than 100 people) are the source of about half of non-government employment in Britain.[36] Other trends, such as the growth of home working, also suggest that people will be less likely to work in large establishments in the future.[37] Of course, these developments do not mean that the mass private property thesis is irrelevant. Although smaller workplaces are undoubtedly increasing, most employees continue to work in large workplaces. However, it does provide some counter-balance to the notion of employees concentrated in 'mass' work communities, watched over by the private police of security companies.

Comparative data on another example of mass private property—leisure parks and complexes—are also hard to find. In recent years, Europe has experienced the appearance of the classic 'leisure' example of Shearing and Stenning's 'mass private property', with the opening of Disneyworld in Paris. Britain has seen a number of significant developments such as Centreparks, Alton Towers, and other large privately-owned leisure areas. In 1991, there were fifty-seven leisure parks in the UK, the majority of which have opened since 1970. On average, these had a greater number of visits than country parks, farms, steam railways, and visitor centres put together.[38] Thus, there is some evidence of the growth of 'mass private property' in the leisure field, although this appears to amount more to gradual change rather than 'quiet revolution'.

The final kind of mass private property that has been mentioned is residential accommodation. It is this which Shearing and Stenning suggest provides the most direct example of the decline in the sphere of the public police. There have undoubtedly been substantial developments of this kind in North America. The growth in privately-owned residential complexes has been so great, probably accounting for the most significant privatisation of US local government responsibilities,[39] that it has led to discussions about 'private governments'. Lavery[40] notes that the central development of this kind is the 'community association' (CA) in which each owner is a member of a prop-

---

[36] Department of Trade and Industry (1995) *Small and Medium Sized Enterprise Statistics for the UK, 1993*, Small Firms Statistics Unit, DTI, June 1995.

[37] Office for Population, Census and Surveys (OPCS) (1994) *Social Trends* 1993, London: HMSO.

[38] English, Scottish, Northern Ireland and Wales Tourist Boards (1992).

[39] Advisory Commission on Intergovernmental Relations (1989) *Residential Community Associations: Private Governments in the Intergovernmental System?* ACIR: Washington DC.

[40] Lavery, K. (1995) 'Privatisation by the Back Door: The Rise of Private Government in the USA', *Public Money and Management* 15, 4, Oct.–Dec. 1995.

erty organisation, having to comply with its rules and also pay for a number of services provided collectively:

Living in a CA is part of the American way of life. One in eight Americans now live in CAs, some 32 million people. There are over 150,000 CAs in the US with nearly 12 million housing units; the average-sized CA will have around 500 housing units. Over 50 per cent of new house sales in the large metropolitan areas are in CAs, which can range in size from a three unit condominium to a 19,000 unit planned community. CAs are a $20 billion business.[41]

Similarly, the notion of 'private government' has been applied to the development of business districts in city centres. Britain has seen an increasing number of local authorities introducing 'town centre management' in recent years. However, Lavery notes a number of important differences from the US experience, in particular that, in Britain, the majority of town centre management schemes are largely funded by the public purse, and have a narrower remit than the American 'Business Improvement Districts' (BIDs).

Shearing and Stenning provide some limited data for North America, charting the growing number of companies building new residential accommodation, and what has undoubtedly been a concentration of mass property ownership amongst a relatively small number of corporations in one Canadian Province. Mike Davis offers a damning critique of the consequences of what he calls the 'enclavisation' of suburban USA, with the wealthy moving to large, privately-owned residential complexes outside the centre of town, policed by private security.[42] Outside these 'gated communities', the public police are left to face the criminalised poor in 'places of terror'. Partly because of the force and style with which he puts his arguments, Davis's vision has frequently been held aloft as an illustration of what is most likely to be an ineluctable future trend in British urban development, and possibly a partial description of what is already occurring, albeit on a smaller scale than in contemporary Los Angeles. 'The American city', he argues, 'as many critics have recognized, is being systematically turned inside out—or, rather, outside in. The valorized spaces of the new megastructures and super-malls are concentrated in the centre, street frontage is denuded, public activity is sorted into strictly functional compartments, and

[41] Community Associations Institute (1993) *Community Associations Factbook*, Alexandria, Va: CAI.
[42] Davis, M. (1992) *City of Quartz,* London: Vintage, p. 244.

circulation is internalized in corridors under the gaze of private police'.[43] Although there are self-evidently many profound differences between the North American and British experiences, one is frequently struck by the degree to which some commentators, especially in the media or in the police, appear to believe that something approximating Mike Davis's vision is already at large here.

It is difficult to obtain firm evidence about the extent of such developments in Britain, although what evidence there is shows important differences from the North American situation. As Bottoms and Wiles have argued, one of the significant differences between metropolitan development in many North American cities and those in post-war Britain is the massive intervention by local government in housing markets.[44] This perhaps prevented the pattern of 'enclavisation' appearing as strongly in Britain, although there are undoubtedly some places where the process is apparent. In London, for example, such kinds of housing are visible in the newly developed Docklands areas, and many of the new riverfront developments are apartment-style dwellings. However, finding evidence of a dramatic transformation in popular residential dwelling is much more problematic. Data from the General Household Survey (GHS), for example, do not show a huge increase in the proportion of households living in flats or apartments, at least in recent years. In fact, the proportion of households in the survey which were described as detached, semi-detached or terraced house, was about the same in 1993 as it was in 1971. Of course, the main move towards large residential blocks in British cities occurred during the 1960s, but these developments mainly involved public housing, rather than the appearance of mass private property. Few of these developments, if any, were policed by private security, although recent years have seen some local councils introduce private security patrols of council housing estates and blocks, and CCTV surveillance is increasingly installed in public housing estates. Finally, although there may be a move towards more of these US-style developments in the future, this, as Lavery noted, 'would have limited impact as there is relatively little new development in the UK, especially when compared to the US'.[45]

    [43] Davis, M. (1992) *City of Quartz*, London: Vintage, p. 226.
    [44] Bottoms, A. E. and Wiles, P. (1994) 'Understanding crime prevention in late modern societies', Paper presented to the 22nd Cropwood Round Table Conference: Preventing Crime and Disorder: Targeting Strategies and Community Responsibilities, Cambridge: Institute of Criminology.
    [45] Lavery (1995), pp. 49–53.

Mass private property in Britain—an overview

The argument that the growth of 'mass private property' is the significant development underpinning the rise of private security is an intuitively attractive one. Important developments have indeed taken place, although it appears that these are not as far-advanced as is the case in the USA. The empirical data about the extent to which mass private property has increased, and what type, has yet to be gathered in the context of arguments about private security in the UK. Shearing and Stenning provide a crucial contribution to our understanding of private policing by relating it to the changing structure of property relations, in particular to the increasing visibility of the guarding sector. However, we should be careful not to over-emphasise this development in explanations of the rise of private security more generally in Britain. First, the empirical evidence suggests a gradual transition rather than what Stenning and Shearing have termed a 'quiet revolution'.[46] Second, as we move into the late 1990s and beyond, the focus will arguably shift away from staffed services—security guards in caps and uniforms. Future developments suggest that the electronic and physical security equipment sector will be of growing importance. It may well be that future developments are 'privatising' life (at least for some people) to a more extreme degree than the move to public–private space, particularly with the development of home-shopping, home-working, and increasingly, home-based leisure activities.

There are some further important differences between the North American and the British context. In particular, there have been far fewer privately-owned developments in the housing and educational sectors. For example, in the USA the housing market has traditionally been free of government controls, and there has been very little public provision in the housing market.[47] This has allowed a greater development of large privately-owned residential estates and complexes, and the development of 'gated communities' policed by private security rather than the public police.[48] In North America many universities are privately-owned, in strong contrast to the UK in which only a small minority of higher education institutions are

---

[46] Stenning and Shearing (1980).

[47] Boleat, M. and Taylor, B. (1993) *Housing in Britain*, London: The Building Societies Association.

[48] Benson, B. L. (1990) *The Enterprise of the Law: Justice without the state*, San Francisco: Pacific Research Institute for Public Policy.

private concerns. In addition, despite the growth of private health care in Britain, the majority of people are still treated in publicly-funded National Health Service hospitals.

These differences in context have important implications for the mass private property argument. In particular, as we shall see when we come to look at the situation in Wandsworth—the focus of our local area study—many of the relevant properties (shopping centres and superstores, gated communities/large residential complexes, parks and open spaces, educational establishments, office and industrial complexes, and hospital sites) are in fact either state-owned, or have an ambiguous sectoral status.

Other explanations

Both 'fiscal constraint' and 'pluralist' theories place the rise of private policing in the context of structural changes in capitalist societies. However, although both raise what have undoubtedly been important developments in the growth of private policing, by themselves they remain inadequate conceptualisations of what is happening. This is particularly the case when we consider the development of what Johnston terms 'hybrid' forms of policing. The rise of non-Home Department forces, and the growth of bodies carrying out regulatory and investigative functions are related to the rise of the 'welfare complex', and the growth of local government responsibilities over the twentieth century. This would suggest that the most substantial period of growth of employment in such bodies in Britain occurred during the 1950s and 1960s. This is a strong theme of Hoogenboom's analysis of 'grey policing', which outlines the concept of a 'police-welfare' complex, in which the growth of welfare state provisions created new categories of crime, and corresponding methods of enforcement and regulation.[49] In this sense, the rise of Johnston's 'hybrid' policing bodies, preceded both the period of heightened financial control which led to 'fiscal constraint', and the period which saw the widespread appearance of mass private property. In Britain, special police forces, such as the British Transport Police (BTP), appeared as a direct alternative to private policing. When the rail networks were nationalised, the BTP became responsible for the policing of what became mass 'public' (in terms of ownership) property. This introduces some doubts about how far we can

[49] Hogenboom (1989).

explain the rise of both private security and 'hybrid' policing bodies by the same factors.

These anomalies, however, are also present in Johnston's third category of explanation of the rise of private policing: what he refers to as 'restructuring and late modern social change'.[50] In the economic sphere, post-Fordist techniques of production, increased fragmentation and specialisation, increasingly flexible work practices, and the division of the labour market into core and peripheral jobs are phenomena common to many economies. The growth of the service sector, the incidence of contracting-out non-core functions, and the paradoxical pressures of decentralisation of service delivery responsibilities and concentration of management controls are all witnessed in British policing. Such explanations provide a way of reconciling the conflict between the strong impression that private security guarding has expanded dramatically over the last decade, and the fact that this does not seem to be borne out by the figures illustrated in Figure 4.1. The increasing tendency for companies to contract-out non-core services in general[51] and security in particular[52] means that a growing proportion of the people employed in these functions are employed by specialist security firms, rather than 'in-house'. This makes for a much more *visible* security guarding industry, and one which might be more clearly measured by indicators such as numbers of firms, rather than total employment.

Johnston also highlights growing diversity in the social and cultural fields, in which increasing social and ethnic divisions have fragmented the societies which are being policed. Finally, he points to the growing body of work on state restructuring, which is occurring as a result of the dual pressures of globalisation and localisation—described as the 'unravelling'[53] or the 'stretching'[54] of the state—which has impacted in important ways on the structure and functioning of the police.

This is an interesting and attractive approach for ordering what has been happening not only in the policing sphere, but also in other spheres of economic, cultural, and social life. The growth of 'non-public' forms of policing, for example, can be accommodated within a framework which stresses fragmentation, diversity, flexibility, and

[50] Johnston (1996).
[51] Ascher, K. (1987) *The Politics of Privatisation*, London, Macmillan.
[52] British Security Industry Association (1994).
[53] Crook, S., Pakulski, J. and Walters, M. (1993) *Postmodernization: Change in Advanced Societies*, London: Sage.   [54] Bottoms and Wiles (1994a).

specialisation. What is less clear, however, is exactly how far this *explains* what is happening to policing, rather than simply describes the developments. It is difficult to disagree with Johnston when he argues that it is: 'clear that many of the changes identified are, in fact, by no means peculiar to the sphere of policing'.[55] Nevertheless, the fundamental dynamics which lie behind the specific changes in policing remain partly unidentified in the 'late modern change' thesis.

Concluding comments

We have examined the available evidence about the growth of private security (and other forms of policing) in Britain. The only source of information currently available about change in levels of security employment over the longer period is the Census of Population. These figures should be treated with caution for two reasons. First, as with other estimates they cover only part of the wide range of activities covered by the term 'private security', the security guarding sector. Second, because of changes in definitions and occupational classifications over time, the estimates are rather rough approximations. However, the data suggest that employment in security and related occupations has undergone a steady rise over the last forty years. This rise has perhaps not been as recent a phenomenon as we are sometimes led to believe and, what is more, employment in these occupations appears to have exceeded sworn police officers during the 1960s. The growing attention paid to private security may thus reflect a growing visibility and pervasiveness (due to developments in contemporary society), rather than a sudden explosive rise in total numbers of people employed (although numbers employed have clearly risen).

In recent decades crime has risen and general levels of insecurity have gathered pace, at the same time as increasing financial constraints have been placed on all public services, including the police. One might expect that as the police become increasingly stretched so other service providers would enter the frame to 'take up the slack'. Given the fact that the government of the time was ideologically committed to privatisation in many spheres, it might seem likely that fiscal constraint, or even 'crisis', might be one of the key developments behind the rebirth of private security. However, although this is persuasive, it is by no means a complete explanation for recent

[55] Johnston (1996) p. 56.

trends in private policing. Something much more fundamental is occurring. To take one key example, there is some evidence to suggest that the site of greatest expansion in the private sector has been in electronic surveillance equipment. The development of this market, however, has by no means been dependent upon the alleged shrinking capacity of the police, except insofar as the police have arguably been increasingly unable to meet public desires for security.

A further notable development in contemporary society has been the emergence of 'mass private property' guarded, in the main, not by public constabularies but by private security. This has been a particular feature of North American society, although it is possible to detect a similar trend in Britain. However, although intuitively it may seem reasonable to argue that there has been a dramatic increase in the amount of public life taking place on mass private property, it is difficult to find evidence of revolutionary change in Britain. There have been significant developments in the retail sector, with the rapid growth of shopping centres and out-of-town retail parks, particularly during the 1980s. However, there is some evidence that the rapid growth of the 1980s has slowed down dramatically. Similarly, the development of 'mass private property' in the residential and employment sectors has been more limited in Britain. The average size of workplace is falling, and there is an increase in home-working. In the residential sector, Britain has not seen a large-scale shift towards large residential blocks patrolled by private security. Thus, whilst there are useful elements in all these theories about the rise of private security and other forms of policing, by themselves they are insufficient explanations of what is happening. In the following chapters we use a case study approach to look in detail at the growing complexity of policing bodies on the ground. Among other issues, this will allow us to consider how such 'global' theories of the rise of private security correspond to the reality of policing at the local level.

5
Policing Bodies in Wandsworth

In the two preceding chapters we focused on the first main objective of this study; that is, to gather indicative data about the size and shape of the private security industry in Britain. In this and the following two chapters we address the second broad objective of the research. This was to analyse the actual operation of so-called 'hybrid' and private forms of policing 'on the ground', and examine their relationship with Home Department police forces. Clearly this requires applying a considerably more circumscribed geographical focus—the London Borough of Wandsworth—to the subject matter of private security and public policing. The second objective was addressed by way of a detailed local study of the variety of 'policing' activities going on in one particular locality, and the relationships and boundaries between them. In this chapter we look in some detail at the nature of the policing organisations on the ground—their functions, powers, and geographical remit. Prior to considering the policing of the Borough, however, we first need to consider some of the background features of the Borough itself—a borough which has undergone significant changes over the last twenty years or so.

The London Borough of Wandsworth

It is important to remember that the local study is a case study. The intention is that it should therefore be illustrative rather than representative. Its worth lies more in the depth and quality of the data that can be collected, rather than the extent to which one could argue that what is observed there is necessarily transferable elsewhere. This is a particularly important point, because of course Wandsworth is in many ways a highly unusual local authority. As one of the Thatcherite 'flagship' boroughs, the local authority was at the forefront of innovation in terms of privatisation and liberalisation during the 1980s.

Wandsworth was chosen as the site for our local study for a number of reasons—its status as an innovative and radical supporter of privatisation made it in some ways ideal for research on public and private policing. Because of this history, there was perhaps no better place to study the dynamics of the relationships between the public and private sectors. In addition, the Borough presented a good mix in terms of socio-economic profile, ethnic minority group, housing type, and use of urban space. This last point was particularly important for the research, as it was vital that the local study include a variety of types of 'space'. As well as the array of 'private spaces' of offices and dwellings, the site chosen for the local area study had to include a number of 'public spaces' such as town centres and parks, as well as some examples of what Shearing and Stenning have termed 'mass private property'. The Borough includes a number of examples of such space, including shopping centres, a number of educational complexes, large office developments, and even a few large residential complexes. Thus, the Borough presented a variety of 'policing' problems for the range of 'policing' agencies operating within it. An additional reason for basing the local study in Wandsworth was related to the very range of policing agencies that were operating there. As well as the Metropolitan Police and a variety of 'private security' firms offering either staffed services, security equipment, or both, there were a variety of other policing bodies. Perhaps the most interesting of these was the Wandsworth Parks Constabulary, the largest and perhaps best-known example of a municipal police force currently in operation in Britain.

Wandsworth has been described as 'clearly the most privatised borough in London and probably the most privatised local district in the country'.[1] The Council was one of the first to apply the process of contracting-out to local government services, and the policy dates back to 1978 when the Conservatives won the Council from Labour, and pledged to reduce local rates by attacking bureaucratic inefficiency. In the early 1980s, in-house contracts for street cleaning services were compared with outside tenders with the result that there were fewer jobs and a more flexible work schedule for the in-house workforce. Despite such savings however, it was not long before contracts began to be awarded to outside tenders. Following the street cleaning contract, the Council announced its intention to invite

[1] Ascher (1987).

tenders for the refuse collection service. This led to a major programme of industrial action by Council employees, although the
return of the Conservatives to power in the local elections of 1982
dealt a body blow to the campaign of resistance. The Council successfully contracted-out the refuse collection service, and followed
this with the award of the contract for mobile gardening to an outside provider. Ascher described the significant problems which the
Council experienced with its first three privatised services.[2] However,
its enthusiasm for the policy did not abate, and by the end of 1984 a
further five services had been put out to contract. The overall effect
was a dramatic reduction in Council employment, which fell from
3300 to 1600 in the first half of the 1980s.

The Borough has seen major changes over the last twenty years or
so. In particular, a large proportion of the council housing stock was
sold off, and this is reflected in striking changes in tenure patterns in
the Borough. The policies of privatisation and contracting-out have
continued into the 1990s. Recent developments have included putting
housing management out to competitive tender. The Borough has set
up nine housing cooperatives, and two estates are currently privately-
managed. During the later years of the community charge, through a
combination of expenditure cuts and privatisation, the Borough was
able to levy a minimal charge; the contrast with neighbouring borough of Lambeth being huge. However, although this has been
clearly welcomed by large sections of the population within the
Borough, it has laid it open to charges of 'social engineering'. This,
it has been argued, has been an important contributing factor to
significant falls in recorded crime in the Borough over recent years.[3]

According to the 1991 Census the Borough had a population of
about 235,000, which represented a fall of almost seven per cent from
1981 (although all inner-London boroughs have experienced broadly
similar falls in total population). In terms of surface area, it is the
second largest inner-London borough, measuring 3,488 hectares. Like
other urban areas during the 1990s, it has suffered high unemployment rates, the male rate of unemployment as recorded in the Census
being 12.3 per cent. Compared to other inner-London boroughs
though, it rates relatively highly in terms of measures of affluence.

---

[2] Ascher (1987).
[3] This was mentioned in a speech by Professor David Downes at a conference
organised by Wandsworth Council in March 1995; the European Urban Delinquency
and Crime Conference 1995.

For example, its proportion of households which are owner-occupied, at 54 per cent, is the highest of all inner-London boroughs. The proportion of households with more than one person per room is about 4 per cent (the lowest in inner-London). The proportion of households owning two or more cars is over a tenth, the highest in inner-London, and although 44 per cent reported no car, this was one of the lowest proportions of all inner-London boroughs.

Who Polices Wandsworth?

In answering this question we will provide a general overview of the nature, status and organisation of the major policing bodies to be found in operation in the Borough. We have divided them up into two broad groups: public (in the sectoral sense) policing bodies and private security organisations. Public bodies we subdivide into three categories: the Metropolitan Police; other bodies of constables (such as Wandsworth Parks Police); and other public policing bodies (such as the Post Office Investigation Department[4]). As will be clear from the discussion in the earlier chapters, we have resisted using a third category—hybrid policing—for those bodies whose sectoral status others have argued to be ambiguous. We explain our position in relation to this particular 'boundary' in more detail in Chapter Seven; for the time being we locate such bodies under the general headings of 'other bodies of constables' or 'other public policing bodies'. In a similar manner, and for ease of understanding, we have also continued with the five point subdivision of private security that we first set out in Chapter Three. Table 5.1 illustrates the range of policing bodies which were operating in the Borough at the time of the study. It should be noted that this list is by no means exhaustive.

Home Department police forces—the Metropolitan Police

Wandsworth Borough is currently divided between two divisions of the Metropolitan Police: Wandsworth and Battersea. On those occasions when we refer to police officers in Wandsworth, this covers the whole of the Wandsworth Borough Council area, and not just the Wandsworth Division of the Metropolitan Police. Whilst the local

---

[4] Now reorganised into Post Office Security and Investigation Services (POSIS).

Table 5.1: Some policing bodies in the London Borough of Wandsworth

Home Department Police Forces
- Metropolitan Police (Battersea and Wandsworth divisions)

Other bodies of constables/special police forces
- British Transport Police
- Wandsworth Parks Police
- Ministry of Defence Police
- Atomic Energy Authority Constabulary

Other public policing bodies
- Environmental Health Officers
- Benefit Fraud Investigators
- [a] Housing Patrol Service
- Health and Safety Executive Investigators
- Post Office Investigation Department

Private security operations
- staffed services (e.g. site guarding, door supervisors, shopping centre security guards)
- investigatory (e.g. professional witness scheme, credit investigation services)
- alarm installation and security equipment

study was designed to include activities across the whole of Wandsworth, given the large size of the Borough, we focused in particular on two sectors, one in the west of the Borough and the other in the east. In 1994/95, the Metropolitan Police staffing of the two divisions covering the Borough totalled about 572 sworn police officers, plus about 200 civilian staff (see Table 5.2).

Sector policing

During the last three years, 'sector policing' has replaced the 'relief' system in the two divisions covering the Borough. The former system divided the day into three eight-hour shifts. The police divisional staff were divided into four large teams called 'reliefs'. One consequence of the relief system was that about the same number of constables were on duty at any given time. A relief was also responsible for policing the entire division for its shift. Dixon and Stanko noted how reliefs came to develop particular characteristics reflecting the beliefs and ethos of the officers and the approach of the relief inspector.[5]

---

[5] Dixon, B. and Stanko, E. A. (1993) *Serving the People: Sector policing and public accountability*, London: Islington Council.

Table 5.2: The Metropolitan Police staffing of Wandsworth
Borough 1994/95

Rank	Number of staff
Constables	437
Sergeants	100
Inspectors	25
Chief Inspectors	6
Superintendents	2
Chief Superintendents	2
Total police officers	572
Civilian staff (including Traffic Wardens)	251
TOTAL POLICE STAFF	823

Source: 1994/5 Annual Reports of Wandsworth and Battersea
Divisions of the Metropolitan Police

They found that under the old relief system any contact with the
public and agencies outside the police (other than responses to calls
for assistance) were the responsibility of specialist officers outside the
reliefs. These included crime prevention officers, schools liaison
officers and neighbourhood beat officers.

Sector policing has its roots in the 1980s experiments in 'neighbourhood policing', and is intended not just to change the organisation of operational policing, but to bring about more fundamental
changes in style as well. In particular, it is supposed to encourage
more localised policing by small teams of officers responsible for a
particular geographical area, and a more proactive and problem-
solving approach. Thus, when Sector Policing was introduced to the
Wandsworth and Battersea divisions, they were divided into a number of local areas or 'sectors', and smaller teams of officers (usually
a sergeant and between four and six constables) were given specific
responsibility for those areas. The aim was to promote greater knowledge of local areas and local people, as well as promoting 'ownership' of problems. The proactive approach was to be encouraged by
the development of new forms of consultation with the community.
These take the form of 'Sector Working Groups', within which problems may be raised and information shared with the local sector
inspector. These are like mini-police community consultative groups
within sectors (though they are not statutory), and they tend to
include representatives of local organisations as well as councillors.

Under Sector Policing, police divisional management can devise their own shift systems, with the overall aim of ensuring that most officers are on duty during the period of highest demand, whilst retaining adequate cover for response to calls for assistance from the public.

There was some feeling among Metropolitan police officers in Wandsworth that sector policing had yet to work out as planned. A good deal of police time was spent doing what was described locally as 'core policing', namely, responding to calls for assistance. The shift systems incorporated 'sector days' which were days intended to be devoted to the development of the proactive sector-based work. However, these days were often eaten into when there were staffing shortages, or during periods of high demand on police resources. This led to a widely-held perception of under-resourcing, both within the police organisation, and within bodies associated with the police, such as the community consultative group.

The sectors carry out a range of policing tasks: responding to calls from the public, investigating minor crime (major crime investigation is a divisional CID function), uniformed patrol, traffic, and some crime prevention/community relations-type activities. The divisional crime prevention office organises an annual summer activities scheme for young people on the local housing estates, in which sector officers participate. The local police have been active in raising sponsorship from local businesses to help fund such schemes. Each workteam has a designated 'neighbourhood beat officer' (NBO) who is tasked with establishing longer term contacts with the particular beat, and developing proactive projects. In practice, however, the NBOs find themselves taken off these duties to take part in response policing. Sector officers have taken part in organised policing operations jointly with the Parks Police and the New Covent Garden security force.

Other bodies of constables—National non-Home Office Police Forces

Although most police research in Britain has focused upon the 150,000 or so police officers in Home Department police forces, there is a range of other special police forces and bodies of constables. In 1977 it was estimated that there were 10,000 personnel with constabulary powers employed by nearly forty such forces in England and Wales.[6] Mason provided a list of thirty-five special police forces

---

[6] Miller and Luke (1977).

across the UK, and a further list of sixteen investigation departments for national public bodies.[7]

The British Transport Police

Perhaps the most visible of these 'special' police forces is the British Transport Police (BTP), the non-Home Department force which the general public are most likely to come across. The BTP trace their origins back to the 1820s when railways first began to be established in Britain.[8] Railway police were sworn in as constables under the particular Act of Parliament which created a new railway company, eventually resulting in a situation where there were over one hundred separate railway police forces. These police forces had two main functions. First, to protect the staff and property of the railway companies, and to deal with crime and order on the network. Second, to deal with public order problems involving the 'navvies' in towns near to the railway. At first, jurisdiction was limited to the railway premises and lines occupying a single county, but it was then extended to the whole line and a distance on either side. The BTP came into its current form with the nationalisation of the railways, and were created by section 53 of the British Transport Commission Act 1949. Until recently, approximately 80 per cent of the funding for the BTP came from central government, the remainder from the British Railways Board, although this balance has changed since privatisation. Now the majority of the income of the BTP comes from the private operating companies running the rail network.

The current legislation gives BTP officers constabulary powers 'in, on or in the vicinity of trains and premises belonging to or used or leased by users of BTP services and elsewhere for matters relating to those premises'. Thus, BTP officers can pursue, arrest and detain suspects using full police powers in the case of a crime committed on the railways. The Police and Criminal Evidence Act 1984 also enhanced the powers of the BTP, giving them police powers of search in goods areas in relation to vehicles as well as to people. There remain interesting grey areas in the jurisdiction of the BTP. Over the last thirty years or so they have been transformed from a largely static force towards an occupationally and geographically mobile police force with, for example, officers travelling from station to station in marked police vehicles. However, unless they deal with matters

---

[7] Mason, D. (1991).

[8] Appleby, P. (1995) *A Force on the Move*, Malvern: Images Publishing.

affecting railway premises, they only have the same powers as any member of the public. The BTP recruitment and training procedures are the same as their Home Office counterparts, with BTP officers undergoing additional training in matters specific to policing of the railways. Since the early 1980s, the BTP has used the same promotion examination system as is used by Home Office forces, and officers take the same examination papers. The rank structures are the same as those of provincial police forces in England and Wales, and there is close operational liaison with Home Office police forces. Joint operations, for example in the case of VIP protection, are common, and there are secondments of BTP officers to Home Office forces and vice versa. The close relations of the BTP with Home Department police forces are illustrated, for example, by the fact that chief officers of the force are members of various ACPO Committees. They are also all associate members of ACPO.

The BTP are a particularly interesting police force in the context of our focus on the different boundaries between policing agencies. First, there appears to be a significant degree of ambiguity surrounding the proper function of BTP officers when outside their jurisdiction. Second, government privatisation policy and its impact on the railways has potentially far-reaching implications for the continued operation and accountability of the BTP. In relation to jurisdiction, it appears that BTP officers are expected to continue to act as police officers even when outside their jurisdiction, and they will act as constables when requested to do so or in an emergency. Nevertheless, questions remain about the extent and strength of the legal safeguards for such practices under the current legislation. One reported incident occurred after the Bishopsgate bomb in the City of London when some BTP officers were helping their colleagues from the City of London and Metropolitan Police to hold back crowds. Businessmen wishing to cross police lines to return to their offices were prevented from doing so by BTP officers, and at least one well-informed worker challenged the BTP officer's right to prevent him from crossing the barrier that had been erected.

Government policy in relation to privatisation originally impacted on the BTP after the selling off of ports and harbours which, when they had been in public ownership, were policed by the BTP. The privatised Associated British Ports decided not to use BTP services, and made their own security arrangements. One case which received much attention was the privatisation of the Harwich port, which on becoming a Sealink port no longer employed the services of the BTP. However, escalating crime problems led the port authority to contract in a private security company, and using an old Act allowing the appointment of special constables in ports, they swore in the security guards as special constables. Recent years have seen privatisation extending to the very heart of the operations of the BTP, with the privatisation of the rail network itself. Since 1 April 1994, the British Railways Board has been the sole employer of BTP officers, and any of the new holding companies associated with the railways who wish to have BTP services must be party to a legal contract, called a 'police services agreement'. For most of these companies, the rail line operators, the agreement will not be optional, and so the threat to the BTP of being directly replaced by private security companies is not yet a real one. The standard agreement will lay down the core policing services to be offered by BTP as part of the contract. To operate under the new system, private companies must obtain a license from the Rail Regulator, one of the conditions of which is that they enter into a policing agreement with the BTP. This is not to say that private security companies have not been seen on the railways, for example the London, Tilbury and Southend line has a number of uniformed security personnel on patrol. But these are complementary to, rather than instead of, the BTP services. Thus, the BTP remain in a very central sense a 'public' police force (this theme is further developed in Chapter Seven).

In terms of our local study, the BTP police the various London Underground and South West Railways lines and stations in Wandsworth. The Borough of Wandsworth is covered by two large areas of the BTP, one operating out of Victoria and Waterloo stations, the other operating out of Stockwell station. It is not possible to estimate the exact staffing levels for the BTP in the Borough, because officers cover a much larger area. For example, the Waterloo police station has over forty police officers but they have the job of policing railway lines and property down to the South Coast. Thus, although BTP officers are clearly active within the Borough, it is not possible to isolate how many staff would be there at any one time. The chief inspector in charge of the Waterloo BTP office reported that BTP officers dealt with a range of policing problems in Wandsworth. A number of operations had been staged against graffiti and vandalism, as well as criminal damage and trespass. In addition they deal with actual and threatened violence on or in the vicinity of BTP property, as well as fraud and attempted fraud. The area covered by Waterloo has its own response cars, although there is an area car which will also respond to calls. Area HQ has sniffer dogs, which the BTP often use to search for suspect packages or to track suspects. The station staff are organised into five reliefs, each headed by a sergeant, providing 24-hour cover, seven days a week.

One development in the Borough which had involved quite extensive input from the BTP was the Safer Stations Scheme. In early 1992 the Council joined the Metropolitan Police in a formal partnership to launch a crime-fighting Charter. A local study showed that much street crime was centred around railway and tube stations in the Borough and, indeed, there had been an increase in crime of approximately 60 per cent at the stations in the borough between 1991 and 1992.[9] As a result of the activities of the Safer Stations Working Group in the Borough a wide range of initiatives were implemented, including CCTV at several stations, the installation of new lighting and, as their 1994 report put it, the 'development of a very close working relationship, (to an extent not previously achieved), with British Transport Police and Metropolitan Police'.[10]

A further, more maverick 'partner' in policing work around the stations has been the Guardian Angels. The BTP chief inspector reported that there had been a great deal of concern some years previously when the Guardian Angels were introduced to London. However, she had heard little of them for some years, although BTP officers still occasionally came across them on the underground system. In the early days, the BTP monitored the movements of Guardian Angels, and kept intelligence about prominent members, but it seems that they are no longer perceived as a threat. Moreover, in interview, one of the senior members of the London chapter said that some years previously the Guardian Angels had taken a policy decision to move their focus away from public transport.

The Ministry of Defence Police
Another important special police force, though one that is relatively invisible in Wandsworth, is the Ministry of Defence Police (MDP). MDP officers have full police powers at MOD establishments and on

---

[9] *Safer Stations*, Report and Action Plan prepared by the Wandsworth Partnership Safer Stations Working Group, London: London Borough of Wandsworth, February 1994.
[10] Ibid, p. 30.

Royal Navy ships. The MDP has been reduced in size over recent years. In 1992, Johnston noted a total MDP strength of about 5,000 officers. However, this has since fallen to a complement of about 4,500, and there have been suggestions that cuts in defence expenditure will lead to further reductions in staff.[11] The Metropolitan Police district and therefore Wandsworth, are covered by the G division of the MDP, which comprises over 1000 officers. This division also covers a further nine Home Department police forces to the east and north of the capital. Since there are no MDP bases actually in Wandsworth, it is reasonable to assume that it is rare for MDP officers to venture into the Borough. Nevertheless, recent reports have highlighted the fact that MDP officers do undertake policing operations away from MOD property. For example, MDP officers on vehicle patrol move between nine Metropolitan Police divisions whilst patrolling defence property in the capital, and are from time to time called upon for assistance by members of the public who do not differentiate them from Metropolitan Police officers. This led to calls by the MDP Federation for a review of legislation, and the granting of full constabulary powers for MDP officers dealing with 'emergency situations'.[12]

The force is responsible for the prevention and detection of crime within their jurisdiction, the protection of defence establishments, and the security of Crown property. As Johnston points out, 'the general rule is that offences committed against the MOD by members of the public, or by MOD civilians, are dealt with by the MDP. Offences committed by service personnel are the responsibility of the service police'.[13] The MDP are particularly visible in garrison towns such as Aldershot where they operate as a general police force, investigating all crimes, except the very serious categories like murder or manslaughter which are transferred to the local Home Department force. The MDP was established in 1971 from a merger of the former separate forces constabularies. As with the previous service constabularies, officers of the MDP had full constabulary powers over Crown property, and service personnel within fifteen miles of military installations, as well as on premises occupied by visiting forces. The Ministry of Defence Police Act 1987 extended the jurisdiction of the MDP to 'any place in the UK' under limited conditions.

---

[11] Ministry of Defence Police (1995) *Chief Constable's Annual Report,* 1994/95.
[12] 'MDP calls for full 999 powers' *Police Review* 26 Apr. 1996.
[13] Johnston (1992) p. 24.

Importantly, the Act also authorised the MDP to respond to requests for assistance by Home Department forces in the vicinity of military bases.

Questions about the jurisdiction of MDP officers may be of special concern given that all MDP officers are routinely trained in the use of firearms. Questions have been raised both about procedures for arming MDP officers when operating in public space, and the nature of the rules of engagement.[14] Government privatisation policy also has some potentially important implications for the MDP. For example, in 1984 the Royal Ordinance Factories were privatised and, despite stated intentions to keep the MDP in their role at these factories until an in-house security company had been recruited and trained, in 1988 the MOD announced intentions to introduce contract private security guards at some factories. Johnston noted the problems associated with the MOD policy of employing unarmed private security guards on routine guarding tasks.[15] The IRA bombing of the Deal barracks in 1989 focused attention upon the effectiveness of using private security for defence establishments, and in particular on the issues of vetting and pay of security staff.

Atomic Energy Authority Constabulary
The other main non-Home Department police force is the Atomic Energy Authority Constabulary (AEAC), to which the same issues of jurisdiction, accountability and legal powers apply. Again, such officers are not particularly visible in Wandsworth—accompanying trains with nuclear cargo being the most likely reason for their presence. The force, which was formed in 1955, has constabulary powers within UK Atomic Energy Authority (UKAEA) establishments, and within a fifteen mile radius of them in respect of offences against UKAEA property.[16] The Atomic Energy Authority (Special Constables) Act 1976 extended the geographical jurisdiction of AEAC constables carrying out escort duties of nuclear matter to any place where this task would make it 'expedient' for them to go. The Act also authorised constables to carry firearms without the necessity of obtaining a firearms certificate. Johnston noted that there had been a general lack of information about the structure, function and accountability of the AEAC, although by the end of 1988 the force establishment stood at nearly 700 officers. The same issues about

---

[14] See Johnston (1992).   [15] Ibid.
[16] See Johnston (1992) for a fuller account of the history and nature of the force.

operations within public space apply to the AEAC, although as with the MDP, ultimately it is the local Home Department force chief constable who has operational control.

Municipal policing

The development of 'municipal policing' is one of the most interesting developments of the 1980s. In terms of small policing bodies operating, under certain circumstances and within certain areas, with the powers of constables, municipal policing is a phenomenon largely confined to London. However, one of the most significant recent developments was the establishment of a 'community force' by Sedgefield District Council in Country Durham. This was set up in 1993, and consisted of a group of ten uniformed officers, with a remit to patrol housing estates and villages across the district. In addition to the patrollers, there are two administrative assistants and three control room staff, with full radio communications and a computer database. The patrol force has six vehicles and patrols 24-hours a day. The patrollers have no police powers, and are intended as a crime prevention force, to deter criminal and anti-social activity, and be 'extra eyes and ears' for the police. However, their uniforms are similar to police uniforms, and the patrol cars, whilst distinguishable from police panda cars, are similar enough to give them added authority.

In London, however, a number of local authorities have developed local municipal forces which are qualitatively different from the Sedgefield development in that they involve bodies of people who have, within certain jurisdictions and certain circumstances, constabulary powers. This has arisen from local authorities making use of the powers given to them in the Local Government and Housing Provisional Order Confirmation (Greater London Parks and Open Spaces) Act 1967, which allows local authorities to swear in employees as constables for the purposes of enforcing by-laws or enactments relating to parks and open spaces. This has been used by several London councils to set up Parks Constabularies, including the Royal Borough of Kensington and Chelsea, Greenwich, Brent (although the experiment was short-lived and the Parks Police were disbanded), Barking and Dagenham and, perhaps most notably, Wandsworth.

The Wandsworth Parks Police

History   The Wandsworth Parks Police was created in 1985, prior to which council-employed park-keepers had responsibility for the enforcement of council by-laws in the parks and open spaces of the Borough. By the mid-1980s, growing problems of crime and incivility in the parks suggested that this approach was no longer adequate, and the Council decided to establish its own Parks Police. When the Greater London Council was abolished in 1986, and the Borough Council took over responsibility for Battersea Park, the work of the Parks Police was significantly extended.

By 1995 the Parks Police employed thirty-five full-time staff plus a further twenty-five part-timers (the Parks Police version of 'specials'). The full-time staff undergo a six-week training course, and then spend a year on probation. The Parks Police largely rely on its own personnel as trainers. At the time of the research, the training officer was an ex-Metropolitan Police chief inspector who had had responsibility for training whilst a police officer. The basic training course covers legal matters relating to by-laws and the criminal law, arrest and restraint, first aid, and various more specialised courses relating to use of a radar gun to detect speeding cyclists, and getting into locked cars.

Legal powers   There is a good deal of ambiguity surrounding the legal status and jurisdiction of the Parks Police, even within their current activities. For example, Counsel's opinion provided to New Scotland Yard was that the 'constabulary powers' of the Parks Police are restricted to use inside the parks, and to cases involving infringements of council by-laws.[17] However, Counsel's opinion to Wandsworth Council was that Parks Constables, duly sworn-in by a magistrate, have the powers of police within the Council's parks and open spaces. Accordingly, the Parks Constables take the view that they have the powers of any police officer within the parks, and also have the power of 'hot pursuit' off the parks in cases of by-law infringement. This view is certainly confirmed by the 1995 report by the Director of Leisure and Amenity Services to the Council Committee of the same name. It states that the above-mentioned Act

---

[17] C. S. Porteous (1990) *re*: The Constitutional Position of Bodies such as the 'Wandsworth Parks Constabulary'. Unpublished legal opinion provided to the Metropolitan Police.

'gave the constables the powers of Police within the Council's parks and open spaces'.[18] Officers have carried out arrests for a wide range of offences other than simple by-law infringements, as the arrest statistics given below illustrate. Parks Police officers wear uniforms which are not dissimilar to those worn by Metropolitan Police officers, and their vehicles are clearly marked with the words 'Parks Police'.

In April 1994 Wandsworth Council announced that they were considering an extension of the operations of the Parks Police to include routine patrol of housing estates. The Metropolitan Police expressed strong concerns about such a proposal, and highlighted the dangers of allowing relatively less-trained uniformed officers to carry out general patrols in the public sphere.[19] However, it was unclear whether the supporters of the proposal envisaged that the Parks Police officers would be operating with the full powers of constables or would simply rely on citizen's powers. Elected councillors appeared to support the full use of constabulary powers, whereas council officers suggested that citizen's powers might be used in some cases if the proposal was implemented.

This confusion appeared to revolve around the legal definition of 'open spaces'. Although there were those who were prepared to argue that council-owned estates could come under the definition of 'open spaces', legal opinion appears to be agreed that such places would not be 'open spaces' under the Act, and thus Parks Police officers would have no extra powers over and above those of ordinary citizens. In addition, there were few by-laws which applied to the council estates, although recently the dog control by-laws were extended to cover them. The proposal to extend the remit of the Parks Police arose from a discussion about breaking up the service charges to residents on particular estates. Residents in the Borough are increasingly required to 'contract-in' particular services, rather than paying one block service charge covering cleaning, repairs, decoration, caretaking, and other functions. The idea was raised (in the main, it seems, by the Deputy Leader of the Council) that extra patrols by Parks Police officers would be a useful additional service to offer. Clearly, it was recognized that there would be a number of issues to be

[18] Wandsworth Borough Council (1995) *Report by the Director of Leisure and Amenity Services on the Wandsworth Parks Constabulary*. Paper 95/39, Jan. 1995.
[19] See 'Council "cops" to be banned', *Observer*, 29 Oct. 1995; 'Police look to protect image with copyright', *Independent*, 1 Mar. 1995.

addressed given the 'public good' characteristics of such a patrol service. For example, one of the issues to be resolved would be the proportion of an estate's residents that would need to agree before patrols were instituted. The details of such discussions disappeared, however, in the furore which ensued when the news of the Council's idea hit the press. It seems that official opposition to the proposal has, for the time being at least, been successful, and the Borough Council have instead put their support behind a drive to recruit 'neighbourhood special constables'. In interview, however, a number of senior Council members said that the idea remained on the 'back-burner'.

Duties   The Parks Police patrol 70 individual open spaces covering an area of about 850 acres in the Borough. They also provide security patrols for twelve libraries, eight leisure centres, four cemeteries, fourteen Play Service facilities, and eleven Youth and Recreation Facilities. They carry out keyholder duties for twenty-two buildings controlled by the Administrative Department, and provide a full alarm call service for all Leisure and Amenity Services buildings. On a number of occasions Parks Police officers have carried out arrests using citizen's powers of arrest, when they have come across a crime being committed away from the parks. For example, one such incident involved an assault outside a public house near Battersea Park. Parks officers witnessed the incident, left the park and arrested the assailant who was subsequently convicted of assault. Similarly, when travelling between parks and open spaces in the Borough in their marked vehicles, Parks Police have been stopped by the public and asked to assist in a range of incidents.

Parks officers also act as in-house security officers for the Borough Council, occasionally maintaining a visible presence at housing advice offices to deter unruly clients, escorting cash deliveries to banks, and maintaining a presence at the council chambers when public demonstrations are expected. The broad remit of the Parks Police is illustrated by the list of 21 duties in the appendix to the 1995 report.[20] The fact that the Parks Police officers are acting in a manner broader than would be expected from the official Metropolitan Police view of them is illustrated by their arrest statistics for 1994, as illustrated in Table 5.3.

---

[20] Wandsworth Borough Council (1995).

Table 5.3: Arrests by the Wandsworth Parks Police 1994/5 (by percentage)

Offence category	Arrests 1994	Arrests 1995
Dishonesty (including burglary, theft and robbery)	44	22
Criminal Damage	18	17
Public Order (including assault on police)	5	7
Drunkenness	10	6
Drugs offences	10	29
Other	18	53
Total	105	134

Source: Wandsworth Parks Constabulary

Although Johnston initially categorised municipal police bodies such as the Parks Police as 'hybrid', or sectorally-ambiguous,[21] we wish to argue that, in two important ways, the Parks Police are best considered as a public body.[22] First, its officers have, under particular circumstances and within a particular jurisdiction, constabulary powers (although as we have suggested there is some legal ambiguity surrounding this point). Second, they are a local, but nevertheless publicly-funded, organisation and are directly employed by the Borough Council. They are directly accountable to the Chair of the Leisure and Amenity Services Committee (which has responsibility for the parks and open spaces in the Borough). The chief officer has no 'constabulary independence' of the kind traditionally enjoyed by the chief constables of Home Department police forces. The chief officer of the Parks Police must provide an annual report to the Committee and answer any outstanding questions.

The Parks Police are subject to the same kinds of 'internal market' reform that are being applied across many areas of public service provision. In 1993, all security functions were transferred to the Amenity Services Division under the new post of Chief Security Services Officer. In keeping with Council policy, a client–contractor relationship was established between the Security Services Section, and clients within the Leisure and Amenity Services Department. A formal agreement came into force in April 1994, and states terms and conditions under which the security services should operate, and lays down expected of service. The Head of Security Services is subject to 'penalty payments' like any other contractor, should his department fail to meet required service levels.

[21] Johnston (1992).
[22] Johnston agrees with this point in a later article, see Johnston (1996*a*).

Other public policing bodies

The Health and Safety Executive

The Health and Safety Executive (HSE) describes itself as a 'non-departmental government body'. It is the operational arm of the Health and Safety Commission, which was established by the Health and Safety at Work Act 1974. Prior to this there was a complex regulatory system relating to different laws in different industry sectors. The 1974 Act imposes general duties on employers designed to protect the health and safety of both employees and customers.

Health and Safety Inspectors (of which there are about 1,500 in the UK) have a significant array of powers under a range of statutes. The main powers include powers of entry to premises, at any reasonable time or at any time at all if an inspector considers a situation to be dangerous. If they expect to be refused entry inspectors may ask a police constable to accompany them. They have the powers to carry out examinations and investigations within premises, and can take measurements or photographs. They can seize goods or samples for analysis or evidence, and can demand access to internal records or files. They can require information from an employer, and if necessary will interview under caution, as all investigators are trained in Police and Criminal Evidence Act (PACE) regulations. Representatives of the HSE stress the non-confrontational approach to regulation which underpins the philosophy of the Robens Report which preceded the Health and Safety Act 1974. The central finding of the report was that the previous complex system fostered a culture in which society relied on regulators to enforce health and safety, and absolved employers from taking action unless unlucky enough to be caught by an investigator and face the possibility of sanctions. The aim was to foster a culture in which the inevitably few inspectors (relative to the number of industrial premises) could be part of a culture aimed at general improvements in health and safety. Of course, the threat of sanctions is still an important part of this, although inspectors prefer to obtain voluntary compliance. There are, in theory, three levels of sanction available to HSE inspectors. First, an improvement notice which explains to the business what the problem is and requires some action within a negotiated period of time. The second level is prohibition notices, which explain the problem and require the business to stop a particular action or process until remedial action is taken. Failure to comply will lead to prosecution (there were about 2,000 prosecutions in 1994). The power to bring a prosecution is invested in the HSE inspector by statute, and in England and Wales it will be the HSE inspector personally who brings the prosecution (on behalf of the HSE). The norm is for the inspector involved personally to present the case.

Environmental Health Officers

Local authorities also have a range of regulatory and investigatory staff working in various functions. The Environmental Services Department at Wandsworth Council includes thirty-four Environmental Health Officers (EHOs) who have a significant range of powers under statute to gain entry to premises and carry out investigations. Within the same department are six Trading Standards Officers who also carry out a range of investigatory functions. The head of Environmental Services described his department as the 'health police', and outlined the complex range of legislation which empowers EHOs to investigate and, if necessary, bring prosecutions. In some cases, the powers reside with the EHOs as employees of the council, in others the powers reside with the EHO. When the EHO decides to enforce a case via prosecution, it is the individual officer who brings the prosecution, and not the Borough Council. The Department also operates the licensing powers for the Council, and has powers under the London Government Act 1963 to revoke entertainments licenses. The licensing function was an important power in the hands of the Council when, as we describe later, the door-supervisor registration scheme was brought in. Some of the powers under the Health and Safety at Work Act 1974 give fairly wide ranging powers to EHOs to enter premises, carry out investigations, and seize equipment. Some admittedly rarely-used powers are interesting in their quite extensive nature. For example we were told that the Public Health (Control of Disease) Act 1984 would, in some circumstance, allow an EHO to 'remove' an unwilling but infectious person to hospital, if the person had a particular disease which was endangering public health. The roles and functions of the EHOs mirror some of the roles of Health and Safety Executive Inspectors, and Housing Patrol Officers. The Health and Safety at Work Act empowers HSE inspectors to enforce legislation in some sites, but local authorities via EHOs in others. The EHOs and the Housing Patrol Service both respond to noisy parties, although the EHOs' deal with the private sector only (in fact the Housing Patrol Service gave extensive advice when this unit was set up). The police now routinely pass on complaints about noise to the EHOs or the Housing Patrol service. On some occasions when police back-up is required, for example on the rare instances when equipment is seized by EHOs, they will be accompanied by police officers.

The Housing Patrol Service

Since 1985 the Council have operated a mobile Housing Patrol Service, which at the time of the study consisted of 48 patrollers and six supervisors. This developed from the old Council caretaking service, and appears to have been an off-shoot of the Council's policy of contracting-out of services to the private sector. With the awarding of contracts for cleaning and maintenance of council-owned estates, there was a need for some kind of monitoring of the performance of the contractors. This was a major factor behind the creation of a mobile caretaking service, as well as broader considerations of the effectiveness of the old static caretaking function. The Housing Patrol service now runs 24-hour patrols on council estates as well as responding to calls from residents. Their primary function remains a housing management one, with the officers acting as mobile caretakers who respond to calls about burst pipes, lift-trappings or people who have locked themselves out of their flats. Of the twenty-three main duties listed in the Council documentation concerning the Housing Patrol service, only three or so relate to 'security' type functions. These are the 'noisy party patrol' wherein patrollers investigate reports of noise nuisance and, where appropriate, complete the necessary forms for action to be taken under the Environmental Protection Act 1990. Another listed duty is that of responding to 'major emergencies' and Housing Patrol officers told researchers how they were amongst the first 'emergency services' to reach the site of the Clapham Rail Crash, and to major gas-explosions which occurred in the Borough. Another listed duty is to patrol estates 'to provide a presence to deter vandalism and encourage responsible behaviour'. Most of the other duties are concerned with general caretaking functions, the monitoring of cleaning and maintenance contractors, lift-trappings, inspection of play areas, graffiti removal, checking on doors, windows and lights in council blocks, and other housing management duties.

However, the service is clearly perceived by many residents on housing estates as having important security elements, and patrol officers complained that residents sometimes expected them to turn up 'mob-handed'. The fact that patrollers travel about in marked cars and vans, wear uniforms with 'Housing Patrol' written clearly on the back, and are in constant radio contact with a central control room, reinforces the impression of there being a significant security element in their service. Many of the calls to Housing Patrol concern low-level 'policing' problems which are often of central concern to residents. A researcher accompanied housing patrol officers on two shifts, and observed a number of such duties being carried out, including requesting crowds of youths who were behaving in a rowdy way to move on, and responding to calls about noisy parties so that the offending tenants could be warned about their behaviour (and if necessary fined at a later date). Although Housing Patrol officers have the same legal powers as any other citizens to undertake 'citizen's arrests' of suspected offenders, in practice they have not used them. The patrollers are strongly encouraged always to act with their own safety in mind. Where a situation appears threatening Housing Patrol officers are not be expected to intervene. This is particularly important given the fact that the officers patrol alone. During observations of Housing Patrol shifts, officers emphasised that they would never be confrontational in their approach, a feature which was central in their training. Nevertheless, the fact remains that they do perform important, if relatively low-level, 'policing' tasks.

Benefit Fraud Investigators

Wandsworth Borough Council pays out the equivalent of more than £100 million a year in benefits (although some of this is notional expenditure, council tax benefit is in the form of lost income). The largest direct pay-out is in the form of Housing Benefit payments to private tenants in the form of rent allowances. This area of expenditure almost doubled in two years, with the 1991/92 total of £27 million expanding to £51 million in 1993/94. Most of this money is ultimately reclaimed from central government, and this has meant increasing attempts by central government to influence local authority policies towards countering benefit fraud. Central government now pays subsidies on 'recovered benefits' over a certain threshold level, which has increased the incentive for local authorities to detect fraud, and shifted the balance from prevention towards investigation.[23] Like other local authorities, Wandsworth has recently

[23] Rowlingson, K., Whyley, C., Newburn, T. and Berthoud, R. (1997) *Social Security Fraud: The role of penalties*, London: Stationery Office.

increased the resources which it puts into benefit fraud investigation and, at the time of the study, the three posts dedicated to fraud investigation were about to be supplemented by a further two. Representatives of the investigation section in the Housing Department reported that the main problem experienced in Wandsworth was benefit fraud from private tenants, and the transient nature of this population added to the difficulties of successful detection. Investigators had, for example, carried out one operation in which in the chosen target area 30 per cent of claims from the area were found to be not valid. The investigation methods included home visits, which sometimes found that the 'claimant' no longer lived at the address. Council staff reported that targeted investigations on particular geographical areas which were perceived as having higher than average concentrations of benefit fraudsters were being increased.

The benefit fraud investigators have no special legal powers over and above those held by ordinary citizens. When investigators interview suspects, they must make it clear that they have no police powers and the interviewee is free to leave at any point, though they do interview under caution. Investigators have a fair degree of discretion in how they go about their job. The usual sanction that is applied is the repayment of benefit obtained fraudulently. Prosecution is a fallback method generally used when people fail to repay or are involved in persistent or organised fraud. It remains a rarely-used method, with only about fifteen prosecutions per annum in the Borough. Prosecutions are undertaken via the police, and the Council tries to obtain maximum publicity for successful cases in the local press, to try to heighten what it believes to be the deterrent effect of prosecutions. The local authority benefit investigators have a close relationship with the Benefits Agency investigators. The investigators usually have long experience of working within benefits administration, and there is no identifiable preference for former police officers.

POID and Royal Mail Investigators

The Post Office Investigation Department (POID)[24] is the oldest law enforcement agency in Britain (and possibly in the world), dating back to 1793 when Anthony Parkin, the Secretary to the Post Office, set up a unit to investigate offences and apprehend and prosecute

---

[24] Now reorganised into Post Office Security and Investigation Service (POSIS).

offenders for crimes against the Post Office. Ever since that date, the Post Office has had its own investigation branch, although this has gone by various names and taken various different forms. At the time of the study, the POID had about 250 detectives, although with administrative support there were about 330 in the department in total. The POID were not a 'statutory' law enforcement agency, but were 'recognised' by the Home Office, and thus expected to comply with measures such as those laid down by PACE. POID investigators have no constabulary powers, and thus can be held personally liable in law for what they do in the course of the job. The POID deal with every crime which affects the Post Office, carrying out full investigations, if necessary arresting suspects (using citizens' powers of arrest), interview suspects under caution, and act as prosecutor (rather than the CPS). The POID, and then POSIS, has a long tradition of working closely with Home Department police forces, and with branches of other agencies such as the investigations departments of British Telecom and Mercury Communications, and also investigators from banks and insurance companies. POID reported that investigators had limited access to the Police National Computer. The organisation is another 'public' policing body affected by the onset of privatisation. With the breaking up of the old General Post Office into new separate operating companies, the POID must sell its services to the Royal Mail, Post Office Counters, and Parcelforce. In noting these developments, Johnston describes the POID as a 'public' body selling its services to private companies,[25] although for reasons laid out in Chapter Seven, we again feel that the sectoral status of the POID is not ambiguous. At the time of our research, the POID was just about to be reorganised into a broader unit, to be called 'the Post Office Security and Investigation Service' (POSIS), which was to combine the investigative function with the site security functions at Post Office and Royal Mail depots.

At the time of the study, the POID had a team of investigators based in Wandsworth, although undertaking work across South West London. Pending reorganisation of the POID, at the time of the research there were two POID investigators working alongside five Royal Mail investigators doing similar work. Investigators reported that their work from Wandsworth was much like the rest of the London South area. The majority of the local work was connected

[25] Johnston (1996).

with benefit fraudsters, the high level of counter crime (particularly pension book fraud) taking up to 85 per cent of investigator's work. In connection with this, POID and Royal Mail investigators work closely with Benefit Fraud Investigators from the Benefits Agency, and from local authorities. Prior to undertaking surveillance operations, for example, they check whether they are covering the same ground as one of these other agencies. Investigators reported that they also deal with employee theft, and robberies. Much of the work involved desk investigations, audit trails, and looking for ways to tighten up the system and prevent fraud. However, the specialist squads of the POID undertake a range of activities, sometimes operating within public space. One central body, 'the mailbag squad' deals with theft from mailbags and assaults on delivery workers, and they carry out covert surveillance, and undertake citizen's arrests of offenders. If a mail-bag theft results in lost benefit cheques, co-operation with the Benefits Agency and local authority allows POID investigators to identify the likely post offices where they may be cashed, and surveillance is carried out in order to catch the offenders. The fact that this squad is more likely to undertake arrests is illustrated by the fact that they have routine access to handcuffs, unlike most other 'policing' bodies described here.

'Private policing'—the private security industry

For Shearing and Stenning the essence of the private security function is visible patrol and surveillance. This, they argued, replicates in some ways the original purpose of the 'New Police' in Britain. However, as Johnston has argued, this is clearly an overly-narrow view of the multiple functions carried out by non-public 'policing' bodies:

[P]rivate security carries out virtually all the tasks undertaken by the police, plus rather more besides; guarding and protection, surveillance, intelligence and undercover work, preventative activities, investigation and detection, custodial functions . . .[26]

Such a view of the complex functional nature of the private security industry is borne out by the research in Wandsworth, although, as noted above, this involves a rather superficial and undifferentiated notion of 'private security'. The functional range of private security can be illustrated by considering some of the security operations in the Borough. The activities of the industry cover elements of all five

[26] Johnston (1994) p. 18.

major sectors of the industry outlined in Chapter Three: staffed services (guarding and patrol), investigation, and the installation and maintenance of electronic and physical security equipment. Analysis of the British Telecom Business 1994 Database entries for the Wandsworth postal code districts found fifty-nine private security company establishments (following the definition adopted in Chapter Three). This total reflected the range of private security companies on the ground, although it did not cover all the security firms operating in the Borough, because many of these had bases elsewhere. The fifty-nine companies were distributed between the five private security sectors as indicated in Table 5.4.

Table 5.4. Distribution of private security firms in Wandsworth

Security services and equipment	19
Electronic security equipment	14
Investigative services	4
Bailiffs and debt collectors	6
Mechanical security equipment	16

In order to build up a more comprehensive picture of private security in the Borough, each of these business establishments was sent a brief postal questionnaire.[27] Certainly in comparison to our national survey, there was a relatively low response rate to the survey—despite two follow-ups and assurances of confidentiality—though this is perhaps not a surprising result given previous experience of postal surveys of private security companies.[28] Twenty-five firms completed questionnaires, a response rate of 42 per cent.

Because of the relatively low response rate, the information from the twenty-five local private security firms is of limited use. However, it is worthwhile perhaps quickly summarising some points of information. Nearly all the businesses that returned questionnaires began trading after 1979 (in fact only four reported that they had begun prior to this). Businesses were asked how many people they employed

[27] Looking at companies with business establishments in Wandsworth itself only gives a partial picture of the private security industry locally. The reason for this is that, as in many other urban areas, many of the industrial sites or vacant offices in the Borough which were protected by a security company, bought in the service from outside the immediate area.

[28] Shearing C. D., Farnell, M., and Stenning, P. C. (1980) *Contract Security*, Toronto: Centre of Criminology, University of Toronto.

in total, and how many worked in Wandsworth. It is interesting to note that the twenty-five replies totalled 8241 employees altogether, of which over 450 actually worked in Wandsworth. This is an interesting baseline figure given that it represents *under half* of the total private security businesses listed in the Business Database. Furthermore, firms based outside the Borough were responsible for many security operations within Wandsworth. This strongly suggests that the private security industry (on our earlier definition) employs well in excess of the Metropolitan Police in the Wandsworth Borough.[29]

Staffed services

A range of examples of security guarding and security patrol were found in the Borough. Some of these were the traditional 'site security' operations, including some of the following examples.

The New Covent Garden Market Security Force

At the time of the study, the New Covent Garden (NCG) Market was running a security force consisting of thirty-five security staff. The security staff are employed from an outside contractor, a medium sized guarding firm; however, the operation is clearly run by the market security manager. There is an interesting history of 'policing' the market, as up until the late 1980s it had its own 'beadle' force, which had a number of powers to enforce the market by-laws. The market covers an enclosed area on a sixty acre site, although there are a number of public highways crossing its grounds. In general, the Metropolitan Police have responsibility for policing these highways, although there are provisions in the Act of Parliament which created the market for the market security force to enforce certain provisions of the Road Traffic Act 1972 in the same way as the police. The beadle force was replaced with a private security firm for reasons of financial efficiency. The market is run by a Quango set up by the Ministry of Agriculture, Fisheries and Food, which appoints a chief executive and a board of members. Even though the security manager described the security force as having the role of the 'village bobby', it was an unambiguously private security force, whose members were not required to use additional powers. Even though in theory they

---

[29] It should be noted that companies were asked how many people they employed in total, not just those on security-related matters. Thus, the total will include managerial and administrative staff.

had access to some extra powers, it was not policy for the security officers to use them. In fact, they rarely made arrests.

The main duties were traditional guarding duties, although the operation was more tightly controlled and directed than many others. The main duties included: staffing the toll booths at the entrance to the market and taking the entrance fees, locking and unlocking various gates and doors, routine patrol, responding to calls for assistance, responding to alarm activations, acting as guides for the emergency services if they should be called, responding to a range of incidents (criminal damage, burglaries, fights), monitoring the CCTV system and taking responsibility for changing tapes, initial investigation of crimes, undercover surveillance, and reporting for offences under the by-laws.

As noted above, the security operation is tightly controlled by the market authority management. The site manager, an ex-army officer, has developed a detailed list of Market Standing Orders, which specify the exact nature of functions to be undertaken in the market. This is a huge volume, with at least 500 pages, covering every aspect of the market's existence. They include the provision about security officers having extra powers; for example:

[V]ehicles using market roads are subject to the provisions of the Road Traffic Acts. Security officers appointed as Law Enforcement Officers are empowered to enforce specific sections of the Road Traffic Acts with the same authority as the civil police.

However, as noted, these powers are not used in practice, and the standing orders give clear procedure to be followed in cases where there have been serious infringements of Road Traffic Acts. This includes informing the neighbourhood beat officer covering the market, and telephoning details to the nearest police station (if the offender is still on site). The level of detail of the list of tasks for security officers is quite striking. The guards patrol using an electronic swipe which proves attendance at key points. There is a CCTV system covering the market site, with a control room monitored by security officers. There is a particularly sophisticated CCTV system in the flower market hall involving over ninety cameras. The traders paid for the system themselves and, according to the security manager, it 'paid for itself' very quickly as theft (a significant problem prior to the appearance of the CCTV system) was all but wiped out from the hall.

Shopping centres and supermarkets

The Borough includes two privately-owned shopping centres both of which contract-in security staff (one has eleven staff members, the other nine). The older of the two shopping centres is very much the larger, including over 100 retailers, and seven large service yards. The guards in this centre work to a shift pattern, carrying out the range of guarding duties. This includes basic unlocking and locking up, surveillance, visible patrol, intervention in various incidents, arrest and detention of offenders, joint operations with the police, the monitoring of the centre's CCTV system, first aid, giving directions to the public and dispersing crowds of youths. Given the nature of the clientele of the centre, the contract specification lays down that half the security officers must be black and at least one must be female. This centre takes a fairly high profile approach towards its private policing. This is because it has experienced a number of significant crime problems, including drug-dealing, serious assaults, gang problems, and even armed robbery. The centre management decided on a much more proactive approach to security in order to reclaim the centre. Heavily-built men in military style uniforms were employed, and told to be proactive in breaking up groups of youths, and generally pre-empting trouble before it started. This approach was perceived to have been very effective, and the centre manager reported that the approach of the security was now more concilia-tory. The centre still suffers from a high level of shop-lifting, and reported between 750 and 1000 thefts per year. The policing of 'anti-social behaviour' (in the centre manager's words) is still a major part of the security function, which means speaking with, and if necessary escorting out, rowdy youths, persistent drunks, beggars, etc. Because the centre is a well-known local meeting place, it tends to attract chil-dren playing truant from local schools. The centre management have a good relationship with local schools, and will detain suspected truants while they call the schools to locate the relevant one. It is fairly frequent for the schools to send a representative down to fetch the child when a truant is located.

The contrasting style of the other shopping centre security opera-tion in part reflected the different problems which it faced. It was in a more upmarket part of the Borough with lower crime rates, and its security force had a lower profile. They wore blazers and slacks (rather than military style pullovers), and in the words of the centre

manager were seen as 'PR people for the property owners'. Their purpose was primarily to provide general security against 'fire, theft and
flood', and not, the centre manager emphasised, to act like police
officers. Their main function was to help the public, give advice and
directions, make people to feel safer, and take action when the need
arises. They were asked to deal with problems in a conciliatory and
low-key way, and the manager felt strongly that a more enforcement-
minded approach would simply foster trouble. The security force
carry out visible patrols, monitor CCTV, respond to alarm activations, respond to calls for assistance, carry out general security and
fire safety checks, and are fully trained with first aid skills. Despite
the different approach to security in this centre, security officers here
also carried out formal citizens arrests when required. They were also
contracted-in from a security company rather than employed in-
house.

We also spoke with representatives of two large supermarket
chains about their security arrangements in their shops in the
Borough. Many supermarkets now employ uniformed security guards
(almost invariably contracted-in from security firms), as well as
employing 'store detectives' inside the stores. The supermarkets concerned would not reveal information about numbers employed on
these tasks. Many of the problems experienced by shopping centres
are also experienced by supermarkets. They find they must process a
large number of minor offenders, usually shoplifters, with whom the
formal criminal justice system does not have the capacity to deal.
They also have developed their own systems of sanctions, the main
one of which is banning. If necessary, this can be backed by a court
order.

Colleges

Educational institutions in the Borough have undergone a number of
reforms over recent years. Firstly, after the abolition of the Inner
London Education Authority (ILEA), responsibility for education fell
to the Borough Council. Since then, there have been further reforms
in further and higher education, taking institutions out of local
authority control, and expecting them to act as independent institutions under the direction of a chief executive and a board of direc-
tors. In effect, this has made some colleges quasi-private concerns,
although in practice most of their funding still comes from the public purse in the form of the Further Education Funding Council. Both

colleges visited in the Borough had a number of sites, some of which were outside Wandsworth. Some of these sites were patrolled by uniformed private security guards. Both colleges inherited guards which were introduced by ILEA during the 1980s. When ILEA was disbanded in 1990, the colleges used the security contractor used by Wandsworth Council. Independence from local authority control has given them more freedom to develop their own security measures.

One of the colleges reported great difficulties in finding a satisfactory security firm for its purposes. The estates manager of one college reported that in the eighteenth month period prior to the current security firm arriving on site, he had employed, and subsequently dismissed, four separate companies, which he described as 'absolutely bloody useless'. All the usual problems associated with the private guarding sector were mentioned: fierce price competition, very low wage rates, unreliable guards, and poor standards of service. Things had improved when the current firm was employed, a firm which specialises in body-guarding, although it has branched out into college security and security at rock concerts and festivals. The other college employed security guards from a larger guarding company, with long experience of guarding colleges and similar institutions. The private security personnel working in the colleges carry out a range of 'policing' tasks: visible patrolling, surveillance, access control, responding to alarm activations, public order, assisting with enquiries from students (their public), as well as monitoring CCTV. In limited circumstances they investigate incidents and collect evidence. They also spend time running and enforcing the internal regulations at colleges, such as rules against smoking on site, and making noise in corridors.

Pubs and nightclubs

All the nightclubs in the Borough employed 'door supervisors'. At the time of the study, the Council was setting up a door supervisors registration scheme, and this listed nine entertainment venues in the Borough known to use such services. From information provided by these venues, it appears that on any given Friday or Saturday night there may be up to seventy door supervisors working at different places in the Borough. The main functions of door supervisors included access control, applying dress rules, preventing entry to drunk people, or known trouble-makers, carrying out routine searches of all customers entering clubs (for concealed weapons or drugs), breaking up fights and restraining violent people, escorting people off the premises, detaining suspects until the police arrive, carrying out routine sweeps of the premises (and lavatories) searching for drug dealers, and general surveillance of what is going on inside the club.

The door supervisors registration scheme is a joint initiative of the local police and the Borough Council. This came into effect in April 1995, although for premises with licenses existing on that date, the scheme would only come into effect on the date of their first license renewal after this. Most entertainments licenses are annually renewable, although premises with a 'problem' reputation may have shorter licenses to give the Council flexibility. There are several nightclubs in the Borough, all of whom have expressed support for the registration scheme. The scheme applies to any door supervisor having a security role, not simply ticket collecting or taking entrance fees. The procedure works via the licensing system, the sanction being that any club employing unregistered door staff would not be granted a renewal of their entertainments licenses.

Any person who wishes to work as a door supervisor in Wandsworth must fill out a registration form, part of which requires them to indicate whether or not they have a criminal record. The prospective door supervisor must also have attended a training session (run by a number of recommended companies—the Council has a list of nine 'approved' training companies). The training courses are between fifteen and twenty hours in length and usually take place over a weekend. They cover four main elements including first aid, fire safety, training in criminal and licensing law, and protocol search and restraint techniques. The course fees vary between £75 and £135 per person depending on the establishment. The person's application is forwarded to the local police, who have the opportunity to raise objections. This almost certainly involves a criminal records check, although no representative of the Council explicitly confirmed that this was the case. This scheme follows that set up by a number of other boroughs in London, notably Westminster and Croydon. One problem for door supervisors is that, at the time of the study, most local authorities did not recognise registration with other borough's schemes, with the consequence that a door supervisor wishing to work in more than one borough would have to go through the whole registration process more than once. The London Local Authorities Act 1995 makes provision for the introduction of such schemes across the Capital.

A Council representative referred obliquely to 'problems' with door staff at certain nightclubs in the Borough, in connection with drug dealing in particular. A Council report to the licensing sub-committee in December 1994 referred to allegations about door staff involvement in drug dealing, and reports of assaults on customers. However, there was no reliable evidence about the extent of these. During the course of the study, there were a number of events involving nightclubs in the Borough which would have had implications for their security. In late 1995, there was a well-publicised police raid on one of the largest clubs in the Borough, which was reported in both national and local press. It was a major police operation, involving over 100 officers, and apparently was planned without the prior knowledge of the club management. The main aim was to catch people in possession of drugs, and all people in the club were searched leading to a number of arrests. Not long after this, a young man died after reportedly taking ecstasy in the same night club. The club was later closed by order of the council. Another incident which was reported in the local press involved a door supervisor from another club, who allegedly assaulted a customer whom he suspected of causing trouble.

Prisoner escort and parking controls

The Borough provided two clear examples of direct privatisation, in terms of functions which were transferred away from state bodies and given to private companies. During 1994, two previously 'public' policing functions were contracted-out to private firms. First, the prisoner escort service is now undertaken by Securicor Custodial Services. This contract covers the whole of South London, though coincidentally the main Securicor Depot is based at Nine Elms, in the east of Wandsworth. The main prisons served by this depot are Wandsworth and Brixton, although most activities within the Borough relate to transporting people to and from the South Western magistrates court at Lavender Hill. There are over seventy staff employed by Securicor on vehicle escort duties, and about 100 court staff. About thirty vehicles operate from the depot. The fleet of vans is electronically monitored, the control room in the central office identifying where each van is and how fast it is travelling. Estimated arrival times at court and explanations for any delays can also be provided to courts.

Secondly, the enforcement of parking regulations away from the 'red routes' is now a responsibility of the Borough Council, who have contracted it to a private company who employ twenty-eight parking wardens across the Borough. These private traffic wardens enforce parking regulations in a similar manner to those employed by the Metropolitan police, they simply do it in different places. However, as one police officer pointed out, they are more driven by the need to raise revenue rather than traffic control, and some believed that this perhaps led to a more zealous approach to parking enforcement than that taken by the Metropolitan Police wardens in the Borough. This kind of transfer of function has generally been welcomed by the public police, faced with burgeoning demands upon their resources. In addition, the natural increases in demands upon the police have led to a *de facto* abandonment of certain lower level tasks. For example, the issues of harassment on housing estates is now seen as a council problem, and noisy party complaints are immediately referred to EHOs or Housing Patrol.

Neighbourhood patrols

It is worth emphasising that we did *not* come across any examples of private security personnel being contracted to carry out patrols of public streets or open residential areas. Developments of this type have received much attention in the press, and are often cited as evidence of the fact that the private sector is increasingly impinging on the domain of the public police, or privatisation is occurring 'by the back door'. The nearest thing to this we encountered were one or two temporary mobile patrols of private residential estates (one of which was conducted by Securicor Guarding), whereby a security guard would periodically visit the site during the day and night. Representatives of Securicor informed us that they do not undertake patrols of public space, although the company has moved into the area of patrolling business parks. The owners of a business park in the east of the Borough employ a security firm to carry out periodic mobile patrols on the site.

The Council clearly wished to take a highly proactive role in the development of crime prevention initiatives, as was shown by the proposals surrounding the extension of the Parks Police remit. Another proposal which was considered by the Council arose from the Home Secretary's suggestion to the 1993 National Neighbourhood Watch conference about 'streetwatch' schemes. This envisaged an 'activated NW' approach, by which members of watches would undertake surveillance patrols of their areas, to act as the 'eyes and ears' of the police. This clearly raised fears about untrained, inexperienced, vigilante-type street patrols, and has been strongly opposed by the police service nationally. In April 1994 the Deputy Leader of the council announced in a report to the Policy and Finance Committee that he wished to 'gauge the range of views about the desirability and perceived effectiveness of non-Police neighbourhood patrols'. In the event, such patrols were never activated, largely, it seems, because of strong opposition from the local police, though a number of Neighbourhood Watch schemes within the Borough do patrol informally as part of their watch duties.

Site security

There were a range of other industrial and commercial sites in the Borough employing security guards to protect their property including the large industrial park in the east of the Borough. There were a number of different operations, many of whom employed small teams of security guards. It was relatively rare to find such guards employed in-house, with most firms reporting that contracting out gave them more flexibility. The firms employing guards included a large publishing warehouse, the depot of a national parcel delivery company, the security vaults of a large auction house, car showrooms, and telecommunications companies.

Investigatory

There are a number of private investigation firms based in the Borough, and undoubtedly more which actually work within the Borough. Such firms are the most difficult to track down. First, there are the practicalities of locating them; they are more likely than any other kind of firm within the private security industry to be small one-person concerns operating from home addresses. Second, the practitioners tend to be more suspicious of external enquiries than others—especially from researchers. In the event, we were only able to speak with one private investigation company working within the Borough (and none of the investigation firms actually based in the Borough responded to our questionnaire).

The professional witness scheme

One interesting example of the use of private investigators within the Borough was in the 'professional witness' scheme piloted by the council. Three firms of private investigators were contracted to carry out covert surveillance on council estates where there had been reports that tenants had been subject to harassment, but witnesses were too intimidated to give evidence to council officials or the police. Professional witnesses were employed to keep watch, witness events, and record events using photographs or video-equipment, in order to provide the council with evidence. It was not possible to estimate the number of people employed in these operations, although from general discussions with a representative of one of the companies involved, we anticipate that it is fairly low (small teams of one or two people). At the time of the study, the project was in its very early stages, and no clear results had become apparent.

The company to whom we spoke was particularly interesting because they employed ex-police officers exclusively, and were a growing company nationwide. Some years ago the managing director had the idea of setting up a company employing the services of retired police officers, and as a consequence set up a register of available employees. They are paid per job, and so income from the work is somewhat intermittent. The firm offers services in the professional witness field, but also can offer commercial fraud investigation services employing highly-experienced ex-fraud squad officers. The company had developed a register of 'hundreds' of former police officers of all ranks and of all service specialisms. This allowed a high degree of flexibility and specialisation—the Managing Director claimed that he could put together a fraud squad consisting of former senior detectives that would be 'larger and more experienced than that of the Met'.

Security equipment

There is a range of suppliers and installers of security equipment, both mechanical (locksmiths, safemakers, grills and shutters) and electronic (CCTV and intruder alarms). The majority of the businesses identified in the Business Database were primarily involved with the provision of electronic or physical security equipment (30 out of 59).

The local authority and crime prevention

As outlined in Chapter One, and again at the beginning of this chapter, the focus of this study is somewhat narrower than some previous studies of 'policing' which have examined a wide range of formal and informal social controls. We did not, for example, include the activities of neighbourhood watch groups, teachers, and parents under the rubric of 'policing'. However, although this section departs somewhat from our narrower definition, it is important to note that Wandsworth Borough Council has become increasingly active in developing and co-ordinating crime prevention policies locally. In 1987, the Council established a Crimewatch unit, which established a Borough-wide programme aimed at reducing crime, mainly through environmental design. Two developments were particularly important for the subsequent emergence of policy. First, with the abolition of ILEA (see earlier), the Council became responsible for education and youth services. Second, the Government's circular 44/90 was published, which encouraged local agencies to enter into a partnership approach to crime prevention. An increasing amount of local co-operation was eventually formalised in 1992 with the Wandsworth Partnership.

This is essentially a strategic information-sharing forum, through which all the agencies involved in crime prevention can communicate and agree joint action. The Partnership has launched a number of initiatives, and perhaps the most significant one is the development of crime-pattern-analysis within the Crimewatch team. A joint working group of council and police officers reviewed a range of crime-pattern-analysis software packages. The Council has recently purchased the NETMAP system, which allows a detailed mapping of local crime patterns. One obstacle which had to be overcome was the matter of local authority access to information held on the Police National Computer (PNC), and to Metropolitan Police records of incidents, crime reports, and crime intelligence. Because of the restrictions imposed by the Data Protection Act 1984, the data passed to the Borough Council is provided in a depersonalised form, with simply the nature of the incident, the place, and the time. Although at the time of writing, crime pattern analysis is in its early stages, this is a particularly significant development because the police have in the past jealously guarded their information.

The partnership also sought to address differences in working cultures between various local agencies by arranging exchanges and 'shadow days', when, for example, a council officer will shadow a police officer for a day, or vice versa. The Partnership established a campaign to recruit more neighbourhood special constables locally, and one approach has been to encourage council staff to enrol as specials—indeed, the first neighbourhood special constable to be recruited was a council officer. The Partnership set up a range of working groups to address specific topics. At the time of the study, the groups covered CCTV, information sharing, training, emergency planning, traffic accidents and drug abuse. These led to a number of developments, such as the 'appropriate adult scheme' by which a register of vetted people are available to act as appropriate adults during police questioning of juveniles.

Crime prevention remains high on the political agenda in Wandsworth. The council leader reported that a range of public attitude surveys carried out in advance of local elections strongly indicated that crime and the fear of crime were top of local residents' priorities. At the time of the research, CCTV systems were present in two of the 'town centres' of the Borough, Wandsworth and Tooting. However, it was shortly to be extended to Putney, Clapham Junction, and Earlsfield, so that all five town centres in the Borough would be covered. The system is monitored at a major control room in Wandsworth, though there was some difficulty in finding the staff to carry out the monitoring (for much of the time, the screens were unmonitored, although video-taped).

Neighbourhood Watch (NW) is actively supported by the Borough Council, who have provided funding for equipment, and administrative support. In the west of the Borough the council have taken over administration of NW from the Wandsworth Division of the police. There is a NW support unit of four staff in the council, led by a retired Putney police officer. They would like to take over the administration of NW for the east of the Borough also, but this was strongly opposed by the Battersea police who felt that NW should be police-led.

Conclusion

In this chapter we have provided a broad description of the range of policing bodies that are visible in contemporary Wandsworth: from the Metropolitan Police at the 'public' end of the spectrum, via bodies such as the Wandsworth Parks Police and the Post Office Investigation Department who occupy what might appear to be an ambiguous status, to site guarding, alarms, CCTV and investigation at the unambiguously 'private' end of the spectrum. In Chapter Six we look at the work of these policing bodies in greater detail, and consider the relationships between them. In Chapter Seven, we then return to the issue of 'boundaries' and, using the example of policing in Wandsworth, consider how best 'policing' is to be theorised, and how the differences between different 'providers' are to be conceptualised and understood.

6

Policing Wandsworth in Practice

In the previous chapter we outlined the basic organisation, purpose, methods, and style of the various 'policing' bodies operating on the ground in the London Borough of Wandsworth. The purpose of this chapter is to look in more detail at some of the relationships that develop between these bodies in practice, and how 'collectively' they police the Borough. In building up a picture of policing in the Borough the material is arranged around three sets of key issues that have been raised in previous chapters. The first of these concerns the competing explanations for the rise or 'rebirth' of private policing. The explanations, we argued, generally fall into two camps: 'fiscal constraint', and 'structuralist' or mass private property theories, and in this chapter we look at the extent to which these approaches help us make sense of the policing of Wandsworth. The second set of issues concerns the relationships between public and private sectors in policing or, more particularly, the extent to which the 'junior partner' or 'economic' models of these relationships approximate to the observed realities of contemporary Wandsworth. We look at the degree of competition, co-operation and co-existence between policing organisations on the ground. Finally, we reconsider some of the debates about the nature of public and private justice in the light of the previous discussion of the nature of policing relationships in the Borough.

Theoretical explanations of the rise of private policing

In Chapter Four we considered several alternative theories about the development of private policing in the light of empirical evidence about Britain. We grouped these broadly into two categories: 'fiscal crisis' theories and 'structuralist' or 'mass private property' theories, though we also considered a third set of ideas grouped by Johnston under the banner of 'late modern change'.[1] Although clearly a local

---

[1] Johnston (1996a).

area study is unlikely to provide the empirical basis for a full-scale testing of these ideas, it nevertheless allows us to examine the extent to which some of the implications of these theories stand up in a local context.

Fiscal constraint theories

Budget constraints

In this approach, the rise of private policing is explained largely in terms of restrictions on the resources of the public police. As we suggested in Chapter Four, even at the national level there are significant limits upon what it is possible to do in terms of testing this theory. In essence we are limited to looking at broad indicators, such as trends in expenditure and employment in public policing and private security, and drawing implications from them. At the local level these difficulties are even greater. First, it is questionable how meaningful even these indicators would be at the local level of analysis. Second, such data is largely unavailable in any case, as we have only limited data about trends in private security employment or expenditure. Moreover, and unlike the national level, even information about trends in public policing over time is inadequate. Periodic reorganisations have ruled out any detailed analysis of trends in Metropolitan Police resourcing of Wandsworth over time. Thus, for example, although the Borough is currently divided between two Metropolitan Police divisions, prior to June 1994 there were three divisions. This in itself makes the collection of time series data about resources almost impossible. Such difficulties are compounded by the fact although the two police divisions (and previously the three police divisions) are coterminous with the Borough boundaries, this has only been the case for about a decade. Similar problems apply to the recorded crime and other workload statistics over time. Furthermore, in order to develop an accurate picture of local public policing resources we would also have to make adjustments for the time spent by 'local' officers carrying out duties in other parts of the Metropolitan Police District (MPD), or even other regions of the country (and also reverse adjustment for the operation of officers from central non-divisional squads within the Borough). The best that is possible in the circumstances is to make assumptions based on trends in police resources nationally and within the MPD in particular. From these, however, it is reasonable to assume that, in broad terms, expenditure on public policing in Wandsworth has seen fairly significant increases over the last decade (although not as great as during the early 1980s). Such increases have almost certainly been outstripped by increases in police workload, in particular as evidenced by crimes reported to the police, incidents attended, and public calls for assistance.

The local perception, perhaps not untypical of the country as a whole, is one of persistent under-resourcing. One of the dominant themes in discussions in the local Police Consultative Committee (PCC)[2] concerned alleged 'restrictions' on the resources available to local divisions of the Metropolitan Police. For example, in 1995 the PCC offered to write to the Home Secretary making out a special case for Wandsworth Borough. Indeed, the local police tend to encourage this perception that they are starved of resources. For example, in a discussion of the Home Office Inquiry into Police Core and Ancillary Tasks,[3] one senior police officer speaking at the PCC argued that all police work should be regarded as 'core' duties, and the police be 'properly-resourced' to carry them out. However, there was no evidence that the local police had experienced any fall in resourcing in real terms over time.

The perception that demands on the police were outstripping resources was echoed by some of the people involved in private security. For example, one of the shopping centre managers said that at one time the local beat officer was often seen patrolling the shopping centre, but that this was largely a thing of the past. This was, in his view, due to police resources being stretched by 'response policing'. An inevitable result of this, he suggested, was that the security guards in the shopping centre were dealing with more and more incidents which would once have been considered the job of the police.

Although observers of local policing in Wandsworth might find it difficult to apply the term 'fiscal crisis' to what has happened to local public police resources over the past decade or so, it is nevertheless

---

[2] New forums for police-community consultation were recommended by Lord Scarman in his report after the Brixton riots. The recommendation was later made more formally in a Home Office circular in 1983 and given statutory force by s.106 of the Police and Criminal Evidence Act 1984. Section 106 forums go under a variety of names; in Wandsworth it was called the Police Consultative Committee.

[3] An inquiry conducted by the Home Office between 1993–95 with the aim of establishing which were the core tasks of the police and which were ancillary. One of the inquiry's key objectives was to consider to what extent ancillary tasks could be performed more efficiently by other policing bodies.

clear that there remained a widespread perception that the resources available were inadequate. This may in itself, however, be very significant. The demand for security and protection is clearly driven in part by a fear of crime and an assessment both of likely risks (however inaccurate) and of the means of minimising risk. To the extent that the police have presented themselves as a key institution in 'the fight against crime', so they have been judged in these terms. The significant and sustained rises in crime over the past twenty or more years have, consequently, seen declining confidence in the ability of the police to tackle crime. Despite increased resources—albeit increases that are outstripped by demand—those concerned about crime have increasingly sought means other than the police for dealing with it. In this sense, although it would be hard to argue that the public police have faced a fiscal crisis in this period, there may be some force in the suggestion that the fact that police finances have not kept pace with public demands on the service has contributed to the long-term process of declining confidence in the police, one consequence of which has been the search for alternative sources of security.[4]

Transfer of tasks

This is one mode of privatisation which, it is argued, occurs in response to fiscal crisis. There were two types of transfer of tasks away from the Metropolitan Police in Wandsworth. The first involved the direct and explicit transfer of responsibilities to other agencies, the second the progressive withdrawal of police resources from certain types of work and their replacement by other providers. Two examples from Wandsworth have already been mentioned in previous chapters: the transfer of responsibility for the prisoner escort service for London South to Securicor Custodial Services in January 1995, and the transfer of responsibility for parking enforcement (except for the red routes) to local authorities in November 1994 and, in Wandsworth, the contracting out of this service by the Council to a private company, who now employ twenty-eight traffic wardens in the Borough. We discuss the 'deliberate' transfer of tasks in greater detail in the next chapter.

---

[4] This process can be seen outside the UK. There are, for example, a number of 'new agents of social control' visible in Dutch towns and cities in the 1990s. See Hauber, A., Hofstra, B., Toornvliet, L. and Zandbergen, A. (1996) 'Some new forms of functional social control in the Netherlands and their effects', *British Journal of Criminology*, 36, 2, pp. 199–219.

The second type of transfer occurs when the police withdraw from certain tasks because of resource constraints (or other considerations) and other agencies step in to fill the gap without there ever having been an explicit agreement about this. Two examples of this include the 'policing' of noise pollution, which has become the responsibility of council employees (EHOs for private accommodation and Housing Patrol for council property). The police are now more than happy to pass on complaints about noisy parties (or other forms of noise pollution) to the council units concerned. The second example concerns the growth of the 'professional witness scheme' contracted by the council to private investigation firms. A representative of one of these firms strongly emphasised that they did not 'wish to be seen as an alternative to the police' and were not looking to take tasks away from the police. It was his perception, however, that the police service was being 'down-graded' and budgets held back, which had necessitated their move out of lower level functions such as harassment on estates. It was the perception of some leading Council members that, given current workload and resources, the police are unable to offer a regular visible patrol service to council estates, and it was this which led to the suggestion that the Parks Police patrols should be extended. Similarly, the Council looked to take on some other responsibilities more usually associated with the Metropolitan Police. One example was the administration of Neighbourhood Watch, which was a Council responsibility on the west side of the Borough, but remained a police responsibility on the east. The Council argued that the police should concentrate their resources away from administrative and clerical work, and the Council consequently expressed an interest in running NW across the whole Borough. The Battersea police division, however, remained of the view that NW should be a police-led scheme, and were careful to guard their role within it.

Changes in the nature of urban space

As we noted in Chapter Four, Shearing and Stenning argue that 'the modern development of mass private property controlled by vast corporate conglomerates, and so frequently consisting of essentially 'public places', is the critical change that has paved the way for the modern growth and influence of private security'.[5] Their argument

---

[5] Shearing, C. D. and Stenning, P. C. (1981) 'Modern private security: its growth and implications', in Tonry, M. and Morris, N. (eds.) *Crime and Justice: An Annual Review of Research*, Vol. 3, Chicago: University of Chicago Press, pp. 193–245.

concerns changes both in physical space and in peoples' use of time. They argue that people now tend to live in private blocks rather than traditional street-facing housing patterns, shop in privately-owned malls rather than in high street stores, and spend leisure time in large private complexes rather than in 'public spaces'. In sum, people are spending more work and leisure time under the 'watchful gaze' of private security. It is almost certain that the people of Wandsworth have been affected in some way by the types of change identified by Shearing and Stenning, and the extent to which this is the case provides a useful method of reflecting on the efficacy of transferring their North American view of the rise of private security to the British context. To this end, it is interesting to identify the examples of 'private–public space' in the Borough and to look in some detail at the ways in which they are policed.

As we argued in Chapter Two, applying the public–private dichotomy to the notion of space is far from unproblematic. In practice, we found that a range of spatial types existed between open 'public' spaces and enclosed 'private ones'. In Wandsworth there exist multiple forms of urban space which cannot unambiguously be defined as public or private. Attempting to conceptualise space, using the two dimensions of ownership and access, leads to a number of difficulties, and there are a number of forms of 'hybrid space' which exist on a continuum between 'public' and 'private':

- Space which is state-owned (national state or local state) and open to groups of people engaging in social interaction, e.g. the high street, market square, parks and open spaces
- Space which is owned/funded by 'state' bodies with more limitations to access, but on which the large groups of people congregate, e.g. colleges, hospital sites
- Space which is privately-owned, where access is generally open to groups of people, e.g. shopping malls, out-of-town retail parks, large private residential complexes
- Space over which there is public right of way, but which is developing the appearance of being 'private' through deliberate design attempts to discourage access, e.g. some riverfront developments, cul-de-sac residential areas
- Space which is owned by 'state' bodies (either national or local), but which is extremely restricted in terms of access, e.g. police stations, MOD establishments

• Space which is both privately-owned and restricted in access to a small group, e.g. small workplace, household.

The above list serves to illustrate the difficulties in providing concrete definitions of types of space and reinforces the view that a straight-forward dichotomisation of space into public and private categories is insufficiently subtle to capture the spatial distribution of policing. Although in Chapter Seven we discuss in greater detail the 'spatial boundaries' between policing bodies, at this stage we will examine how the development of 'mass private property' and other forms of mass space have impacted on the policing of the borough.

Shopping malls

Wandsworth Borough has only two shopping centres of the type identified by Shearing and Stenning, and the predominant feature of shopping in the Borough remains the traditional 'high street'. One of the shopping centres opened in the early 1970s, and the second one opened in 1990. Both have employed small teams of private security guards since opening, and the number of guards has changed little over the years. The two shopping centres are situated in contrasting parts of the Borough, and reflect this in their differing styles. The older mall is much larger and generally more crowded. It is situated in a high crime area, and has a harsh-looking concrete exterior, a more functional design, and few decorations and plants. The newer mall is found in a more 'upmarket' part of the Borough. Its high ceilings and more intricate design involving plants and ornate furnishings contribute to a more genteel atmosphere.

As we have already indicated, there are clear contrasts in the approach to security adopted by the two shopping centres. In the older shopping centre the security force is highly visible, consisting of large and slightly intimidating-looking men wearing military-style uniforms. A set of handcuffs are kept in the security control room in order to help restrain violent people, although it was reported that these are only used very rarely. In the newer, more upmarket shopping centre the security guards are, in the words of the centre manager, viewed more as 'public relations staff for the property owners'. It was emphasised that they are not expected to behave like police officers. The security officers wear blazers and slacks, and appear to be less confrontational in their approach. Nonetheless, despite their very different styles, from time to time security officers in both centres are required to make formal citizens' arrests, and therefore receive training in the use of such powers.

The different approaches may reflect the different problems experienced by the two centres. The older mall is situated in a high-crime area—it has experienced drug dealing, violent assault, armed robberies and organised shop-lifting. The main security problem for the newer mall has been petty shop-lifters, and in the five years since its opening there had yet to be a serious violent incident on the site. In some ways, this contrast mirrors the contrast in public policing styles, between high crime inner-city areas, and the policing of more comfortable suburbs. However, the manager of the newer mall argued that some of the more serious problems experienced in the other shopping centre were actually related to having a more 'enforcement-minded' approach to security—arguing that this exacerbates tensions, and provides a challenge for local youths.

In so far as both shopping centres are privately-owned, and thus entry is at the discretion of the owners, they are the natural domain of private security rather than the public police. However, this is not to suggest that the Metropolitan Police are excluded from these spaces. On the contrary, both centre managers reported that they would welcome routine patrols of their centres by local police officers. According to the manager of the older centre, a few years prior to our study, the local neighbourhood beat officer (NBO) was often seen patrolling in the centre, and had a regular liaison with the security guards: 'It was a general two-way flow of intelligence which has by and large stopped now'. The NBO also used to carry out training sessions for the centre security guards, covering subjects such as crime prevention, legal powers of arrest, control and restraint techniques, and general security matters. In contrast, the manager noted that 'you rarely see a police officer on patrol now'. In his view this was the inevitable result of increasing demands upon police resources. As a result, the majority of incidents of crime or disorder which occurred in the centre were now usually dealt with by the private security guards, at least in the first instance. Elements of both the fiscal contraint and mass private property arguments can thus be detected in the way that policing of the centre has developed. The fact that the centre is privately-owned has not prevented the Metropolitan Police having routine access and, until some years ago, carrying out regular patrols. However, since this time increasing demands on police resources led them to withdraw from routine policing of the centre. The presence of private security—ubiquitous on such mass private property—arguably made it easier for them to do so.

The newer centre also had a close relationship with the local police. The centre manager chaired the local crime prevention panel and was also a member of the police consultative committee. Although police officers did not regularly patrol the centre, there was (in the words of the manager) an 'open invitation' for local officers to come in for a cup of tea and a chat in the security control room. During a publicity campaign to recruit more Special Constables, the local police had been invited to set up a stand in the centre, and the centre management were pleased to have the opportunity to have uniformed police officers on site. Thus, although in theory the centre management had the right to refuse routine access to the Metropolitan Police, in practice this did not happen. It remains possible of course that the centre management might have taken a different view had Metropolitan Police officers made a habit of adopting a high-profile policing approach within the centres. Anything which could be interpreted as discouraging shoppers, and which would therefore be in conflict with the property-owners' objectives, would clearly be discouraged. The reality was quite the contrary, with both centre managements reporting that they would actually welcome more routine 'public' policing, but realising that under current circumstances it was unlikely to occur. This was not to suggest that increased police patrols would allow them to reduce their private security bill, merely that the police presence would add to general feelings of security. In sum then, the policing of the shopping centres by private security reflected not so much a deliberate displacement of public policing by centre managements, but a practical 'gap-filling' response to a perceived lack of police resources or a change in police priorities.

Gated communities and enclavisation

We found no examples in Wandsworth of the privately-patrolled 'gated communities' of the type characteristic of many North American cities. However, an examination of developments in the built environment within the Borough provided a number of points of interest.

The Borough includes some examples of gated residential developments, although it would be stretching the imagination to describe them as 'gated communities'. Few, if any, are completely gated-off from the outside world, and few, if any, employ private security guards. However, several large private residential apartment blocks on the riverfront are equipped with CCTV, and at least one has a security guard on duty in the reception area. Security has, of course, been a growing area of concern for private housing developers, and this trend has been encouraged by such schemes as 'Secured by Design' which promotes the incorporation of crime prevention features into the basic design of housing estates. A representative of the Borough Planner's department reported that this has contributed to a growth in the number of 'cul-de-sacs', with restricted 'through routes', which leads to the development of an inward-looking 'self-policing' effect. Whilst informal surveillance inside the development is facilitated, such developments result in 'dead space' outside, and an atmosphere of increased isolation and, it is argued, insecurity. The Borough Planner's Department representative reported that the Council are actively opposing such enclavisation-type developments in the private residential sector. When the Department considers planning applications for residential development, the broad aim of 'revitalising public space' informs its decisions.

Although the Council took steps to prevent the development of 'enclavisation' in the private housing sector, on council-owned estates there have been trends in the opposite direction. Many of the Borough's older public housing developments, dating from the 1960s and 1970s, are large and rambling estates, with rather incoherent layouts. The representative of the Borough Planner's Office reported that it was now Council policy to try to divide such estates into manageable segments, by introducing road barriers, low fences, and clearly marked paths, which are intended to discourage general access. The opportunities for unchecked movement through the estates have, in the view of the Council, encouraged petty crime and vandalism. The aim is to introduce subtle design features, which divide areas of 'public space' from semi-public and private spaces. One example of such action followed complaints by residents of private houses backing onto a council estate about youths throwing stones over the walls at their windows, and also climbing into their back gardens. The Council responded by building a higher and stronger fence between the gardens and the estate boundary. In one site which had a complex labyrinth of small alleys and streets linking an area of terraces, semi-detached houses, and a block of purpose-built flats, there were extremely high rates of property crime, in particular theft of and from motor vehicles, burglary, and vandalism. Crime pattern analysis suggested that most of these crimes were being committed by people from outside the immediate area. The Council therefore erected a series of gates at the main points of entry to the area. Only residents were given keys to these gates. The area experienced a dramatic decrease in recorded crime following this development.

One of the most obvious ways in which 'private' space increases is when large multi-residence blocks replace more traditional rows of terraced houses. This effectively transforms a single public 'street' into a mass of private 'streets' (i.e. the stairs and corridors of huge high rise blocks, or the pathways of multiple town house complexes). The developments of this kind in Wandsworth occurred mainly during the 1960s, and in the public rather than the private housing sector. The housing department reported that the Borough has the third largest number of high-rise blocks of all the boroughs in the UK. The development of large council housing developments during the 1960s involved a switch from high street, traditional street-facing residences, to multiple-residence blocks. However, these were patrolled neither by private security, nor routinely by the public police, although some properties were serviced by council-employed caretakers who lived on-site. The development of a mobile 'housing patrol' service arguably reflected a formalisation of the more informal social control undertaken by caretakers, into a more formal 'policing' function, although it was undertaken by the 'local state' (i.e. the Council) rather than private security companies.

Public parks and open spaces

The Borough has about 850 acres of open parkland in all, and the physical extent of these spaces has changed little over the years. Some of these are just small play areas, although there are four very big parks, and three other main areas of parkland. As we described in Chapter Five these spaces have been policed by the Wandsworth Parks Police since 1985, although the Metropolitan Police are by no means excluded from these areas and are, from time to time, involved in significant policing activities in them. It is difficult to extend the mass private property argument to the parks, because they are in an important sense 'publicly-owned'. However, it is important to consider to what extent the Metropolitan Police have been displaced by the Parks Police.

Prior to the establishment of a Parks Police service, the parks and open spaces of the Borough were not routinely patrolled by the Metropolitan Police, but by Council-employed park-keepers. The introduction of the Parks Police thus signalled a higher profile form of 'policing' of the parks, but represented a formalisation of the social control previously carried out by park-keepers, rather than a displacement of Metropolitan Police. In fact, the by-laws relating to parks and open spaces make it quite clear that the Metropolitan Police still retain the right to operate within the parks should they think fit:

Nothing in these by-laws shall take away, abridge, or limit any remedy now existing by way of indictment, or shall interfere with the powers of the Metropolitan Police, or any authority legally existing or in force for preventing or punishing offences, or with the powers of the Council as having the control of any Park, Garden, or Open Space.[6]

The expansion of the Parks Police activities onto other kinds of council property, and in other parts of the Borough, is not related to any shift in the structure of property relations. It would thus be hard to sustain the argument that the Parks Police have displaced the Metropolitan Police from an area which was previously their 'domain'.

Educational institutions

There have been important developments in the funding and organisation of educational institutions over recent years. The government's 'social market' approach to education has, for example, resulted in colleges of further and higher education increasingly being required to act as individual businesses. In London, this was compounded by the abolition of ILEA and the subsequent independence of some colleges from local authority control. This has created a form of 'hybrid' space, not privately-owned in the sense of 'mass private property' but again, not publicly-owned in the sense that parks and streets are. As we noted in previous chapters, a number of colleges of higher and further education in the Borough have contracted-in private security guards. Like the example of the parks, though, this cannot be represented as a displacement of the public police from areas and functions they previously dominated.

Of course, the fact that colleges were once directly under local authority control did not imply that there was ever free public access

---

[6] Wandsworth Borough Council, Parks and Open Spaces Committee, By-Law 27.

to such sites. As our brief discussion of 'hybrid space' earlier showed, spaces which are 'public' in terms of ownership can sometimes be the most 'private' in terms of access. Thus, there was never total public access to the college sites. The increasing use of private security is therefore unrelated to the issue of the colleges being run independently of local authority control. Similarly, even when the colleges were unambiguously 'publicly-run' by the local education authority, their sites were not routinely patrolled by the Metropolitan police. The fundamental change that has taken place has been that informal and less visible forms of internal 'policing' have been perceived as decreasingly effective, and therefore have been supplanted by more visible forms of 'policing' represented by private security guards. For example, the estate manager at one of the colleges outlined how surveillance and other forms of 'low-level' social control had previously been part of the everyday job of staff such as receptionists, caretakers, and gardeners. They would, for example, take note of suspicious strangers, ask people if they needed help, and open and lock gates and doors. These functions had been taken on by a more formalised 'policing' presence in the form of uniformed security guards.

Overview

There have, then, been some interesting developments in property relations in the Borough in recent decades. In a relatively minor way these have involved the growth of mass private property. More significant, however, has been the emergence of a variety of types of 'hybrid space' and the formalisation of security arrangements on such sites. This process of formalisation came about partly as a result of changes in the nature of the security problems experienced in such places (schools, hospitals, parks). However, it would be wrong to assume that the increasing visibility of private security on such sites represented a move from public to private policing. Rather, in most cases this was indeed a formalisation of security arrangements involving the replacement of staff such as caretakers, wardens, and park keepers by uniformed security guards. In most cases the presence of the public police on such sites would always have been unusual.

Relationships between different 'policing' organisations

The various theories about private security bring with them a set of assumptions about the nature of the relationship between public and private policing bodies. One kind of theory might suggest a largely co-operative relationship. For example, the 'junior partner' theory suggests that a complementary relationship exists between the public police and private policing bodies. In this model, state police forces, faced with expanding demands on time and resources, are actually helped by other organisations which take on 'non-core' tasks. Another viewpoint would see a competitive relationship between state police and other policing bodies. For example, a radical strand of the fiscal crisis argument highlights the threat of privatisation to state police forces. This focuses on the transfer of police tasks to the private sector, with the resulting encroachment of private security on functions and territories which were once considered the sole pre-serve of the 'public' police. Under such circumstances, we might expect a relationship between the police and other policing bodies which was characterised by mutual suspicion, competition, and even hostility. A third view would suggest that the relationship is neither complementary nor competitive. If, as suggested by the mass private property thesis, the growth of 'private' policing is largely an indirect result of wider changes in the respective domains of private and pub-lic policing, then public and private policing bodies would generally be seen to be operating in largely distinct spheres. This would sug-gest a relationship characterised by co-existence. Wandsworth pro-vided interesting examples of all these kinds of relationships, although in the main it seemed that most relationships came into the 'co-existence' category.

Co-operation

Representatives of local private security companies with whom we made contact generally reported that, where there was a relationship with the police to comment on, it was a good one. Co-operative rela-tionships took a range of forms, including the following: swapping of general advice or information, specific intelligence sharing, sharing of equipment or facilities, passing over of cases, joint operations, social contacts/'old boys' networks', and police response to calls from private security.

There were a number of examples of the police and other agencies carrying out joint operations. This most usually involved private security firms carrying out the early stages of investigations, and call-ing the police in when enough evidence had been gathered, in order for them to 'feel collars'. It appears that this role was one that was frequently welcomed by the local police. A police sergeant in the sector containing the New Covent Garden Market reported that they had had some 'good arrests' from such cooperation with the market security force. The market security force had also co-operated with operations carried out by the investigations branch of HM Customs and Excise, and with 'sweeps' of casual workers at the market by Benefits Agency fraud investigators. There had also been contact with Immigration Officers, who occasionally detained suspected illegal immigrants working in the market's casual workforce. The nature of this 'co-operation' was not clear, other than exchanging information and, possibly, providing back-up in case of trouble.

Other similar examples occurred in one of the shopping centres, where the security force would gather CCTV and surveillance evidence of drug-dealers. The security force in one of the colleges had co-operated with an operation in which plainclothes officers came on site to observe and eventually arrest suspected crack dealers. Once again, the actual enforcement function was largely left to police officers. The role of private security was to gather the preliminary evidence and pass it on to the police.

More direct 'joint operations' occurred between the Metropolitan Police, and other 'public' policing bodies. For example, Health and Safety Executive (HSE) inspectors and Environmental Health Officers (EHOs) reported that a police constable would be asked to accompany enforcement officers on calls where serious opposition or other trouble was expected. The Head of Environmental Services described one operation in which EHOs wished to seize stereo-equipment following an illegal rave party. EHOs were accompanied to the scene by eleven police officers. In the same vein, Post Office Investigation Department (POID) representatives reported that they have close working relationships with the Metropolitan Police and undertake joint investigations with them. In the same vein, Parks Police officers undertake joint operations with Metropolitan Police officers in the parks and open spaces of the Borough. One example involved the surveillance of suspects in and around the parks; another was the policing of major public events such as fireworks displays and the annual Battersea Show. In the latter case, the Metropolitan Police generally take charge of the crowd and traffic control on the public roads outside the parks, and leave the operation inside the parks to the Parks Police (although there is close liaison, and should the Parks Police feel the need they can ask for Metropolitan Police help inside the parks as well). The British Transport Police (BTP) have a great deal of experience and expertise of policing football crowds, terrorism, and VIP visits. The BTP chief inspector in charge of Waterloo police station explained that there is 'very close liaison with the Met', and joint operations had undoubtedly taken place on the railway lines crossing the Borough.

One aspect of co-operation between the public police and 'private policing' highlighted in Britain by Johnston[7] and in the USA by Marx[8], is the existence of an 'old boys' network' of former police officers working in the private security sector. Few direct examples of this were found in Wandsworth. However, a high proportion of the security managers interviewed were former police officers. For example, a former Crime Prevention Officer from one of the divisions was working for a local alarm company which was centrally involved in setting up a project run by the local crime prevention panel which provided cut-price alarms for the elderly. A more striking example involved the private investigation firm employed on the pilot for the council's professional witness scheme on housing estates. This company hired out specialist teams of ex-police officers (and exclusively ex-police officers). The company had a register of hundreds of former police officers of all ranks and from all specialisms within the service. The managing director claimed that within a few days he could 'put together a fraud squad of former senior police officers which would be bigger and more experienced than the Metropolitan Police Fraud Squad'. A small team of ex-police officers working for this company had carried out some covert surveillance on a problem housing estate as part of the council's 'professional witness scheme'. The chief security officer of the council (who was head of the Parks Police) is a former senior army officer with extensive experience in Northern Ireland. The training officer is a former Metropolitan Police chief inspector, and a number of former police officers and former special constables are found amongst the ranks of the Parks Police. However, the POID was not, it seems, dominated by ex police officers. The organisation has a long history, and a distinct culture and identity. Thus, although police-style language characterised discussions with some POID investigators, it was clear that the majority of POID personnel are recruited from within the branches of the

---

[7] Johnston (1992).

[8] Marx, G. (1987) 'The interweaving of public and private police in undercover work', in Shearing and Stenning (eds.) (1987).

Post Office. Although there are some ex-police staff, it was reported that these represent a decreasing proportion of POID investigators.

Personal contacts with the local police organisation, whether done via 'old boy's networks' or not, were important in determining the nature of local relationships. Some contacts were long-standing. For example, the manager of the security operation at New Covent Garden Market was a prominent member of the local Businesswatch, and developed close contacts with the local police officers. There was a regular contact, and a two-way flow of information about local troublemakers and crime trends. This informal exchange of intelligence also occurred between the local police and the security forces in the shopping centres, a development actively encouraged by the centre management. One of the private investigation firms undertaking 'professional witness' work on council estates reported that it is company policy to discuss such operations with the local police prior to beginning them. Advice and informal information exchange also occurred between some local nightclub managers and the local police. The manager of one local public house with a late license reported that it was a familar 'watering hole' for CID officers from the local police station, a number of whom he had got to know personally. The local Crime Prevention Officer occasionally gave informal advice about known local trouble-makers. It seems that this kind of informal information exchange is not always one way. For example, some private security operatives are able to develop a highly specialised knowledge of particular fields. One example of this from Wandsworth was the security manager of Christie's Fine Art Security Services (a former senior detective in the Metropolitan Police) who had given training seminars to police officers on the investigation of the theft of fine art and antiques.

Evidence from the USA suggests that private detectives (many of whom are former police officers and retain close contacts with the force) have almost routine access to police data through informal contacts.[9] Johnston[10] referred to 'well-publicised cases of police officers trading information from the Police National Computer to contacts in the industry' in Britain and, moreover, to the allegation that the police were the source of information provided to 'vigilantes' in one highly publicised case in 1993.[11] Perhaps unsurprisingly, we

---

[9] Cunningham and Taylor (1985).   [10] Johnston (1992).

[11] Johnston, L. (1996) 'What is vigilantism?', *British Journal of Criminology*, 36, 2, pp. 220–36.

did not come across any specific examples of such information-transfer from Wandsworth. Informal discussions with security personnel suggested that it almost certainly goes on, though we discovered little about the circumstances or the extent. That such a transfer of information occurs is certainly unsurprising given the number of former police officers working in the security business. One such security manager (another ex-police officer) strongly implied that he used in-force contacts to carry out criminal records checks on prospective employees when he remarked, 'if I played the game as it should be played I would stand a very good chance of employing a criminal'. The loss prevention manager at a depot in the Borough (again, a former police officer) reported that in his experience, police information was quite frequently available to private security personnel in this way, although he gave no specific examples. A senior manager of one site described an incident when a company came and set up an illegal parking operation on the company's land. He made a complaint to the local police who refused to act on grounds of it being a civil matter. He then telephoned a senior officer in New Scotland Yard whom he knew well. The consequence of the call, according to this manager, was that the police arrived promptly to make inquiries, and a Police National Computer (PNC) check was carried out on the vehicles of the parking company staff. Such a check would not normally be available to somebody outside the police service. The 'parking company' were moved on quickly as a result.

At the point in one interview with a security manager when we were discussing the issue of checking the appropriateness of staff to undertake security duties, the security manager, who was looking through his staff files, picked them up and showed them to a local police officer who was also part of the meeting. He said, pointing at the file, 'can I show them [the researchers] this?'. The police officer shook his head to indicate that he could not and the file was put away. Given the stage of the interview, and the fact that it was a personnel file that the manager was holding, it seemed to us highly likely that what he was thinking of showing us were 'unofficial criminal records checks' that had been carried out on his behalf, though we could not confirm this subsequently.

Police information was a central element to the door supervisor registration scheme which was set up by the Council during the study. People applying to be registered as door supervisors in the Borough needed to be ratified as 'suitable' by the local police, who presumably were running Criminal Records Office (CRO) checks on applicants before clearing them for registration. In a similar way, we were told that, although the Parks Police do not have direct access to PNC information, if they see a suspicious vehicle they simply ring up a contact in the local police and have a vehicle check carried out. Some organisations had a limited right of access to PNC information. For example, the POID has the right of access when required for particular investigations, although this does not allow routine vetting of staff. The exception to this is the recruitment of Christmas casual labour, which we were told by a POID representative were subject to Criminal Records Office checks, 'either by precedent or by law'.

Although this does not relate directly to 'policing' bodies as such, the issue of information exchange is particularly relevant to the local authority role in crime prevention. There has been an increasingly close relationship between the local police divisions, and the Borough Council, an important part of which was the formalisation of the 'partnership' in 1992 (see Chapter Five). Information-sharing forums now exist in the shape of a number of topic groups, comprising police, councillors, council officers, and members of relevant groups. The groups include ones on car crime, CCTV, youth crime, and street crime. A key one is the information sharing topic group. Council officers reported that they had just reached the culmination of five years of negotiation with the police, and the police had agreed to release police crime statistics by electronic transfer to the Council. There had been a lot of hold-ups concerning data protection issues, and problems with the Metropolitan Police software contractors, who had delayed developments. Nevertheless, this agreement allowed the Council to begin crime pattern analysis, using the NETMAP software system which allows the merging of datasets and detailed analysis of crime trends by postcode area. The council described this kind of access to police information as 'absolutely central' to local authorities taking a proactive approach to local crime prevention. The police had been somewhat nervous about releasing this kind of confidential information to local authorities, especially in light of the data protection legislation. Council officials also reported that the police feared that crime statistics would come to be used in party political disputes. Nevertheless, there is an increasing acceptance on the part of the police of the notion of routine data transfer to local authorities, and Wandsworth was the first London Borough to have such access.

There were a few examples of equipment or facilities sharing. One private security force working on a site next to a large estate allowed the Metropolitan Police to use their CCTV system to carry out surveillance of the estate. Parks Police officers reported a case from some time ago when they were undertaking a number of joint operations with the Metropolitan Police, which were inconvenienced by having to maintain contact via telephone. A Metropolitan Officer lent them a Metropolitan Police radio to provide access to police airwaves. After the Data Protection Act, the police became concerned about the Parks Officers having this radio, and it was returned. The Parks Police carry out interviews and fingerprinting with arrestees in Metropolitan Police stations. Businesses may help the Metropolitan Police by loaning them property for particular operations. We were told of cases in which the police had been loaned marked vans of express delivery or electrical repairs firms, in order to carry out undercover surveillance. It is not unusual for businesses to allow police officers access to their property to carry out surveillance on adjoining areas. The POID reported that they use police facilities when they need to arrest and charge a suspect. In the police station, a POID investigator is treated 'like any other police officer', is given access to the custody suite, and is able to sign the charge sheet him or herself.

Despite differences of opinion about their legal status, the Parks Police appeared to have an excellent working relationship with the local divisions of the Metropolitan Police. Indeed, one of the divisional commanders described them as 'an invaluable resource'. The chief security officer confirmed this good relationship, describing it as 'very, very close'. The Parks Police take people they have arrested to Metropolitan Police stations, and in the majority of cases, custody officers accept and process the arrests. The only problems arise when there is a new custody officer who is unfamiliar with the Parks Police, or where the police feel that arrests have been made in cases where the exercise of powers may not be lawful. The Metropolitan Police are willing to pass on cases to the Parks Police. One example concerned an event in the parks when a child complained to her mother about a steward who, she claimed, had indecently assaulted her. The mother rang the Metropolitan Police, who contacted the Parks Police with a description of the suspect, and also advised the woman to report the matter to the Parks Police office. Parks Police officers arrested the man, who was subsequently convicted for assaulting the child. It emerged that this man had a number of convictions for sexual assault. The Parks Police will defer to the Metropolitan Police in appropriate cases, although this will not prevent them from becoming involved should the Metropolitan Police not make it a priority. One example of this was quoted by the Chief Security Officer, who said that certain parts of the parks are used for drug taking or dealing. When this is serious, the Metropolitan Police are informed, but if they are unable to provide staff to deal with it, plainclothes Parks Police officers carry out surveillance to deal with the problem.

Competition

There was little evidence of any major conflict between the public police and other policing bodies. One significant area of tension, however, surrounded the proposal by Wandsworth Council to extend the remit of Parks Police patrols to council-owned housing estates. Some Parks Police officers reported that a few Metropolitan Police officers had made clear their displeasure at this, and the proposal was strongly and successfully opposed by New Scotland Yard. In fact, from the perspective of Parks Officers, there was a qualitative difference in the perspective of the local Metropolitan Police divisions as compared with senior officers and others at New Scotland Yard. It is clear that New Scotland Yard took a more defensive or negative view of the Councils's proposal, and several of the Parks Constables took the view that this position was overly defensive, particularly given their feeling that relationships with local police officers were very positive. That said, we did come across some reports of problems. For example, one Metropolitan Police sergeant told us that 'as far as we are concerned they are not police officers' and said that it was occasionally irritating to have Parks Officers bringing in people arrested 'for all sorts of silly things'. Parks Officers themselves said that a minority of Metropolitan Police officers were somewhat dismissive of the Parks Police, although this was confined a few officers at one or two particular police stations.

The local police reported no major conflicts in recent years between themselves and private security companies. One (acting) sector inspector stated that some years previously the private security company who had had the contract for a local shopping centre had (apparently) opposed the police coming into the centre unless called. However, this company no longer held the contract, and a good working relationship had been established with the current contractors who encouraged the police to come into the centre when on routine patrol.

One might expect to find the greatest likelihood of difficult relationships between public and private police bodies in relation to the particular functions which had been 'hived off' from the public to the private sector. As noted earlier, Wandsworth provided two notable examples of 'contracting-out' in the area of policing. The first was the privatisation of the prisoner escort service in January 1995. Prior to 1995, prisoner escort services were the responsibility of prison officers and Metropolitan Police officers based in a central unit, not part of either of the Metropolitan Police divisions covering Wandsworth. Senior police officers at the divisional level reported a very high level of satisfaction with the new service. One divisional commander described it as 'an excellent example of privatisation', and added that his custody officers were positive about the contractors' performance under the new system. The negotiations surrounding the setting up of the new system had been smoothed by the fact that the Securicor management team included a number of senior ex-police officers. However, the positive view of privatisation was not held equally in all parts of the police organisation. Unsurprisingly, we heard reports that police and prison officers who were returned to the beat or to prison wings respectively by privatisation of prisoner escort and court duties, were not keen supporters of the policy. In fact, a few (and it was stressed that these were a small minority) had been deliberately unhelpful to Securicor staff. Problems with the new service had occurred, but the majority were seen as 'teething troubles'—caused for example by the different custody records systems in different stations—rather than resulting from deliberate sabotage. The same situation applied to relationships between Securicor staff and prison officers. Reportedly, there had been problems with a small minority of prison staff 'making life difficult' for Securicor staff in the short term, but the system was running smoothly within a relatively short period of time.

In late 1994 local borough councils in London became responsible for the enforcement of parking regulations on all roads the which were not 'red routes'; Metropolitan Police traffic wardens retaining responsibility for parking enforcement on red routes roads and small areas (approximately 30 feet) leading onto red routes. In Wandsworth, the Council contracted-out the service to a private company, a development supported by the Metropolitan Police. The local police anticipated some difficulties because the new parking control system is largely 'revenue driven' rather than 'traffic control driven', but saw this as a matter for the local authority. The boundaries between jurisdiction of Metropolitan Police traffic wardens, and those of the local council, were marked by a small white triangle, painted onto the pavement. These, it was felt, represented the points at which conflict might occur, although no examples of 'boundary disputes' came to light.

The lack of strong opposition to these developments partly reflects the fact that neither example of privatisation resulted in significant staff losses for the local police. The Metropolitan Police prisoner escort service was not a divisional resource, and the reorganisation of Metropolitan Police traffic wardens out of central London, where red route policing is minimal, to outer boroughs, actually resulted in a substantial increase of Metropolitan Police traffic wardens working in the two divisions covering the Borough. The lack of opposition may also reflect the somewhat peripheral nature of the tasks that were 'privatised'. It is notable that the Council's proposal to extend the Parks Police's work in that most symbolic of policing tasks—visible patrol—was greeted with significant and successful resistance by the police, even though this had no immediate or apparent implications for local policing resources.

Co-existence

In the majority of sites where private security was employed there was little contact between them and the local constabulary. For example, on a large business park in the east of the Borough, although a number of businesses employed (or contracted) security guards to patrol their sites, these guards had only irregular contact with local police officers. Not untypical was a large warehouse, the site manager of which reported that he rarely saw the police. He estimated that during the previous twelve months, the police had not been called more than three times. As noted above, the Borough's shopping centres were now much less likely to be included in routine Metropolitan Police patrols. The notion of the police and private security operating largely in different spheres was also suggested by the college security guards. The police rarely came on site unless called, apart from the occasional undercover operation. Management at one college saw a very different role for security guards from the police. They had introduced a rule that staff should call security in the first instance when there was an incident, because this would be more likely to defuse any conflict. The site manager said that they had experienced problems through staff calling the police too early, and the uniformed officers turning up 'mob-handed' which had actually exacerbated matters.

In the nightclubs and public houses which used door supervisors there was again only irregular contact between these staff and the local police. This was usually restricted to particular incidents where the police were called. However, it was noticeable that the Sector Inspector for one sector which included a number of nightclubs expressed sympathy for the difficulties experienced by door supervisors, and reported a generally good relationship between police and 'bouncers' in that area. As noted above, the Council and police recently introduced a registration scheme.

Relationships between policing bodies—an overview

Examples of good relationships and co-operation between the public police and other security bodies can be interpreted in a number of ways. Such relationships may be seen as evidence of what Johnston described as a 'benign integration of civil society and the state' in which 'policing becomes a single unified system'.[12] A more pessimistic view is that of Flavel who argued that a co-ordinated and coherent 'policing' complex was developing, which posed serious threats to civil liberties.[13] As Johnston noted, the fragmentation and variation in relationships that exists on the ground suggest that neither model satisfactorily explains what is going on.[14] He moved on to two other models, one being that in which the function of maintaining order is increasingly transferred into corporate rather than government hands. Finally, there is Mike Davis's dystopian vision in which the middle classes gate themselves off in fortress communities, protected by private security, whilst the public police are left to embattle the criminalised poor and dispossessed in the 'places of terror' that remain.[15]

None of these models accurately fits what is developing in Wandsworth. There appears to be a range of relationships between

[12] Johnston (1992).

[13] Flavel, W. (1973) 'Research into security organisations', Paper presented to Second Bristol Seminar on the Sociology of the Police (unpublished).

[14] Johnston (1992).

[15] Davis, M. (1990) *City of Quartz*, London: Vintage.

different bodies, and it was difficult to generalise across the diverse private security operations, and the range of public policing bodies other than the Metropolitan Police operating in the Borough. The closest forms of co-operation appeared to have developed between the public police and bodies with some statutory source to their powers or existence, such as the Parks Police, British Transport Police, and the Post Office Investigation Department. Close working relationships also developed with the larger private security operations such as that at the New Covent Garden Market. However, in many cases, the police and *private security companies* operated in largely independent spheres. They would come across each other sporadically, and the relationships were transitory and shifting. Generally, the relationship between the police and these smaller security companies was one of benign co-existence. They were mutually tolerant, operated in spheres that tended to keep them apart and yet overlapped, and indeed co-operated when the occasion demanded. There was, however, no clear evidence of the development of a co-ordinated 'total policing' system as such. The Metropolitan Police, stretched by an increasing workload, appeared to be forced into an increasingly responsive style of policing, close in style to Bayley's model of 'honest law enforcement' in which the police concentrate on 'authoritative intervention, symbolic justice and traffic regulation'.[16]

In many ways, however, although private security and other forms of policing were arguably taking an increasing role in policing the Borough, it is clear that many of them effectively have their activities partially underwritten by the Metropolitan Police. Thus, if things go badly wrong, whether it be for the Parks Police or a shopping centre security force, they have the safety-net option of calling the police. However, whilst this model may be developing in practice, it is doing so within the context of the sector policing initiative, which is intended to develop another of Bayley's models—'stratified crime prevention'—in which responsibility for crime prevention is concentrated on uniformed frontline personnel who are tasked with determining the form of policing best suited to particular areas.[17] How the models of 'honest law enforcement' and 'stratified crime prevention' play themselves out in police work in years to come will not only be intrinsically interesting for students of the police, but will also have important implications for the role of private and other 'public' policing bodies.

[16] Bayley, D. (1994) *Police for the Future*, New York: Oxford University Press.
[17] See Bayley (1994) ch. 7.

Private and public justice

An important theme in discussions about private policing, concerns the degree to which it operates within the context of 'private' justice systems, which are qualitatively different from formal legal regulations. As we described above, Shearing and Stenning argue that the public police and private security operate in fundamentally different contexts.[18] More particularly, they argue that whilst the public police operate within the formal criminal justice system, private policing is undertaken in the context of systems of 'private justice'. They further argue that recent decades have seen an 'unobtrusive but significant restructuring of our institutions for the maintenance of order, and a substantial erosion by the private sector of the state's assumed monopoly over policing and, by implication, justice'.[19] Henry defines private justice as '. . . the localised non-state systems of administering and sanctioning individuals accused of rule-breaking or disputing within groups or organisations'.[20] Private justice includes the practices of disciplinary bodies, boards and councils of industrial and commercial organisations, professional and trade associations and unions, as well as peer sanctions undertaken by relatively amorphous voluntary associations, and at the very informal level, the personal morality that one individual may impose on others. Henry noted that 'private justice . . . comprises those institutions of social control that maintain the normative order'.[21] The argument is that the ultimate goals of private justice and those of public justice may be in conflict, and that the former is far more pervasive than the latter. In this view, the public justice system is often seen as a 'last resort'; something used as an adjunct to 'private' means of conflict resolution.

We confront similar difficulties when trying to define 'private justice' as we do when considering 'social control' and indeed, 'policing'. That is, the inherent complexities of the concept lead to a temptation to define it so broadly as to render it meaningless. Henry argues that 'private policing' is but one component of the wider phenomenon of private justice, which itself is part of the 'totality' of

[18] Shearing C. D. and Stenning P. C. (eds.) (1987).
[19] Shearing C. D. and Stenning P. C. (1983) 'Private Security—implications for social control', *Social Problems*, 30, 5, p. 496.
[20] Henry, S. (1987) 'Private justice and the policing of labor: the dialectics of industrial discipline', in Shearing C. D. and Stenning P. C. (eds.) (1987) pp. 45–6.
[21] Henry, S. (1983) *Private Justice: Towards integrated theorising in the sociology of law*, London: Routledge and Kegan Paul, p. 89.

social control.[22] He thus makes a strong distinction between private justice and the *destructuring* of state control, which, he says, includes methods of dispersing social control (decarceration, decriminalisation, etc.) and simultaneously widening the state net in times of fiscal and legitimation crises. He also distinguishes the concept from *privatisation*, using Cohen's[23] definition, whereby 'the state ceases to supply a particular service and it is then supplied by private sector enterprises which are directly paid by the public as customers'. In this approach, Henry follows the legal pluralists such as Pospisil who argue that 'any human society . . . does not possess a single legal system, but as many such systems as there are functioning groups'.[24] Thus, a single institution may contain a variety of social forms, each with distinct 'legal systems' of social rules, norms and sanctions, with varying degrees of informality. These forms may well conflict with each other, or with 'state law'. A final aspect of Henry's argument concerns the relationships of the different forms to each other, and to state law. He argues that 'state law' is constituted through a dialectical process, in which the law gains identity and support through the incorporation of several forms of private justice, but at the same time loses identity and generates opposition through fostering semi-autonomy of other private forms. The same 'mutually constitutive' dialectical relationship exists between forms of 'private justice'.

An important point for our consideration of private justice in our local study is that Henry sees private security guarding as 'straddling the boundary' between private and public justice. When the state contracts a private security company to patrol public areas, or a private company contracts a security company to protect property from the threat of external crime, then this forms part of Cohen's 'destructured' social control.[25]

But when the private security company is contracted by groups or organisations to perform a policing function on its own membership, then it becomes part of what I call, private justice . . . It will then be a component of an administrative chain in which deviants from the rules or principles of the organisation are processed through a private judicial machinery concerned

---

[22] Henry, S. (1983 and 1987).
[23] Cohen (1985) *Visions of Social Control,* Cambridge: Polity Press, p. 64.
[24] Pospisil, L. (1971) *Anthropology of Law,* New York: Harper and Row, p. 98.
[25] Cohen, S. (1985).

with considering their offence and dispensing sanctions to those found guilty.[26]

Chapter Two illustrated the inherent difficulty in using the public–private dichotomy to systematically sort processes or forms into a binary opposition. The same difficulty applies to the concepts of private and public justice. In reality, systems of justice can be differentiated by increasing levels of organisation and formality, with the 'public' forms appearing at the more formal end, and the 'private' forms approaching the informal end of the continuum. For example, in a workplace a particular worker's misbehaviour may invoke informal peer sanctions of reprobation and disapproval by colleagues. However, a more formal level of control may be exerted by the threat of disciplinary procedures laid down by the employer, which can be invoked when an employee is in breach of internal rules. This may eventually result in the sanction of dismissal. If a worker's behaviour is such that the criminal law is broken, then the police may be brought in and a criminal prosecution undertaken.

Henry's 'private justice' systems should not be confused with the civil law, the framework of which is laid down by the state. The civil law is sometimes distinguished from the criminal law in terms of 'private' and 'public'. For example, Finn quotes a seventeenth century judge, Sir Matthew Hale, who divided legal offences into two categories: 'Such as are criminal or public, wherein the wrongdoer is proceeded against criminally . . . Such as are civil or private, wherein at the suit . . . of the party injured, he had reparation or right done'.[27] We should note that the notion of private justice adopts a different version of 'private' than the legal distinction between criminal and civil, with the distinguishing characteristic of private justice systems being that they are in some sense less formal than 'public justice' systems, but more particularly that they are 'non-state' forms of regulation. On this view, both the civil and criminal branches of the law are part of the wider justice system, shaped and regulated by the state. These two distinctions arise from the different broader conceptions outlined earlier. Seeing the criminal law as 'public' is largely concerned with the individual/collective and market/state division. A criminal prosecution is undertaken by public officials on behalf of the collectivity, and paid for by the state. A private prosecution is under-

---

[26] Henry, S. (1987).

[27] Finn, P. (1983) 'Public function-private action: A common dilemma', In S. Benn and G. Gauss (eds.) *Public and Private in Social Life* London: Croom Helm.

taken on behalf of an individual and is not paid for out of taxation. The notion of 'private justice', however, involves quite a different conception of 'private'. Private justice systems are less explicit, less universal and in this sense, more 'hidden' than the public justice systems based on 'state law'.

Private justice and policing Wandsworth

We found a range of systems of social control within groups and organisations, with their attendant 'justice system' which exhibited varying degrees of formality, and interacted in different ways with the public justice system. There is widespread evidence that some organisations prefer to deal internally with rule-breaches which could strictly be regarded as criminal matters. In many cases, private security acts as simultaneously as part of both public and private justice systems.

New Covent Garden Market Security Force
This provided a clear example of the interaction of private security with different systems of justice within one organisation. At one end of the spectrum, there was the largely informal system of 'popular justice' amongst the market traders, who had a strong ethos against stealing from other traders, and an equally strong aversion to involving the police and other agents of the formal criminal justice system. Nevertheless, at one time the flower market had a major problem with theft from stalls, until a sophisticated system of CCTV was installed in the main hall. This closely monitors each stall, and records any activity. The security officers informed us that theft from stalls had been almost eliminated by the system. The security force played a limited but nevertheless important 'facilitating' role in this justice system. Traders who had suffered theft would ask to view the tapes of cameras monitoring their particular stall and, because of the nature of the trade, would usually recognise the thief. It was extremely rare for such cases to be reported to the police—the usual procedure was for the trader 'to sort it out himself'. We asked a security officer if the sanction—the most usual sanction being to sack the employee responsible—might also involve physical violence. He did not reply directly, but grimly stated that most of the traders were 'East End lads', who had strong feelings about stealing from each other. There were, then, various degrees of formality. At one extreme, the 'offender' could receive summary justice which might

involve violence, or perhaps the loss of their job. However, it is also an offence against the market by-laws to steal from other traders, and the security force could take action based on by-laws (which allow the market to fine people, or exclude them for a time, or simply caution the offender). This is, however, a distinct 'private justice' system from that operating in the domain of informal peer sanctions.

As noted above, market traders were often unwilling to involve the 'public justice' system and its agents, the Metropolitan Police, in cases of rule-breaking. This was the cause of some frustration to the market management, who employed a range of tactics to persuade traders to take formal action against offenders, largely without success. However, on occasion the market management themselves are able to collect sufficient evidence to report matters to the Metropolitan Police. The market security force play a very important role in this process, monitoring CCTV footage and carrying out covert surveillance. The occasional symbolic prosecution is undertaken for its perceived deterrent effect. The security manager described a recent case where an offender was convicted and received the maximum fine, saying that it 'sent a ripple through the market'. Although the Metropolitan Police are rarely involved in the day-to-day policing of the market, their symbolic power is clear. When the researchers accompanied market security officers during a night shift, it soon became apparent that the unexplained presence of men in plain clothes with the security officers had been noted by traders. Security officers said that the word would quickly spread that CID officers were on site.

Thus, we have identified at least three systems of justice in operation within the market site. There is the informal system operated by market traders, the more formalised system characterised by by-laws and policed by the market security force, and the formal framework of state justice. Clearly, these systems overlapped in some ways, and were not mutually exclusive. However, they retained distinctive characteristics, which makes it difficult to generalise about how they related to each other. It was difficult to find evidence of Henry's 'mutually constitutive relations', whereby different systems of justice interacted to change each other. One development saw a theoretical 'formalisation' of one part of the market's own formal but internal system of justice, and an increase in the degree of overlap with the public justice system. The by-laws had recently been revised, giving the security force constabulary powers for enforcement of the Road

Traffic Act on the highways crossing the market site. However, in practice these powers were not being used, because the site manager did not think it appropriate that private security guards should be encouraged to undertake arrests. This is perhaps unsurprising in light of the fact that the market security force had actually replaced the previous 'beadles', who had apparently operated much more like a public police force in that they carried out arrests on the market site.

Shopping centres and supermarkets
There are also various levels of 'justice' in operation within shopping centres and supermarkets. Shopping Centres and supermarkets operate systems of 'banning'. For example, any person caught (or strongly suspected of) shoplifting may be banned for life, regardless of whether or not they were prosecuted. Such a sanction does not apply only to shoplifters or those who have committed offences for, as this is private property, as with many other privately-owned premises the 'management reserve the right to refuse admission'.[28] Thus, in theory, the management can refuse admission to any person. This would include members of groups who threaten the 'commercial imperative'[29] including beggars, vagrants, drunks or rowdy youths. As Bottoms and Wiles pointed out '[t]he owners and managers of mass private property are, however, unlikely to be influenced by any considerations of justice for a small number of excluded individuals, being more interested in the utilitarian pursuit of the greatest happiness of the greatest number, and of course their own profit margins'.[30] Thus, a highly effective system of 'private justice' can be used by centre management to prevent certain individuals or groups from entering the property. Recourse to the civil law *ultimately* underpins this particular system of 'private justice' in so far as a banned person who insists on entry can be sued for trespass. In practice, this is rarely necessary, and the banning system operates via security guards refusing certain people entry and goes no further than this. Banned people who manage to enter shopping centres are 'forcibly removed' (in the words of one shopping centre manager) or 'asked to leave' (in the words of another).

[28] Banning can occur for a variety of acts, ranging from criminal offences such as theft or vandalism, to minor acts of 'anti-social behaviour' such as rowdiness, spitting or swearing.

[29] Johnston (1996*a*).

[30] Bottoms, A. E. and Wiles, P. (1994*a*) 'Crime and insecurity in the city', Paper presented at the International Course organised by the International Society of Criminology, Leuven, Belguim, May 1994.

Two anecdotes from the shopping centres in Wandsworth may be of particular interest here. First, a man who had been convicted of shoplifting in one centre paid his fine and some time later sought to enter the shopping centre. He was caught by security guards and escorted from the premises, having been informed that he was banned. He wrote to his local MP, saying that he had paid his debt to society and now wished to be allowed to shop in the centre like many other residents. The MP took a sympathetic view and wrote to the centre manager supporting his constituent. The centre manager however took a different view, and said that the ban would continue. The manager of another centre reported that banned people may approach him to plead their case to be allowed back in. 'Offenders' are sent to see the site manager to 'give an undertaking as to their future behaviour', then the site manager may decide to let them back in the centre. People will have their bans lifted when 'they have learned to abide by our rules'. The sanction is quite effective, particularly against local youths, as the centre is a focal point for meeting and socialising, as well as shopping.

Shopping Centre managers expressed frustration that so few shoplifters are processed through the criminal justice system. Partly this occurs because some shop-owners prefer not to prosecute. Others want to prosecute more offenders but believe the costs to be prohibitive relative to the benefits. Many feel that the formal system of justice cannot cope with a large number of relatively minor offences, and so take them no further. The manager of one centre expressed frustration with one shop manager's refusal to prosecute. She said she 'knew for a fact that they had a huge problem' with employee theft, but still preferred to deal with things internally. The management of supermarkets realise that they cannot possibly prosecute all those people arrested for shoplifting. Although a very large number of people are arrested in British supermarkets each year (by managers, security guards or store detectives), a significant proportion are not prosecuted. Retailers must rely instead on the deterrent effect of uniformed security guards in most stores, the public humiliation in being stopped and questioned by store detectives, the shock of being formally arrested, and perhaps the use of a formal caution by the police. Managers are realistic about the capacity of the criminal justice system which simply could not process all the cases of shoplifting that occur.

Schools and colleges

Schools and colleges are also good examples of institutions which contain a number of distinct but inter-related social forms with their own systems of private justice. Any person looking back on their own schooldays will probably remember the pervasiveness of peer group pressure, the reluctance of bullying victims to invoke the protection of teachers or parents, and the strong emphasis on dealing with problems oneself. However, perhaps more than is the case in many other organisations, educational institutions have their own explicit and detailed framework of internal regulations through which 'offenders' can be processed. In both colleges covered by the study, private security guards are involved in varying ways in a number of different systems of private justice. First, they are clearly an important part of Cohen's 'destructured social control' (i.e. protecting the site from the threat of external crime). Access control and site protection form a key part of their work. However, security guards are also involved in the kind of 'private justice' systems clearly described by Henry, by helping to enforce internal college regulations. They are also involved in a less formal 'peer group' system of justice, which involves implicit or explicit challenges to some of the more aggressive students on their own terms.

On one site, the site manager made a strong distinction within the role of security guards, saying that lecturers are clearly informed of the limits of the security guards' remit. Thus for example, dealing with disobedient students is not supposed to be a responsibility of the security guards. However, in practice, security guards on this site are generally involved in enforcing minor regulations. For example, in one college security guards enforce minor rules such as the prohibition of chewing gum in the library, and ensuring that 'noise levels' in the corridors were kept within 'reasonable' bounds. This neatly illustrates that much of the work of private security guards contracted to work on these sites was concerned with the 'internal policing' problems associated with the students within the college, as much as protecting the college from the threat of external crime. On another college site, as well as checking entrance passes and preventing unauthorised access, private security guards enforce college regulations such as no-smoking rules. The ultimate sanction within these private justice systems is expulsion from the college. Security guards form the first point of contact for college management in enforcing many of these rules. 'Offenders' may appear before the principal and security guards can be asked to 'give evidence' at this hearing. Within the control room at one college, guards keep a log of the details of every incident, ranging from a student being 'cheeky' to serious threats and assaults. Thus, in these capacities, private security operates as the agent of management.

There was some evidence that on occasions, matters which could be subject to criminal proceedings are dealt with internally instead. The head guard at one college gave two reasons for this. First, it is often the decision of the victim whether or not to call the police. In many cases, the victim prefers not to involve the police for fear of reprisal. But a second kind of reason for not involving the police is to protect the image of the college, since calling the police is considered 'bad for publicity'. Despite these reasons, there have been instances when colleges are clearly prepared to take things further than internal rules and invoke the criminal justice system. This depends on perceived levels of 'seriousness'. For example, the security firm at one college reported that a student caught smoking cannabis on site would probably be expelled and the case would go no further. However, should there be evidence of dealing in any kind of illicit drugs, then this is reported to the Metropolitan Police. Similarly, assaults (unless of a very minor nature) are generally reported to the police. In sum, although direct involvement of the private security guards in the public justice system is far from frequent, it can and does happen.

Another interesting aspect of the private security role in 'private justice' arose from discussions with security guards about their experience of the job. Guards in one college had initially experienced some quite serious problems with violence and disorder caused by both students and outsiders. As noted in Chapter 5, as well as being agents of the college, the guards also engage with students in a slightly different context. In the words of one guard, some of the 'young stags' amongst the male students saw the security guards as a target, and wanted to prove a point. It was important for the security guards not to lose face, and we heard several tales of personal stand-offs, which were clearly operating in a different sphere of justice from college rules and discipline. The fact that the guards that had been hired were ex-army, physically large, and had a clear air of menace about them was, in an important sense, partly a recognition of the existence and the symbolic importance of these more informal spheres. In explicit recognition of this, one site manager who was delighted with the success of the security company in reducing incidents on site, made a number of references to the fact that the guards were large, tough-looking ex-soldiers. In his view, this had helped them gain respect (or fear) of the more 'difficult' students.

In the other college, a guard outlined how important it was not to back down when physically threatened. On one occasion this had resulted in the guard removing the pips from the uniform and suggesting that the threatening student step outside the college gates to 'sort the matter out one-to-one'. This constituted the removal of the symbols of college authority, and a willingness to step into another, more informal, sphere of private justice. Clearly, the various spheres of justice cannot be viewed as distinct. The guards argued that, without the respect gained by showing that they were prepared to operate within the more informal spheres of 'rough' justice, they would not be effective in their operations in other, more formal, systems. In addition, the guards could always, in theory, call upon the resources of the more formal systems such as college regulations or even the police.

Parks and Open Spaces

The Parks Police also operate across a number of systems of private and public justice. For example, an important part of their job is to act within the public justice system. The council park-keepers they replaced were perceived as having insufficient powers and authority to police the parks. This is why the Parks Constabulary was created, with its officers sworn in as constables for the purposes of enforcing parks and open spaces by-laws. As the next chapter will explore, there remains some confusion about the extent of the legal powers of the Parks Constables. What is certain though, is that in practice, Parks Officers are acting as full constables within the parks and open spaces in the Borough, carrying out arrests under the Theft Act for example, as well as reporting people for offences under the by-laws. Being part of the public justice system, even within this limited jurisdiction, is clearly an important part of the self-identity of Parks officers. We spoke to several of them who all confirmed that they believe, within the parks, they have the powers of any police constable. This is confirmed by their arrest statistics, and the nature of the work they are involved in.

However, this is only one of the contexts within which they work. Clearly, most of their operations within parks and open spaces involve enforcing the numerous by-laws which apply to these areas. As well as the Wandsworth Council By-Laws (specifying about twenty-seven prohibited activities), the Parks Police also enforce the old Greater London Council (GLC) Parks Gardens and Open Spaces By-Laws (of which there are over fifty covering similar things), the regulations governing public conveniences, and a range of Dog Control By-Laws. There is a regular flow of prosecutions for by-laws offences, and the Parks Police are perceived as a very effective body for enforcing what the Borough Solicitor described as 'quasi-criminal' matters. At another level, the Parks Police act as 'security officers' for the council. In this capacity, they will be required to investigate breaches of procedure, make a symbolic presence within certain council properties, respond to alarm activations from council buildings, and as such be an important part of another private justice system.

In the same way as for the college security forces, the question arises: what relationship exists between the different systems of private justice, and between them and state justice? One striking finding was that the breadth of the responsibilities of the Parks Police gives them quite broad powers within their jurisdiction. A researcher accompanied a Parks Officer on patrol, who described one area which had been subject to complaints about people having sex in public and men exposing themselves to other users of the park. When asked what action he would take if he caught an offender, he replied that he had two options. First, to arrest and charge under the Sexual Offences Act. Second, and more likely, to report for an offence under the by-law which prohibits 'any nuisance contrary to public decency and propriety'. He argued that he would more usually take the second option because the burden of proof was less. Thus, the by-laws, whilst making up a total framework of rules and regulations at a level below the normal consideration of the criminal law, also provide a flexible resource for Parks Officers. When a criminal offence is taking place which also may be prohibited by the by-laws (another example is criminal damage, which is also forbidden by a number of by-laws), the Parks Officer would have a choice as to the mode of action.

Private justice—an overview

We need to give further consideration to systems of private and public justice, in particular the possibilities of the 'mutually constitutive relationship' between private justice and public justice, and between different forms of private justice. However, this would clearly require some more detailed research within a small number of institutions. From our brief consideration of the 'private justice' systems we came across in Wandsworth, a number of points are worth mentioning. First, there is clear evidence that private justice systems, as Henry described them, are alive and well in Wandsworth. This is not in the least bit surprising, for as a number of disciplines have shown us (for example, industrial sociology, the sociology of the family, organisational behaviour, industrial relations), systems of regulation and control, both informal and formal, are central to human organisations. More interesting perhaps are the questions about the nature of these systems and the degree to which they shape, or are shaped by, state law. This takes us back to Cohen's arguments about the reserve arsenal of coercion, and the spreading of the state's control net (although, as we see above, Henry distinguishes private justice from this). It is difficult to explore these questions with our data. However, what they do confirm is that private justice can be much more than an adjunct to the public criminal justice system. There are occasions when groups or individuals actively prefer their own systems of less formal sanctions and rule-enforcement, even in clearly 'criminal' cases. However, this should not be taken as arguing that private and public justice systems are necessarily qualitatively different spheres. In some cases, private justice develops where it is believed that the public system will not be effective (for example, with the shoplifters). In other cases, private justice is simply the preferred method irrespective of the likely effectiveness of formal criminal proceedings (for example, the flower market traders). The relationship between public and private systems of justice is a complex and important one requiring further investigation. Finally, our consideration of private justice systems has some interesting implications for arguments about the rise of private security. As we stated earlier, Shearing and Stenning placed the rise of private security firmly in the context of the growing importance of private systems of justice as opposed to traditional state systems. However, our analysis suggests that the growing reliance on private security and other forms of 'policing' reflect a serious weakening of informal sources of social control, with their attendant, less visible, systems of sanctions and pressures. Examples of this included the replacing of caretakers and gardeners by more explicitly security-oriented personnel (for example, the Parks Police, Housing Patrol), and the private security guards in colleges

taking on social control functions which had previously been undertaken as and when necessary by lecturers, receptionists and gardeners. It seems that more and more matters which would once have
been dealt with informally (within private systems of justice) have
been laid at the door of the agents of more formalised types of social
control. In this sense, it is the decline of the most informal 'private
justice' systems, rather than their growth, which has contributed to
the growing fragmentation of 'policing' bodies.

Concluding comments

In this chapter we returned to three sets of issues identified earlier in
the book: explanations for the rise of private policing; the relationship between public and private policing organisations; and the
nature of public and private justice. What can we learn from the
Wandsworth experience in these areas? First, we must reiterate the
limitations of a local study in this regard. Though we have much to
say about one London borough we cannot assume that what is
observable there has happened elsewhere, or that the conclusions that
we draw from what we have observed there can necessarily be
assumed to be applicable elsewhere. That said, much of what has
been written previously about private security has contained so little
in the way of empirical evidence that the in-depth nature of a local
area study is perhaps particularly valuable.

The first observation to make is that although the Metropolitan
Police are clearly stretched in terms of making their resources meet
the increasing demands placed upon them, it would be difficult to
sustain the argument that some form of fiscal crisis has been the principal driving force behind the growth of private security in London
in general or in Wandsworth in particular. First, there is no evidence
that there has been a fiscal crisis. In the period in which private security has expanded at its fastest, there have also been significant
increases in expenditure on the public police. Second, and we return
to this below, the fastest growing part of the private security industry has been that part concerned with alarms and electronic surveillance; it has not been in areas in direct competition with services
provided by the police. Third, and related to this, there is little evidence of major expansion in the guarding sector—either in terms of
numbers or in terms of the range of functions such guards perform.
Fourth, to the extent that security guards have superseded others, it

has been wardens, park-keepers, caretakers, and others involved in low-level social control activities that have been replaced. In the main it has not been the police.

Whilst the evidence from Wandsworth provides little support for the 'fiscal crisis' theory, it was nevertheless clear that there was a widespread perception in the Borough (and not just among the local police) that resources were increasingly limited. We do not dispute this. Clearly, demand has outstripped supply. This, together with a wider climate in which public confidence in the police has been shaken in a number of ways, has provided what is perhaps a necessary but not a sufficient condition for the private security industry to prosper. With increasing insecurity or fear of crime comes an increasing demand for protection. To the extent that a belief takes hold that the police cannot deal with crime alone (the very fact that people might ever have been encouraged to think otherwise now seems extraordinary) then other means will be sought. CCTV, alarms, security guards, neighbourhood watch, and (though there is no evidence of this in Wandsworth) vigilantism are all part of this process.

The next basic observation is that the changes that have been visible in the policing of Wandsworth amount to gradual change rather than a 'quiet revolution'.[31] Elements of the North American experience can be detected, but no more than this. Of course, there is the possibility that things may change further in the future. However, given the deliberate policies of the Borough planning department (to avoid the 'privatisation' of public space), and the constraints set by land availability and the broader economic position, there would appear already to be significant limits on the extent to which property relations in British cities can mirror those of the US. One of the Wandsworth shopping centre managers—a representative of the British Association of Shopping Centres (BASC)—argued very strongly that the large shopping centre was a phenomenon of the 1980s. In particular, she felt that such developments had been underpinned by the consumer boom and the relaxation of planning controls typical of parts of the decade. She illustrated her point by saying that in the past year she was the BASC judge for the best new centre

---

[31] Philip Stenning and Clifford Shearing argue that 'the post-war years in Canada have witnessed what can fairly be described as a quiet revolution in . . . policing and social control systems . . . At the forefront of the changes which are taking place . . . is the phenomenon of private security'. Stenning P. C. and Shearing C. D. (1980) 'The quiet revolution: the nature, development and general legal implications of private security in Canada', *Criminal Law Quarterly*, 22, p. 220.

in Britain, and there had been only one entry. She felt that land prices, and trends in shopping behaviour, suggested that there would not be a large growth in shopping malls in the future. Ironically, though it has been little focused upon, the growth area arguably involves even greater 'privatisation' than the shift to mall shopping: that is to say, the growth in 'home shopping'—shopping from catalogue or even via 'shopping channels' on satellite TV.

Such developments are more of a threat to the 'public sphere' than are the developments of mass private property. Even in the restricted arena of say, shopping malls, there are opportunities for face-to-face interactions with people, even if these are restricted by the property owners. Walzer has highlighted how new technology is restricting the opportunities for social congregation of all types.[32] The new mass media of communication make it possible to engage with the world at home: '. . . we don't need to go out at all. We can sit, safe and secure, in our own living rooms or family rooms and listen to music, watch the news, see movies, plays or vaudeville shows, tune in to a political debate or a revivalist preacher or a "talk-show" . . .'.[33]

This, like the analysis of mass private property, clearly more accurately applies to developments in suburban North America. Thus, in terms of the actual physical amount of land that is council-owned in Wandsworth, little has changed since the 1960s. Moreover, as we have stressed repeatedly, it is important not to lose sight of the fact that the domain of private security includes more than simply security guards. The data we have been able to present on the size and shape of the industry suggest that its most important sector is that of electronic security equipment. Arguably, therefore, what we should be focusing on is what has been referred to as the 'surveillance society'[34] or the 'maximum security society'.[35]

In Wandsworth there was little evidence of dramatic increases in the numbers of security guards employed, nor any obvious increase in the functions being carried out by such guards. The most striking development in the Borough was the growth of CCTV. Twenty years ago, the few CCTV systems then in existence would have been rather crude by today's standards. Today however, almost every organisa-

---

[32] Walzer, M. (1995) 'Pleasures and costs of urbanity', in Kasinitz, P. (ed.) *Metropolis: Centre and Symbol of Our Times*, Basingstoke: Macmillan.

[33] Ibid, p. 326.

[34] Lyon, D. (1994) *The Electronic Eye*, Cambridge: Polity Press.

[35] Marx, G. T. (1988) *Undercover: Police surveillance in America*, Berkeley: University of California Press.

tion visited as part of the study—from Battersea Dogs Home to New Covent Garden Market—had installed what were sometimes very sophisticated CCTV systems. These systems, although they were occasionally used to monitor the public domain, were primarily directed inwards and designed to secure the private territory of the owners.

Moreover, the Borough Council has invested substantial sums of money in the development of CCTV systems for the five town centres in the Borough. CCTV has also been introduced onto some housing estates and council-owned alleyways. Mobile cameras are available for particular operations. The system in Wandsworth Town Centre was the first in the Borough, and involves state-of-the-art equipment including multi-plex 'touch controlled' cameras, which can be monitored via sixteen screens in a control room at Wandsworth Town Hall. As has been the case with the introduction of town centre CCTV systems in other parts of the country, this development has raised concerns about civil liberties and the rise of a 'surveillance society', and this was the subject of a policy report by the Wandsworth Partnership as early as January 1993. However, as outlined in the previous chapter, both the Council and the police had experienced difficulties in releasing staff to monitor the CCTV system. All the cameras were video-taped and the tapes retained for two weeks. They had been used successfully in evidence, for cases involving assault and drug-dealing, and recorded crime rates in Wandsworth Town Centre dropped substantially after their introduction. The Council maintained that it was their policy to restrict the use of this equipment to anti-crime initiatives in the public domain, and furthermore, that access to the cameras is open only to the police and the local council.

The relationship between the Council and the police locally was extremely strong and co-operative. What of the relationship between the Metropolitan Police and other policing bodies more generally? In Wandsworth much of the time the Metropolitan Police and other security bodies operated in largely independent spheres. The relationships between them were not static, however, and were constantly changing and being (re)negotiated. Though at times there was some mutual suspicion—one might think it odd if bodies involved in 'policing' were not suspicious as a matter of course—in the main, we characterised the relationship between the police and private security as one of benign co-existence. There was little evidence of the development of a co-ordinated system of 'total policing'. The phrase

benign co-existence could also be extended to describe the relationship between public and private systems of justice locally.
Predictably, there was considerable evidence in the Borough of active
private justice systems and that these were much more than merely
an appendage of the public justice systems. However, their relationship with the state justice system was shifting and complex. In part
they were enabled to operate in the way they did because of the existence of a further more formal set of sanctions in the shape of
public justice. In another sense, the weakening of some of the more
informal systems of justice had led to growing demands upon the
public justice system. The activities of many working in the private
security industry and in other policing bodies are underpinned,
indeed underwritten by the police. The police, it is assumed, will
always be there if they are needed when things go wrong.

7

The Boundaries of Public and
Private Policing

The growing focus upon fragmentation and diversity of 'policing' agencies has led to a number of important advances in our thinking about policing.[1] First, it has broadened our focus beyond the activities of that body of state officials commonly known as 'the police'. The work of a number of authors has highlighted a range of organisations and agencies outside the public police whose activities in some way can be described as 'policing'.[2] Thus, it is increasingly accepted that 'policing' should not be simply equated with what 'the Police' do. Second, the existence of a range of agencies involved in policing has brought into question the utility of the public–private dichotomy in policing. In particular, Johnston has highlighted a growing blurring between public and private policing sectors. This is related partly to the existence of a range of so-called 'hybrid' policing bodies whose sectoral status, he argues, is ambiguous. For Johnston, then, 'policing consists of a complex of connections between formal and substantive powers, and between private and public activities, which the sociology of policing has, by and large, failed to address'.[3]

In shifting our gaze beyond an exclusive focus on public constabularies, these authors have made a vital contribution to the way policing is conceptualised. However, whilst they correctly criticise the overly-narrow nature of previous definitions of policing, rarely do they provide a new and more inclusive definition. It is important,

---

[1] See, for example, Leishman, F., Cope, S. and Starie, P. (1996) 'Reinventing and restructuring: towards a "new policing order"', in Leishman, F., Loveday, B. and Savage, S. (eds.) *Core Issues in Policing*, Harlow: Longman.

[2] See Johnston (1992; 1993); Shearing and Stenning (1983; 1987); and South (1988).

[3] Johnston (1992) p. 190.

therefore, that we are explicit about what, for current purposes, we have included under the rubric of policing. In Chapter One, we provided a working definition of policing. This was intended to be broad enough to encompass the activities of 'policing' bodies outside of public constabularies, and yet not so broad as to equate policing with all social control, however informal. Thus, we suggested that it was useful to think of policing as being *those organised forms of order maintenance, peace-keeping, rule or law enforcement, crime investigation and prevention, and other forms of investigation and associated information-brokering—which may involve a conscious exercise of coercive power—undertaken by individuals or organisations, where such activities are viewed by them and/or others, as a central or key defining part of their work.*

The primary aim of this chapter is to develop a conceptual framework which will enable us to analyse the boundaries between the diverse range of bodies involved in policing. We discuss the nature of the boundaries between different policing forms, and we examine the extent to which these have become blurred. This paves the way for a consideration of how far and in what ways the concepts of 'public' and 'private' are usefully applied to policing. In doing so we pay due regard to the body of work outlined in the opening chapter, but argue that none of the extant conceptualisations actually captures the full complexity of the contemporary policing division of labour, or produces the conceptual tools with which to make sense of the essential differences between public and private policing.

Policing as a multi-dimensional concept

Much previous writing, as we have outlined, has focused upon the functional and legal dimensions of policing. The police have either been defined by what the 'public police' actually do[4], or by the special legal powers they bring to their tasks[5]. The fact that this is insufficiently sophisticated to capture the complexity of contemporary policing was noted by Marx, for example, who argued that rather than simply categorising forms of policing as public or private, we need first to ask a series of questions about given forms of policing.[6] These included the following:

[4] See Cain (1979).
[5] Bittner, E. (1980) *The Function of Police in Modern Society*, Cambridge, Mass.: Oelgeschlager, Gunn and Hain.   [6] Marx (1987).

- Where does the policing occur?
- Whose interest does it serve?
- What functions are involved in the policing?
- Who pays for the policing?
- Who actually carries out the policing?
- Who controls and directs the policing?
- Who has access to the data collected as a result of it?
- What popular and self-definitions characterise the policing?
- What organisational form does the policing take?
- To what extent are social control agents linked together in informal networks that transcend their nominal definition as public or private?

Marx acknowledged that it is difficult empirically to answer these questions, and some, such as when is a public or private interest being served, are unlikely to result in consensus. Nevertheless, applying such questions takes us beyond a simple dichotomisation of policing organisations into public and private. The difficulty with this approach is that although it clearly enables important facets of policing to be uncovered, it does little to help in a schematic sense. Using the questions, Marx argued, means that 'an elaborate multidimensional matrix could be constructed from the answers to such questions. The number of empirical configurations probably almost matches the number of logical possibilities'.[7] Whilst engaging in the construction of such a matrix might allow one to get at the complexity of contemporary policing, it would do little for organising and ordering thinking about policing. A way forward can be found by identifying a more limited set of dimensions of policing, each of which potentially relates to more than one of Marx's questions.

Although Johnston does not use Marx's schema explicitly, his theorisation of changes in the policing division of labour points to how this might be done.[8] He reviews the problems of previous analyses of policing based upon the functional and legal dimensions. More particularly, he inserts into the analysis two further dimensions—the 'sectoral' and the 'spatial' dimensions of policing—'First, there is the debate about the relative roles of the public and private sectors in policing and crime prevention. Second, there is dispute about the appropriate spatial level (central state or local state) from which

---

[7] Marx (1987) p. 187.

[8] Johnston, L. (1993) 'Privatisation and protection: spatial and sectoral ideologies in British policing and crime prevention', *Modern Law Review*, 56, 6, pp. 771–92.

police and crime prevention services should be provided and controlled'.[9] The spatial dimension incorporates Marx's questions about what organisational form policing takes, and who controls and directs it. The sectoral dimension includes the questions: who pays for policing and whose interests does it serve?

Johnston noted the growing 'sectoral' complexity in policing, with the operation of 'hybrid' policing bodies which, he argued, cannot be neatly fitted into either public or private sectors. The 'spatial' dimension is also becoming more complex, with the centralisation of control over (public) policing in recent years given an added twist by pressures arising from the European Union. Johnston's use of sectoral here is relatively unproblematic, and this basic distinction between public and private sectors runs throughout what we have to say in the rest of this chapter. However, the term 'spatial' in this context can be confusing. Johnston's use of the term concerns the *geographical level*, on a central–local axis, at which the control and administration of policing is organised. This is clearly an important dimension along which policing needs to be considered, and a number of authors use the idea of the 'spatial' in this way.[10] However, we remain unconvinced that the term is most appropriately used in this way. The primary reason for this is that it is easily confused with another dimension that has hitherto been ignored by most authors: the *type of space* in which policing takes place.[11] The 'spatial' dimension is, we suggest, more accurately used to analyse the nature of the space where policing is carried out (one of Marx's questions); whether this space be 'public', 'private', or somewhere between the two. As a result of the decision to use 'spatial' in this sense, henceforward we will refer to Johnston's spatial dimension—the level, on a central–local axis, at which the control and administration of policing is organised—as the 'geographical' dimension of policing.

There are, therefore, a number of dimensions along which the boundaries of policing are to be analysed, and between which the meanings of 'public' and 'private' will vary:

---

[9] Johnston, L. (1993) 'Privatisation and protection: spatial and sectoral ideologies in British policing and crime prevention', *Modern Law Review*, 56, 6, p. 771.

[10] See for example, Fyfe, N. R. (1991) 'The police, space and society: the geography of policing', *Progress in Human Geography*, 15, 3, pp. 249–67.

[11] Thus, even though he fails to define what he means by the term, Loader recognises the importance of space in this sense to an understanding of contemporary policing in general, and to the policing of young people's use of public space in particular. See Loader, I. (1996) *Youth, Policing and Democracy*, Basingstoke: Macmillan, chs. 3 and 4.

Sectoral: What is the relationship of particular policing organisations to the 'state' and the 'market'?

Spatial: In what forms of 'space' do particular policing organisations operate?

Legal: What legal powers do the staff of particular policing organisations use/hold?

Functional: What functions do particular policing organisations perform?

Geographical: At what level along the local–national–international continuum are particular police bodies organised?

Using the example of Wandsworth as a case study, we explored in some detail the boundaries between policing organisations in terms of the first four of these dimensions. Given the localised nature of the case study, there are limits to what we are able to say about the geographical dimension of policing. Consequently, we limit ourselves in the main to some observations about institutional variation along this dimension. The other dimensions we intend to discuss in detail. We begin with the dimension that is the focus of much of the writing in this field: the sectoral.

Sectoral Boundaries

The essential sectoral distinction between public and private policing is usually framed in terms of the state versus the market. It is the sectoral dimension which actually gives rise to the terms 'public' and 'private' policing, with public policing seen as funded by taxation and provided by state-employed officials, contrasted with the selling of private policing services for profit in the free market. However, as we discussed in some detail in Chapter Two, although this is the dominant aspect of the sectoral public–private distinction, in reality there are a range of institutional forms of service provision on a public–private continuum, with central state control and provision at one end, and market provision at the other.

The 'public' nature of 'hybrid' policing

The most influential recent examination of sectoral complexity is that undertaken by Johnston.[12] As noted above, he argued that there is a

---

[12] See Johnston (1992; 1993; 1996a).

range of policing forms—categorised as 'hybrid' policing bodies—
whose sectoral status is ambiguous. As we were able to show, there
were a number of examples of these 'hybrid' bodies operating in
Wandsworth. However, as we argued in Chapter Two, if one accepts
the necessity of inserting this third category in between public and
private, one obvious consequence is to make simple sectoral distinctions less easy. Indeed, a close reading of Johnston's work shows that
although he created the hybrid category in response to the problems
he and others rightly identified in relation to the use of a crude public–private dichotomy, his hybrid policing category is itself not
unproblematic. Indeed, he accepts that it is impossible to define
clearly what comes into this category. The definition he offers is that
hybrid policing 'comprises a complex morass of agencies . . . whose
formal status and operating territories cut across the public-private
divide'.[13] In fact, the morass is so complex that it seems that 'hybrid
policing' appears to be no more than a residual category comprising
everything deemed to involve 'policing', but which is carried out by
bodies other than private security firms or Home Department police
forces.

Though we agree that there are significant differences between
Johnston's 'hybrid' policing bodies and, for example, the
Metropolitan Police, we wish to argue that the most important differences are not 'sectoral'. Indeed, though it is a highly complicated
distinction, we argue that the public–private divide can still be usefully applied to sectoral boundaries in relation to policing. To explain
the reasoning behind this, it is useful to consider the meaning of the
term 'hybrid' and to attempt to apply it to policing on the ground in
Wandsworth.

The term 'hybrid' suggests something which has a combination of
the features of two distinct species, in this case, 'public' and 'private'
policing. However, closer analysis of 'hybrid' bodies reveals that, in
sectoral terms, there are good reasons for regarding them as 'public'.
The local study revealed that there are a range of 'policing' bodies
operating in Wandsworth, including a number that would fit into
Johnston's 'hybrid policing'. These included the Wandsworth Parks
Police, Environmental Health Officers (EHOs), Benefit Fraud
Investigators, Housing Patrollers, British Transport Police (BTP)
officers, Health and Safety Executive (HSE) Investigators, and Post

---

[13] Johnston (1992) p. 114.

Office Investigation Department (POID) Investigators. This list is by no means exhaustive, and undoubtedly there were other bodies with regulatory or investigatory functions operating within the Borough. However, for the present purposes it is sufficient to analyse the activities of these significant 'hybrid' agencies.

In reality, far from having ambiguous sectoral status, it seems that the one thing which these bodies all have in common is that they are all in important respects 'public' bodies (in sectoral terms). That is, they are nearly all (mainly) *publicly-funded* bodies (whether through national or local taxation, or a combination of both), they are staffed by public employees, and they do not depend for their survival on the selling of services for profit (as would a private security firm). Of course, there are aspects of their operations which have 'private' overtones. Johnston, for example, describes the POID as a 'public body which sells investigative services in the market place'.[14] It is certainly true that the 'privatisation mentality' has been applied to this, as to other services. For example, the various components of the old General Post Office (GPO) (Royal Mail, Post Office Counters Ltd, Parcelforce and so on) 'buy-in' investigative services from the POID. However, this is not the same thing as selling services in the market place. The POID retains important 'public' powers (such as that of access to the Police National Computer). The uses to which such information can be put are strictly controlled, and this limits the circumstances in which the POID can 'sell' its services. To take one important example. When the National Girobank was privatised and sold off to the Alliance and Leicester Building Society, the POID was no longer able to carry out investigative services for the newly-privatised section. There are, on the other hand, some examples of the POID 'selling' services, such as crime prevention consultation to privatised parts of the GPO, but these activities are relatively limited. One further way of considering 'publicness' (in terms of state versus market) is the extent to which purchasers are able to choose between suppliers in the marketplace. In interview, a senior representative of the POID said that it would not be possible for the management of, say, Post Office Counters Ltd to decide to dispense with the services of the POID, and replace them with a private investigation firm. Moreover, even if the management were able to do this, it is highly unlikely that it would, given POID expertise in the area, and their

[14] Johnston (1996*a*) p. 61.

access (as a public body) to PNC information, which would not be available to a private company.

Similar arguments apply to the British Transport Police (BTP). Although some people are in the habit of describing the BTP as a 'private police force', there are good reasons to argue that this is really a term of speech which has developed as a way of distinguishing the BTP from Home Department police forces. Although the BTP historically developed out of railroad 'company' police forces, there is little question that the term 'private police force' is now a misleading description of the BTP. It has (until recently) been almost entirely publicly-funded, and its officers are full-time state officials. The government's privatisation policy introduces some ambiguities, in particular the fact that the private operating companies who now run train services in the various areas, have to draw up 'Police Services Agreements' for core police services, and thus the funding of BTP operations is now from private rail operators. However, this point should be qualified in two ways. First, the purchase of policing services from the BTP is not optional for the rail operators, but is a condition of being given an operating license by the regulator. Thus, although the private railway operators have the option of complementing BTP services with private security officers,[15] there is no question of replacing the BTP with private security staff. Consequently, it is hard to argue in this instance that a real 'market' exists. Second, even though BTP's operations are funded privately, the BTP retains its independence as a public police force. Its officers have constabulary powers, granted by statute, and in this have independence from the direction of the rail operators, even though the operators provide funding. In April 1996, Clare Short MP received a written answer to a parliamentary question to the Minister of Transport on the subject of the BTP. The question asked whether franchise agreements for rail operators would stipulate the use of the BTP, and whether there would be an obligation for operators to contribute to the costs of policing services. The answer confirmed the 'public' nature of the BTP:

The British Transport Police will continue, as *a unified public force*, to be responsible for policing Britain's rail network. Police services will be provided to all licensed railway operators, who will be obliged, through license

---

[15] The private operators of the London, Tilbury and Southend line, and the Network South Central service have both employed private security guards since privatisation, but as well as rather than instead of BTP officers.

conditions, to enter into agreements with the British Transport Police to use and pay for all law and order functions that require the use of professional police resources.[16] (emphasis added)

The third example, the Wandsworth Parks Police, are distinct in a number of important ways from the Metropolitan Police, and other Home Department police forces. However, the crucial differences are not sectoral. The Parks Police are a public body. They are publicly-funded from local taxation, and accountable to a committee of locally elected councillors. The Parks Police are also sworn in to the public office of 'constable' for their activities within parks and open spaces in the Borough. The Parks Constables are public employees in that they are employed by the 'local state' and, also, in so far as they have statutory powers determined by an Act of Parliament. Of course, there are strong reasons why we should distinguish bodies like the Parks Police from Home Department police forces, and these will be considered in more detail later. However, it is important to reiterate that the crucial distinctions are not to be found along the sectoral dimension.

Similar, possibly stronger, arguments apply to the sectoral status of other examples of 'hybrid' policing in the Borough. Those operations who use staff with statutory powers, such as HSE investigators and EHOs, are quite clearly public, in terms of funding and in terms of having statutory powers. Furthermore, developments such as 'selling services' in an internal market are more limited in the case of these bodies than arguably is the case for the Metropolitan Police. This is also true of other bodies whose core function involves regulation, law-enforcement, or order maintenance, but whose members have no special powers over and above those of the ordinary citizen. Housing Patrol officers and Benefit Fraud Investigators are employees of the 'local state', and their activities are almost entirely funded by local taxation. In this sense they are 'public' and not 'hybrid'.

In sum, on the sectoral dimension alone, it is not possible to demarcate between 'public' and 'hybrid' policing bodies. Consequently, we believe the term 'hybrid' to be an unhelpful conceptual tool for distinguishing between different public policing bodies. In Wandsworth, as well as the Metropolitan Police, there is an array of other policing bodies which are also public in terms of funding and staffing. It is only necessary to use a category such as 'hybrid'

[16] Written answer to Clare Short MP, 16 Apr. 1996.

if the 'public police' are defined *a priori* as Home Department police forces. If this is the case, a catch-all category must be found for other 'policing' bodies. Although we recognise that there are distinctions to be drawn between different types of public policing agencies, these distinctions do not, in our view, require the creation of a new sectoral category. In practice, there are a series of 'policing bodies' in operation in Wandsworth all of which can be fitted without difficulty into either the public or private sectors. The most helpful distinction within the 'public' category, is between what we have termed 'public constabularies' and 'other public policing bodies'. This distinguishes those policing bodies whose staff have constabulary powers and describe themselves as 'police', and those whose staff do not. All of these bodies are quite distinct from the 'policing' services provided by employees of private companies and sold for profit in the free market.

Of course, the fact that we do not find 'hybrid' to be a helpful term in this regard is not meant to imply that a blurring of sectoral boundaries is not occurring. Indeed, we found a variety of institutional forms which straddled the sectoral divide in operation in Wandsworth. This is most helpfully illustrated by reference to the purchaser–provider split for policing services. Table 7.1 illustrates the sectoral blurring by plotting 'providers' of policing services ('public constabularies', 'other public bodies' and 'private bodies') against 'purchasers'. The 'public' and 'private' categories of purchaser are self-explanatory. However, we have included a category of 'quasi-private', which covers bodies such as Hospital Trusts and Higher Education Colleges, who although mostly still funded indirectly out of public expenditure, are increasingly required to imitate the behaviour of private concerns.

Public Constabularies

In sectoral terms, the majority of the work of the Metropolitan Police falls unambiguously into the 'public' category. The police are mainly funded by a combination of national and local taxation, they are a (sometimes notoriously) bureaucratic organisation, and the majority of the work-force is made up of full-time state officials. Nevertheless, although this description fits most of the activities of the Metropolitan Police, it is possible to detect areas where there is some blurring of the divide between private and public.

One noted aspect of this blurring has been what Johnston has termed, the 'privatisation mentality', or the growing pressures (com-

Table 7.1: Sectoral boundaries in policing

PURCHASER	PROVIDER		
	Public Constabularies	Other Public Bodies	Private
Public	Met. Police—most activities	National—POID, HSE most activities	National—Prisoner Escort Service
	Parks Police—most activities	Local—Housing Patrol, EHOs, Benefit Fraud Investigators	Local—Borough Parking Enforcement/Professional Witness Scheme
Private	Met. Police—charging fees and selling services	POID—selling of crime prevention advice to National Girobank	Nightclub bouncers Site security
	BTP—police services agreements with private railway companies	Housing Patrol selling services to privately-managed estates	Shopping centre security
	Parks Police—policing of privately-run events in parks		
Quasi-private	Section 24 PMCA—e.g. policing of hospital trusts (not applied in Wandsworth)	Housing Patrol Services sold to Housing Co-operative Estates	College security Hospital security

mon to other public services) on the police to adopt 'consumer rhetoric'.[17] This began with the extension of the Financial Management Initiative to the police service in the early 1980s, which encouraged a concern with the 'three E's' (economy, efficiency, and effectiveness) via the adoption of private sector business management techniques. This process has continued apace, strengthened by the activities of the Audit Commission who have published a series of reports on various aspects of police work during the latter half of the 1980s and the early 1990s.[18] More recently, the Citizens Charter has been applied to the police service, with the publication of 'league tables' comparing police forces on standard performance indicators, and the range of reforms included in the Police and Magistrates' Courts Act 1994 which were mentioned above.

[17] Johnston (1996a).

[18] See, for example, *Improving Vehicle Fleet Management in the Police Service*, (May 1989); *The Management of Police Training* (Dec. 1989); *Taking Care of the Coppers: Income generation by provincial police forces*, (Nov. 1990); *Effective Policing—Performance review in police forces*, (Dec. 1990); *Reviewing the Organisation of Provincial Police Forces*, (Feb. 1991), all London: HMSO.

The effects of such developments are clearly visible in Wandsworth. Both Metropolitan Police divisions covering the Borough publish annual reports detailing performance against indicators, and the published objectives for the previous year. In all police stations in the Borough (a practice throughout the Metropolitan Police District), there are 'customer satisfaction' questionnaires which visitors to the police station are asked to complete. The 1994/5 review for the Wandsworth division shows a striking reliance on crime-related indicators, including graphs and charts illustrating the number of reported offences in the division in the four quarters, and the average clear-up rate per quarter. The four published divisional priorities for the coming year show a similar leaning towards crime-related work, these being: to deliver the standards defined in the Metropolitan Police Charter; to achieve a detection rate for notifiable offences of 20 per cent; to achieve a detection rate for burglary of 15 per cent; and to increase the detection rate for street crime to 15 per cent.

In this manner, the police service, in common with other public services, is increasingly being required to imitate aspects of private business concerns. However, a consideration of the 'purchaser–provider split' in the case of public policing shows more significant blurring of the public–private divide. First, it is possible to identify areas in which the Metropolitan Police provides services to private purchasers. Minor developments of this kind have occurred with the emergence of private sponsorship. Although this is not strictly private 'purchasing' of policing in a contractual sense, it establishes the principle of private funding of public services, and raises questions about what might be given in return. Given constraints on the growth of public resources, and the continued expansion of demands upon the public police, they have increasingly sought out private sponsorship for particular activities. To date, this has been a relatively minor (relative to total resources) development, and confined to a few activities such as police-run schemes for young people, and crime prevention campaigns. Many projects attracting private sponsorship are run under the auspices of agencies outside the police but linked to them, such as crime prevention panels. Examples from our local study include private sponsorship to support an 'alarms for the elderly scheme', a youth summer scheme on council estates, and private funding for CCTV schemes covering public space, and monitored (in part) by the public police.

This, of course, is not a new development. The charging of fees and the selling of specific services has been possible since the 1964 Police Act, although the practice has been growing in importance over recent years. Perhaps the most notable example of this is in the policing of large public order events such as football matches. There have been a number of cases in recent years in which constabularies have pursued commercial initiatives. The South Wales and West Yorkshire police forces, for example, have been reported to be considering setting up their own security firms in their local areas.[19]

Recent legislation will further encourage developments of this kind. In particular section 24 of the Police and Magistrates Courts Act 1994 allows local authorities (and some other bodies such as NHS Trusts) to contract with police forces for the deployment of extra police staff. Such agreements may provide specific definitions of the roles and functions of such designated officers. One of the first examples of this development was the contract between the Royal Devon and Exeter NHS Trust and the Devon and Cornwall Police.[20] A contract worth £60,000 was signed which provided the Trust with two police officers to patrol hospital sites. Within the same police force area, Torbay district council contracted for the employment of extra police constables to patrol the town. Corby Borough Council in Northamptonshire was the first council to pay for extra officers. It agreed to pay the local constabulary an extra £110,000 a year to pay for four additional officers to patrol the streets of the town. Reports of the deal pointed out that the council had 'agreed to pay for the policemen (sic) only if they go out on the beat and are not used for clerical work'.[21]

At the time of writing, there have been no examples of section 24 of the Police and Magistrates Courts Act being applied in Wandsworth. Indeed, a report by the Borough Solicitor in October 1994 stated that although the Act provided a mechanism for local authorities to make extra grants, the Home Office had advised the Council that any grants made to the police would not increase the income for local divisions, because it would be offset by a corresponding reduction in central funding. This position seems anomalous, because it effectively undermines the point of the provision, and brings into question the benefits for local councils such as Torbay in implementing section 24 of the Act. Whether or not this

---

[19] Johnston (1993).   [20] See the *Independent*, 5 Sept. 1995.
[21] 'Sponsored police go on the beat', *The Times*, 2 May 1995; 'Town pays for extra beat constables', *Police Review*, 31 Mar. 1995.

interpretation is correct, it has led to a perception on the Council that there is little to be gained by providing an additional grant to the Metropolitan Police. However, the strong opposition to the proposals to extend the remit of the Parks Police may well lead the local Metropolitan Police commanders to consider this option in the future.

Other bodies of constables such as the British Transport Police and the Wandsworth Parks Police have, like the majority of public services, seen the growth of a 'privatisation mentality' in recent years. As noted above, the implications of the privatisation of rail networks has meant a growth in 'private funding' for the BTP, with the rail operators signing 'Police Services Agreements' for their lines. However, for the reasons outlined above, there is good reason to continue to regard the BTP as a public policing body. The same is true of the Parks Police. The 'privatisation mentality' applies not just to the Parks Police but also, as we argued above, to the Metropolitan Police and other constabularies. The Parks Police, for example, operates its own budget, and charges for its services to other departments within the council in what approximates to an internal market. In addition, they undertake a response service to alarms activations in council buildings. The Parks Police offered this service to council departments at a much cheaper price than could private alarm companies. In theory, the Parks Police could offer a similar service to private firms, although activities like this have yet to develop in practice.

Other public policing bodies

As we have argued, the sectoral status of officials such as HSE investigators or EHOs is fairly unequivocally public. Overall, there has perhaps been less blurring sectorally for the other public policing bodies, whose staff do not have constabulary powers. For example, there were few examples of such bodies providing services for private purchasers. However, it is likely that the kinds of 'market-style' reforms referred to earlier—for example those which encourage client–contractor splits, internal markets, the development of performance indicators, and increasing emphasis on cost-effectiveness—have impacted to varying degrees on all public services, including those under this category. The clearest example from Wandsworth occurred in relation to the Housing Patrol service.

The Housing Patrolling service provides patrolling directly to council-owned estates. This is a case, at least on a general level, of a public provider (the Housing Patrol Service) meeting the demands of a public purchaser (the Borough Council). However, the Housing Department has contracted the management of a number of estates out to private companies (private purchaser), and to Housing Cooperatives (quasi-private purchaser). In these cases, there are a number of options open to management of the estates in question. They can 'buy-in' the services of the Council's Housing Patrol, they can employ their own patrollers, or they can contract the service out to other bodies. One of the co-operatives decided originally to contract the call-out elements of the Housing Patrol service to a private security company, although this was abandoned when the company found itself unable to provide the housing management services that were required. The Housing Patrol service was then given the contract to provide the emergency call-out service on that estate and continues to provide that service.

Private policing bodies

Private 'policing' bodies are defined as profit-making bodies selling services in a competitive market. The majority of private security operations observed in Wandsworth were providing services for private purchasers. There were numerous examples of this, of which only a few appear in the table. For example, in a large business park to the east of the Borough, a number of the firms present have a small number of private security guards, some employing in-house guards, but most contracting in from outside firms. Most of the major supermarkets in the Borough employed both store-detectives (in-house) and contracted-in uniformed private security guards. There are a number of suppliers of mechanical and electronic security equipment in the Borough. As well as providing for commercial premises, many of them deal on a one-to-one basis with private householders. All the nightclubs in the Borough employed door-supervisors.

However, there were also some specific examples where private companies were providing services for public purchasers, in some cases having replaced public providers through a contracting-out process. There were three particular examples of private providers delivering services financed by what were clearly public purchasers. In the first case the public purchaser was the Home Office. Since January 1995, Securicor Custodial Services have operated the prisoner escort service, taking over from Metropolitan Police officers and HM prison officers. The second example concerned a local government public purchaser, Wandsworth Borough Council. Since November 1994, the responsibility for enforcing parking regulations on roads away from the red routes has fallen to the local authority. Wandsworth Borough Council, noted for its radical Conservative policies in a number of areas, contracted this service out to a private company, Control Plus Ltd.

A further example of public purchasing and private provision is provided by the 'professional witness' scheme undertaken by the Council. These schemes are growing in popularity with local authorities confronted with the problem of neighbour harassment of various forms on council-owned estates, where intimidation prevents victims from giving evidence to the police or council officials.[22] In a pilot scheme, Wandsworth Council hired three private investigation firms to undertake covert surveillance on council estates, rather than using directly employed council personnel. The notion of private security companies working for public bodies is, of course, not new. As Johnston noted, the Ministry of Defence contracted private security companies to guard some military bases during the 1980s,[23] and private security companies are also contracted to guard some Home Office establishments, including Metropolitan Police buildings (although no particular examples of this came to light in Wandsworth).[24] Thus, we can identify a number of examples where public funds are used to purchase public services, although in most important respects the providers remain self-evidently private.

Another area of apparent ambiguity concerns private security companies providing services purchased by bodies whose own sectoral status is unclear. One important example in Wandsworth Borough is the New Covent Garden Market Authority. This was set up by statute, is not a representative public body in the sense that the local council is and, in many ways, acts as a private company whilst retaining some public characteristics. The Market Security Force is, however, unambiguously private, being provided by a local private security firm. Similar arguments apply to local colleges of further education. The government's education reforms introduced social

[22] In 'Under private investigation', *Independent*, 21 Mar. 1995, Anna Moore noted schemes in Sunderland, Salford, Manchester, Southwark, Lewisham, Stoke, Blyth Valley, Bury, Leeds, and Coventry.

[23] Johnston (1992).

[24] Recent reports have suggested that the Home Office spent up to £40 million a year employing private security firms. See, for example, 'Home Office £40m private security bill' *Guardian*, 3 Oct. 1994.

market mechanisms into further and higher education. After the abolition of the Inner London Education Authority (ILEA), responsibility for education fell to the Borough Councils. However, further reforms during the early 1990s took the further and higher education colleges out of council control and set them up as independent bodies, in some ways more like private businesses. These colleges are given a set budget, and must balance costs against revenue, raise their own income by way of fee-charging and hiring out premises, and meet certain stated criteria and performance targets. Although the majority of the funding in fact still comes from the public purse (indirectly), these bodies are increasingly acting as 'quasi-private' organisations. Both colleges in the research site had private security guards contracted in from specialist security companies. The same kind of argument applies to the development of NHS Trusts, an increasing proportion of which have private security guards. The ambiguity around NHS Trusts and Colleges arises from the fact that they are basically 'publicly-owned' bodies which are increasingly acting as though they are private concerns.

Despite the undoubted blurring that is occurring on the sectoral dimension, the public–private divide is still a useful one. Even though bodies such as the Metropolitan Police are increasingly encouraged to undertake some privately-funded activities, this still amounts to a small proportion of income relative to the total. The vast majority of its funding still comes from taxation, and this is unlikely to change in the near future. Turning to the other public bodies undertaking policing activities, the same argument applies, if anything more strongly, with the overwhelming majority of funding coming from taxation. Although the contracting-out of services by national and local government has provided a lucrative market for some private security companies, once again, the greatest part of the 'private policing' market is accounted for by private purchasers.

In sum, Wandsworth provides a neat illustration of the fact that a wide variety of bodies are involved in 'policing' over and above Home Department police forces. There is indeed a growing sectoral complexity in the institutional forms which are emerging. However, this applies as much, if not more, to the Metropolitan Police as it does to some 'hybrid' bodies. Indeed, we would suggest that there are strong grounds for arguing that the majority of these apparently 'hybrid' bodies are in fact more accurately described as 'public'. This is not to argue that there are not fundamental distinctions between the Metropolitan Police and these other bodies. It is simply that these distinctions are to be found on dimensions other than the sectoral, and it is to these dimensions that we now turn.

Spatial Boundaries

In the spatial dimension, we are concerned crucially with questions about *where the policing takes place*, rather than who does it or who pays for it. This takes us into a fundamentally different conception of the public–private dichotomy—one which we discussed in some detail in Chapter Two. Whereas sectoral concerns revolve around state versus market, the spatial dimension rests more centrally upon a notion of 'publicness' as openness. It is more fundamentally about the extent to which certain spaces are accessible to people or, alternatively, the extent to which and the ways in which, access is limited or denied. We should reiterate at this point that the way we are using the terms 'spatial boundaries' or 'spatial dimension' in this context is significantly different from, and needs to be clearly distinguished from, Johnston's 'central state–local state' continuum. We elaborate on this below.

Earlier we outlined a variety of interpretations of the notion of space. For present purposes, however, we will lean towards the geographical sense of the term (i.e. that of an interactional and experiential space which has physical attributes although it can be the product of social convention). There is a large body of ethnographic research which shows how police culture informs a distinctive interpretation of the 'territory' encountered by police officers.[25] Holdaway illustrated the strong territorial interests of police officers, in which the 'patch' of a particular police station is seen as 'owned' by its police officers.[26] Rather than consider space in terms of whether services are organised at a national or local level, space is treated here in terms of the 'natural domains' of the different policing bodies. Do they operate mainly on 'public' space, on 'private' space, or some combination of the two?

The first step is to consider how different forms of space can be defined for these purposes. The central importance of 'space' in

---

[25] See *inter alia* Hobbs, D. (1988) *Doing the Business: Entrepreneurship, detectives and the working class in the East End of London*, Oxford: Clarendon; Holdaway, S. (1979) *The British Police*, London: Edward Arnold; (1983) *Inside the British Police*, Oxford: Blackwell; Smith, D. J. and Gray, J. (1983) *The Police in Action*, London: PSI.
[26] Holdaway (1983).

debates about private security arises from Shearing and Stenning's thesis that changes in property relations or, more particularly, the rise of 'mass private property', is central to an understanding of the rise of private security. As we outlined in Chapter Two, the spatial dimension is perhaps the most complex of those under consideration because it is so easy to confuse fundamentally different conceptions of the public–private divide. Shearing and Stenning's analysis of 'mass private property' combines two notions of the dichotomy—the sectoral notion of ownership with the spatial notion of access and openness—and highlights the crucial importance of the spatial dimension in policing.

Although in looking at policing within Wandsworth we will identify a considerable amount of overlap between policing bodies in terms of the types of space in which they operate, it is the spatial dimension which provides one of the most crucial distinctions between some policing organisations. What we seek to do below is to consider the activities of a number of key policing bodies operating in Wandsworth, and to examine the range and nature of 'spaces' in which each operates.

Our analysis of the spatial dimension of policing requires a different categorisation of the 'public' policing bodies from that used in the discussion of sectoral boundaries. Where previously we distinguished between 'public constabularies', 'other public bodies' and 'private policing bodies', we now introduce a fourth category as a result of separating Home Department Police Forces and 'other bodies of constables'. One of the central differences between Home Department police forces such as the Metropolitan Police, and other 'special police forces' or bodies of constables, is that the former are far less spatially-constrained. They are all 'public' constabularies in the sectoral sense, but the way they operate spatially varies considerably. A graphic representation of the spatial boundaries in policing is found in Table 7.2. The analysis presented there not only distinguishes 'providers' of policing services by the kinds of space in which they operate but examines the Metropolitan Police separately from other bodies of constables.

Home Department police forces—the Metropolitan Police

As Table 7.2 suggests, the core policing activities of the two Metropolitan Police divisions covering Wandsworth were clearly located in 'public space'. The responsibility for uniformed patrol, traffic policing, and public order policing in the public spaces of the Borough fell largely to the Metropolitan Police. In cases where other bodies operated in public space their activities were in an important sense underwritten by the Metropolitan Police, in that there was no apparent suggestion that the presence of such bodies somehow superseded the jurisdiction of the Home Department force.

Table 7.2: Spatial boundaries in policing

	PROVIDER			
SPATIAL DOMAIN	*Home Dept. Police Forces*	*Other bodies of constables*	*Other public policing bodies*	*Private security*
Public	Metropolitan Police— Routine patrol Public order Traffic policing	Parks Police/BTP arrests outside jurisdiction	Housing patrol service—visible patrol on estates POID—Mailbag robbery squad	Riverfront development—private security patrolling in public space Parking enforcement
Private	Domestic violence and child abuse investigations Response to calls from the public	Parks Police—actions within council buildings BTP—follow-up investigations may take officers into private space	HSE Inspectors/EHOs—operations within workplaces and privately-rented accommodation	Site security Nightclub bouncers In-house security
Hybrid	Occasional patrols within shopping centres Joint operations in colleges	Parks Police—operations within parks and other open spaces BTP—station forecourts, other railway property	Housing Patrol Service—patrolling stairwells and corridors within council blocks	Shopping centre security College and hospital security

Whilst authors such as Shearing and Stenning have focused on the shrinking of the 'natural domain' of public policing, the Borough provided some examples in which the spatial domain of public policing has clearly expanded over recent years. The Metropolitan Police, in common with other police forces in Britain, have been under increasing pressure over recent years, to intervene more actively in crimes which have occurred within what has traditionally been viewed as the private sphere of the home and family.[27] As a result, the police service has been more likely to take action in cases of domestic violence, and there has been a huge growth in the number of child abuse investigations carried out by specialist police officers working with child protection social workers. The way that such crimes are dealt with is still the subject of much debate and discussion.[28] What is clear though, is that developments have not affected the 'natural domain' of the public police in one direction only. Wandsworth was served by both a specialist domestic violence unit, consisting of Metropolitan Police officers, and a team of specialist child protection officers.

It is also clear that the access that the Metropolitan Police have to private property is considerably more restricted than their access to public property. It remains important, however, not to make assumptions about the degree of correspondence between the nature of space and the nature of policing. Although the 'natural domain' of the public constabularies may be public space, constables have, for example, powers to enter and search premises without a search warrant, and to stop and search persons or vehicles under section 1 of the Police and Criminal Evidence Act 1984 (PACE). Nevertheless, it is perhaps important to note that a number of our sources suggested that much police time continues to be taken up with responding to calls for assistance. These require the police to enter a variety of types of space. 'Response policing' not only makes it difficult to fulfil the aims of sector policing, but also eats into time set aside for routine patrol, which is restricted to public places.

Turning to 'hybrid' forms of space, the examples of 'mass private property' which could be found in the Borough were interesting

[27] Jones, T., Newburn, T. and Smith, D. (1994) *Democracy and Policing*, London: Policy Studies Institute; Sherman, L. W. (1992) *Policing Domestic Violence: Experiments and dilemmas*, New York: Free Press.

[28] See, for example, Radford, J. and Stanko, E. A. (1996) 'Violence against women and children: the contradictions of crime control under patriarchy', in Hester, M., Kelly, L. and Radford, J. (eds.) *Women, Violence and Male Power*, Milton Keynes: Open University Press.

although limited to a few examples. In the two privately-owned shopping centres there was no evidence that the police were discouraged from patrolling and, on the contrary, there was close co-operation between the local police and the centre management. In fact, the police were actively being encouraged to patrol through the centres (although in practice this did not happen often). This might be taken to confirm Shearing and Stenning's observation that 'even when [the police] have had the resources to police privately owned public places—and typically they have not—they have been philosophically disinclined to do so'.[29] Apparently, it had been the case that the first private security company to patrol one of the centres had made it clear that they did not want the public police to come into the centre unless called. By the time of the research, this company had long since lost the contract and relationships with the police were now totally different. Given that the shopping centres are private property, in theory the owners could deny the public police routine access. The centre managers reported that they welcome the presence of Metropolitan Police officers and would, in fact, like to see more of them on their property. The management of one centre, for example, invited the local police to set up a stall in the centre during a recruitment drive for the special constabulary. Generally speaking, however, patrolling officers are rarely seen inside the shopping centres these days, not least because the local police know that private security is present, and therefore are able to use their stretched resources elsewhere.

Similarly, although the intervention of the Metropolitan Police on other kinds of 'hybrid' space such as colleges and NHS Trust premises was less frequent, it was by no means unheard of. As we outlined in Chapter Six, one of the colleges had allowed undercover police officers to undertake surveillance on its site. A representative of another college outlined how the police had recently come on site (uncalled) and arrested a student. The police do undertake operations on hybrid space, sometimes at the request (or with the co-operation of) the 'owners' of the space, as well as on occasion without such a request. In March 1996 in the aftermath of the murder of London headteacher Philip Lawrence, the then Secretary of State for Education and Employment, Gillian Shephard, announced that the Government would introduce legislation to give police extra powers to stop and

---

[29] Shearing, C. D. and Stenning, P. C. (1983) 'Private security: implications for social control', *Social Problems*, 30, 5, p. 496.

search school pupils and students for weapons on school or college premises, thereby extending their powers in 'hybrid' space.[30]

As we noted above, the fundamental distinction between Home Department police forces, such as the Metropolitan Police, and other public constabularies is that the latter are usually spatially specialised. A further distinction to bear in mind is that, in geographical terms, the Home Department police forces are also less specialised. The Battersea and Wandsworth police divisions are, of course, part of a much larger organisation, the Metropolitan Police. Central functions, such as public order problems in other parts of the capital, may result in police officers, who usually work in Wandsworth Borough, being temporarily diverted to other parts of London. Moreover, the Metropolitan Police is itself part of a wider police service which is increasingly undertaking national and international functions. Consequently, officers from the Metropolitan Police District may be, and are, called upon to carry out duties in other police force areas under mutual aid arrangements. A good example of this occurred during the course of the study, when it was reported to the Police Consultative Committee that officers from the Wandsworth division had been on duty at the demonstrations against animal exports in Sussex and were therefore were not available for duty in the Borough.

Other bodies of constables

The distinguishing feature of those bodies of constables which are not part of the general police service is that their jurisdiction is invariably limited in a number of ways, a key one of which is spatial. The Parks Police, as the name suggests, carry out their central functions on the 850 acres of parks and open spaces in the Borough. It is these areas of land to which the Act which creates them refers, and it seems to be generally accepted that their 'constabulary' powers, pertain to these areas only (although there is further disagreement about the extent of these constabulary powers as we explore in relation to legal boundaries below). However, as Table 7.2 shows, in carrying out their routine duties (patrolling and by-law enforcement in the park areas) they are required to travel across the Borough from park to park, as they do when carrying out duties such as responding to alarm activations in Council buildings, and cash deliveries to banks. They do so, as we have said, wearing uniforms which are not

---

[30] 'Police to search pupils at school for weapons', *Independent,* 7 Mar. 1996.

dissimilar to those of the Metropolitan Police, and driving cars and vans marked clearly with the words 'Parks Police'. In the course of these activities in 'public space' Parks Police officers have carried out arrests, usually when they have witnessed a crime taking place. They are clear that when they do so they use the powers of any citizen (under section 25 of PACE), and are not acting as constables. Most of the sorties of the Parks Police into the wider 'public sphere' (i.e. outside the parks) are incidental to their routine activities on council property and in public parks. However, the reported proposal in 1994 to extend the routine patrols of the Parks Police to council estates caused considerable controversy, and the public police firmly and successfully asserted that this was their 'space'. As the next section shows, the question of whether it was within the Council's power to extend the remit of their Parks Police in this manner is legally unresolved. In practice, however, the voice of the Metropolitan Police was strong enough to persuade the council to place the proposal on the back-burner and instead support a campaign for the recruitment of more special constables.

The British Transport Police is another body of constables whose legal jurisdiction is spatially constrained. Their powers extend to the prevention of crime and the investigation of offences on (and in the vicinity of) railway vehicles, stations, and other property. However, in investigating offences committed within this space, they have the legal jurisdiction throughout England and Wales. Thus, for example, a BTP detective would retain the powers of a constable to arrest a person suspected of assault committed in a station, even if this was now some time later and the person was at home. The BTP officers have similar uniforms to those of Metropolitan Police officers, and drive in police cars and vans. The word 'police' is prominent on these, and the words 'British Transport' much smaller. British Transport Police representatives provided us with a list of incidents at which BTP officers were present but their limited jurisdiction meant that the extent of their powers was ambiguous. For example, BTP officers often travel between sites in marked cars, and may be flagged down by members of the public and have their attention drawn to an incident. In most cases, BTP officers respond as any other police officer and take action, but in some rare cases members of the public query their legal powers off railway property. This is a source of great concern to BTP and the chairman of their Federation commented that he had once asked 'the Deputy Chief Constable if an officer who declined to act (in a situation where they had no powers to do so) would be disciplined and he said yes. Our guys are in a Catch 22 situation.'[31] It is highly likely therefore that on occasion the BTP officers who cover the Wandsworth and Battersea divisions move beyond their spatial jurisdiction, and may be required to act as police officers when in 'public space'. However, during the period of the research we came across no specific examples of such events, and certainly no examples where this was problematic.

Other public policing organisations

The natural territory of enforcement officers such as EHOs and HSE investigators is much more specific and restricted than the constables covered so far. It is centred mostly in the 'private' domain of work-places, where they carry out investigations concerning pollution, noise, hygiene, safety, and other matters. However, there can on occasion be a role for HSE and EHO investigations in the 'public areas' of private spaces, for example where there is a danger to the public in a restaurant or a shop. The EHOs in particular have a range of powers which may take them into the public domain. Although the examples given were not specifically from Wandsworth, the chief environmental health officer told us that under the Public Health (Control of Disease) Act 1984, an EHO has the right to remove to hospital persons with certain infectious diseases if they refuse to go voluntarily. This amounts effectively to an arrest, although not carried out with constabulary powers.

The Housing Patrol Officers were usually restricted in their operations to council-owned housing estates. They would patrol the corridors and streets of an estate, and although driving between the estates takes them into the public domain they do not generally carry out any of their duties away from council property. On occasion, the nature of the job took the Housing Patrol into the private domain of people's households (and also to private estates where there was a specific contract for their services). During the research, on one evening shift the Housing Patrol Officer (with the researcher) was invited into the flats of people who had called the housing office complaining of water dripping from their ceiling. We obtained entry to the flat upstairs and examined the toilet cistern which was leaking and causing the dripping into the flat below. Housing Patrol officers

---

[31] 'BTP "forced" to make unlawful arrests', *Police Review*, 24 Feb. 1995.

also enter people's homes to help the elderly or disabled who have activated a 'help alarm' call to the control room. Finally, in major emergencies (for example, the Clapham rail disaster), Housing Patrol officers have played an important role in public space.

Benefit Fraud investigators work in a variety of forms of space. They will seek to gain entry to people's houses, but only with the consent of the owner, and they carry out surveillance of people in the public domain.[32] The POID operate across all types of space. In the course of an investigation, they will have access to Post Office property, as they are the agents of the employers. However, their activities may take them into the private domain of people's houses (they will search a suspect's house, but only with consent), and the public domain of the streets. POID investigators do carry out searches of persons and property, but only with the consent of the person concerned. If they refuse to give this consent, they are generally arrested and a police warrant obtained to carry out the search.

Private policing bodies

The activities of private policing bodies take them into a variety of kinds of space. Much of the extant literature argues that 'private security forces . . . operate primarily in areas of private property to which the public police do not have routine access' and, indeed, even come close to suggesting that it might almost be its defining characteristic.[33] Predictably, therefore, many of the staffed guarding operations in the Borough were restricted to private property and largely private space. For example, the site guards at a number of operations on business parks in the Borough were not only confined to private property, but also had little to do with the public police. Their main focus was on protecting the specific geographical territory represented by the private property. It was rare that private security guards saw their role as extending into public space, unless it was a specific kind of 'mass private property' on which they were employed. Thus, the security guards at one of the colleges spent most of their time controlling access to the property, and enforcing college rules and regulations. However, this activity was clearly demarcated by the college

---

[32] See, for example, Rowlingson, K., Whyley, C., Newburn, T. and Berthoud, R. (1997) *Social Security Fraud: The role of penalties*, London: Stationery Office.

[33] Shearing, C. D. and Stenning, P. C. (1981) 'Modern private security: Its growth and implications', in Tonry, M. and Morris, N. (eds.) *Crime and Justice: An Annual Review of Research*, Chicago: University of Chicago Press, p. 213.

gates. In interview, the head of the security staff illustrated this when he said that the guards would break up fights in the college grounds, and if the students 'want to do that, they can go outside on the pavement to do it'. Once the activity was outside the private space, he saw it as no longer a problem for him or his staff, but rather something that the Metropolitan Police would have do deal with. Conversely, the same security guard proudly recounted the time when a suspect fleeing from pursuing Metropolitan Police officers ran into the college grounds. As soon as the suspect entered the college 'space', he became a legitimate concern for the private security guard, who duly chased and caught the suspect, before handing him over to the grateful Metropolitan Police officers.

In the shopping malls, the outer spatial boundaries of the private policing operation are provided by the centre site. The management of both centres discourage the security officers from pursuing suspects off site, although it is not expressly forbidden. The main purpose of discouraging this is fears for the safety of the guard—once outside, radio contact will be lost, and it will be difficult to send assistance. An important additional consideration is that the guards' insurance cover extends only to operations within the centre. Thus, from the guards' perspective, the area inside the centre, whilst not being a safe sanctuary, is clearly a safer place to be than risking the unknown and uninsured outside. An interesting example of the complexity of spatial boundaries was found in the shopping centres. Whilst the centre management employed security guards to patrol the 'public areas' of the private centre—walkways and malls—the tenants have the option of making their own security arrangements within their rented space. Thus, in both centres, there are shops using store detectives and some which have uniformed security guards. The 'routine patrol' of the centre security guards does not take them into the shops, but they can be called upon by shop managers for help. One of the centre managers explained that within the private space of the shop, these security guards are answerable to the shop management.

There are spatial restrictions on the activities of store detectives in supermarkets. Most of the large supermarkets place a high priority on the safety of staff and, thus, pursuit of suspects or the detention of violent or threatening suspects are not encouraged. This is not to say they do not occur. In general, the store detective is trained only to make an arrest when they are as sure as they can be that the suspect is intentionally leaving without paying for goods taken. This may require them to wait until the suspect is past the check-out, or even just outside the doors of the shop.

Although private security tends to be concentrated in private space, the local study gave rise to some limited examples of private security and investigative firms operating mainly in public spaces. In Wandsworth there are no direct parallels with the large private residential areas which characterise the suburbs of many large North American cities. Although there are a small number of 'gated' developments, and some large private residential apartment blocks on the riverfront, these are generally uncharacteristic of residential buildings in the Borough. One major riverfront development, which at the time of the study was still under construction, consists of office and residential units. Properties are advertised with security as a major selling point— the area is patrolled by uniformed security guards and there is an extensive network of CCTV. This is a particularly interesting development for, in its design, construction and policing, it is clearly intended to 'privatise' what is, in terms of right-of-way, public space. To enter the development there is one entrance only—a large archway which gives the false impression that the roadways inside are private property. The archway is clearly intended to symbolise the move from one form of space to another more restricted one. This impression is backed up by uniformed private security and CCTV cameras. Moreover, the Council has had reports that, despite the fact that there is a public right of way, the private security guards have on occasion sought to make some people unwelcome. We should report, however, that as 'patrolling researchers' we did not actually experience this.

A further example is provided by the private investigation firms which were hired by the Council to carry out a 'professional witness' service. On occasion, these firms carried out surveillance within public space. Some other aspects of the work of private investigators are extremely interesting in spatial terms, although we were unable to obtain much information about the other activities of private detectives operating within the Borough. Some functions, like credit investigation for example, may require very little moving about in physical space, but rather sitting at a desk and accessing various different electronic forms of information. Some of this may be 'public' space, some of it 'private'. Without even leaving the office, it is thus possible for the private investigator to intrude on private space.[34]

---

[34] See Reiss, A. J. (1987) 'The legitimacy of intrusion into private space', In Shearing and Stenning (eds.) *Private Policing*, Newbury Parks, Calif: Sage.

As outlined earlier, the council employed 'private' traffic wardens to enforce parking regulations away from the red routes. These personnel were operating in 'public space', although their jurisdiction was demarcated from that of the 'public' (Metropolitan Police) traffic wardens, by a white triangle painted onto the pavement 30 yards away from the red route. These marks were not particularly visible, creating a grey area in which the boundary between the public and private traffic wardens was potentially problematic. The fact that the local authority-employed private wardens were 'revenue driven', whereas the Metropolitan Police wardens were 'traffic control' driven was raised by one of the divisional commanders as a source of possible difficulty and, perhaps, competition. This, it was suggested, might tempt the private wardens to operate outside their jurisdiction.

Thus, there were some important examples of private providers of policing services operating outside the domain of 'private space'. However, it is important to emphasise the limited nature of these developments. In particular, there were no examples of private security guards undertaking residential street patrols of the kind which have received so much media attention nationally.[35] In general, the natural domain of private security remained largely that of private space.

Spatial boundaries: a concluding comment

Central to one of the most influential theorisations of the rise of private security is the development and spread of 'mass private property' and, as a consequence of this change in property relations, the fact that increasing parts of many people's lives take place on private property which has public overtones and yet is policed by private agents. Not only is this argument extremely relevant to developments in North America, it also seems intuitively attractive when thinking about the situation in Britain, and helps move the debate about private security away from simple considerations of public police funding. However, it remains a somewhat incomplete explanation. Whilst a local area study does not allow full-scale testing of this thesis, our study of private security in Wandsworth raises a number of questions about the 'mass private property' argument. Although there are

[35] Fogg, E. and Brace, M. (1994) 'Private policing cuts crime on Islington estates', *Independent London*, 16 Aug. 1994; Hyder, K. and Victor, P. (1994) 'Hiving off police jobs dangerous, chief warns', *Independent on Sunday*, 14 Aug. 1994.

examples of mass private property (as Shearing and Stenning defined it) in Wandsworth, they are somewhat limited and certainly do not form the fully-fledged basis for explaining the widespread incursion of private security into the Borough (and such an incursion is visible). Moreover, there are several types of 'mass property' whose sectoral status is ambiguous in the UK context, although they would more often than not be privately-owned in North America—in particular, local authority owned land, large educational complexes, NHS Hospital Trusts, British Rail property. None of these can really be described as mass 'private' property, although some do share some of the characteristics of the type of property key to Shearing and Stenning's arguments.

Although it should be clear from the evidence above that there is, ostensibly, a considerable amount of 'spatial overlap' in the policing of the Borough, nevertheless a number of patterns emerge. First, and reinforcing some of the observations made about sectoral boundaries, it is the case that although the 'natural domain' of the Metropolitan Police is public space, their broad remit provides them with access to significant private and 'hybrid' realms as well. Indeed, the majority of public constabularies work primarily in public space, though the jurisdiction of non-Home Office forces is generally significantly more circumscribed. The private sector, as one would expect, operate primarily, though not only, in private space. Crucially in this regard, however, the realities of space are so complicated that they cannot comprehensively be captured by the private–public dichotomy. We have made reference to a series of types of 'hybrid space'; spaces which in some sense are neither unambiguously public nor unambiguously private. The more private they become the more likely they are to be policed by private bodies—or public and private bodies—though how they are policed is determined, of course, not only by the sectoral status of the policing agency or agencies in question, but also by the powers and capacities these bodies bring to their work. It is to these, what we have referred to as the legal boundaries of policing in the Borough, that we turn next.

Legal Boundaries

Concern with legal boundaries has characterised much of the work on policing. Indeed, as we illustrated in Chapter One, the police have often been defined by their legal powers or, more concretely, in terms of their capacity for the legitimate use of force.[36] The previous sections on sectoral and spatial boundaries were structured by dividing them according to the sectoral status of the policing bodies being considered. Comparison between policing bodies is crucial for this section, and the sections which follow deal with distinct 'policing' powers, the extent to which each is available to different policing bodies, and how they are utilised in practice.

Arrest

The tradition in British policing has been to limit the powers of the police. The 1929 Royal Commission argued that the police should have as few powers as possible which are not also enjoyed by ordinary citizens.[37] However, the power legitimately to deprive a person of their liberty is one of the central police powers. It is in powers of arrest that we surely find the essence of the difference between members of public constabularies and other agents carrying out order maintenance and investigative functions. However, as we have outlined, staff from a range of bodies in the Borough outside the Metropolitan Police undertook arrests quite frequently. These bodies included the BTP and Parks Police, store detectives, POID investigators, and the members of private security firms working in the shopping malls. Arrests are undertaken by a variety of bodies, some using citizen's powers, some using the powers of a constable, and some using both, depending on the circumstances.

In general, a constable has the same statutory powers of arrest as any citizen, plus a number of additional statutory powers. Section 24 of the Police and Criminal Evidence Act 1984 (PACE) empowers *any person* to arrest without warrant anyone who is in the act of committing an arrestable offence or anyone whom (s)he has reasonable grounds for suspecting to be committing an arrestable offence. In addition, where an arrestable offence has been committed, *any person* may arrest anyone who is guilty of the offence, or anyone whom (s)he has reasonable grounds for suspecting to be guilty of it. The additional powers held by constables are also provided by section 24 of PACE, and enable a constable (but not an ordinary citizen), who reasonably suspects that an arrestable offence has been committed, to arrest anyone whom (s)he reasonably suspects to be guilty of it. A

---

[36] See Bittner (1980).
[37] Leigh, L. (1985) *Police Powers in England and Wales*, London: Butterworths.

constable also may arrest anyone whom (s)he believes is about to commit an arrestable offence, or whom (s)he has reasonable grounds to suspect is about to commit such an offence. Section 25 of PACE gives police constables access to a *general power of arrest*, which applies to all other offences (not specified under section 24). A police constable has limited powers of arrest if (s)he has reasonable grounds for suspecting that any offence has been committed/attempted or is being committed/attempted, and it appears to her/him that service of summons is impractical or inappropriate because 'any of the general arrest conditions is satisfied'. The first condition is when the officer cannot obtain the name and address of the person concerned, or reasonably believes those given to be false. The second general arrest condition applies when there are reasonable grounds for believing that an arrest is necessary to protect the suspect from harming her/himself or others, to prevent the loss or damage of property, to stop an unlawful obstruction of the highway, or to prevent an offence against public decency. Ordinary citizens do not have access to this general power of arrest.

Thus, an ordinary citizen has the legal power to arrest without warrant the following:

- anyone who is in the act of committing an offence
- anyone whom s(he) has reasonable grounds for suspecting to be committing such an offence
- provided that an arrestable offence has been committed, anyone who is guilty of it, or whom (s)he has reasonable grounds for suspecting to be guilty of it.

Problems most frequently arise where a citizen's arrest occurs on reasonable suspicion that someone has committed an offence, but the arrested person is ultimately acquitted of that offence. The arrest will be *de facto* unlawful if, for example, it is proved that the offence in question was not committed.

Thus, there are clear and important differences between the powers of arrest held by any citizen and those held by a police constable. In practice, however, it appears to be the case that the difference between a citizen's and a constable's arrest are not so significant that they impose undue limitations on public constabularies working outside their jurisdiction. Thus, Parks Police officers make arrests outside the Borough's parks and open spaces and BTP officers will also undertake citizen's arrests when on public rather than Railtrack or

London Underground property. The private security officers and store detectives received training in legal powers of arrest and, in general, made formal arrests, informed suspects that they had been arrested, and read them their rights. The same applies to POID investigators, who also rely on citizen's powers of arrest, and are extensively trained as to when such powers apply.

Despite the clear legal boundary between the powers of police constables and those of citizens, there remains some ambiguity about the legal status of Parks Police officers, with New Scotland Yard and the Parks Police themselves taking different views. This relates in part to the fact that Parks Police officers wear police-style uniforms which may confuse an arrestee about the powers of the person arresting them, a point developed below. Further ambiguity exists about the actual extent of the Parks Constables' powers within the parks. The Metropolitan Police solicitors take the view that the Parks Police have limited constabulary powers which are restricted to use inside the parks and to cases involving infringements of council by-laws. However, the Parks Constables take the view—derived from separate Counsel opinion given to Wandsworth Borough Council—that they have the powers of any police officer within the parks, and also as having the power of 'hot pursuit' off the parks in cases of by-law infringement.

Nevertheless, relationships between the Parks Police and the local divisions of the Metropolitan police are very good, and Metropolitan Police custody officers accept most arrests by Parks Police officers as lawful, and process them accordingly. When the Metropolitan Police have doubts about the particular circumstances of an arrest, they are likely simply to release the arrestees, although this happens very infrequently. One example of such an arrest occurred when Parks Police officers in plain clothes arrested some suspected robbers at their homes and brought them to a Metropolitan Police station. They were released without charge immediately. It appears that such examples are quite rare, and the local Metropolitan Police commanders regard the Parks Police as a valuable resource.

It has yet to be tested in case law what the actual position is regarding the extent of constabulary powers held by the Parks Police. In the majority of the cases in which an arrest is made by a Parks Police officer, citizen's powers suffice. Indeed, the threat of an arrest is often enough to make a by-law offender comply with the request for name and address. There was one case, however, where someone

232   Private Security and Public Policing

who had been arrested challenged the lawfulness of the arrest and threatened to sue the Council. The case did not reach court, an apology was issued, and the Parks Police officer in question was reprimanded by the Head of the Council's Leisure and Amenities Department. There are, in fact, a limited set of potential circumstances which would provide an opportunity for the powers of the Parks Police to be tested, and until such time as there is a legal challenge in court the apparent ambiguity surrounding their powers is likely to persist.[38]

Some difficulties arise from the fact that there are spatial limitations on the use of legal powers, for example in relation to the BTP. They have police uniforms, drive police vehicles and, as we have suggested, may often receive requests for assistance from members of the public who either do not realise, or are not in a position to worry about the fact that the officer is not fully empowered in all circumstances. One example where the legal and spatial limitations led to very real difficulties occurred in one of Wandsworth's neighbouring boroughs. A BTP officer on duty in a London Underground station had his attention drawn to a disturbance in the pub opposite the station. He attempted to break up a fight between two men, one armed with a knife. During the course of this he was assaulted by one of the men, whom he arrested and charged with assaulting a police officer in the course of his duty. The magistrates discharged the accused man, on the grounds that it was not a lawful arrest—the BTP officer having acted outside his jurisdiction.

Although HSE investigators and EHOs have important statutory powers, these do not include any particular powers of arrest above those of any other citizen. The rare exception to this is the statutory power of an EHO to 'remove' to hospital somebody with an infectious disease who insists on being in public, thereby endangering other people. Housing Patrol officers and benefit fraud investigators do not, as a rule, undertake citizens arrests, and clearly perceive this to be the role of a police constable. Housing Patrol officers will simply call in the police if they believe an arrest is likely to be necessary. Private security guards from the New Covent Garden security force had, in theory, access to constabulary powers to enforce certain sections of the Road Traffic Act on the public roads which crossed the market site. However, in practice these powers were not used.

[38] For an extended discussion of the differences of opinion about the status of the Wandsworth Parks Police, see Johnston (1993).

Detention

The police have a number of powers of detention, the condition and duration of detention now being closely regulated by PACE. Prior to PACE, it was quite common for suspects 'voluntarily' to attend police stations in order to 'help police with their enquiries'. Research within some police forces has suggested that voluntary attendance is now used relatively little, although we did not collect any data on this from the police in Wandsworth.[39] When a private citizen makes an arrest, it is his or her duty to take the arrested person before a Justice of the Peace, or to a police station, as soon as is reasonably possible. However, subsequent detention and questioning of an arrested suspect is a matter of degree. For example, while a shoplifter may reasonably be detained for a time while the police are called, and may be asked to justify his or her actions, a store detective is not justified in taking the arrested person back to the scene in order to obtain further evidence.

We found some variations in the degree to which staff of different policing bodies were informed about the legal position on detention. Although members of those bodies for whom arrest and detention were frequent experiences were usually well-versed in the legal position (the police, Parks Police, the POID, and store detectives), members of private security firms were more varied in their knowledge. On the one hand, security guards in the shopping malls received training in citizens' powers, and carried out proper formal citizens arrests when an arrest was required. However, private security guards in some cases appeared to make a distinction between making an arrest and detaining somebody. For example, at one of the colleges, the senior security guard strongly confirmed that guards would never undertake arrests, even if they came across a serious crime taking place. He argued that they were not legally empowered to make arrests, which was the job of the police. Similarly, nightclub managers in the Borough reported that their door supervisors would not arrest a suspect within the nightclub, but would detain them until the police arrived. Section 29 of PACE makes it clear that there is no 'halfway house' between liberty and arrest—either a person is free to go when they please, or they are under arrest.[40] Thus, the legal

---

[39] See, Dixon, D., Coleman, C., and Bottomley, K. (1990) 'Consent and the Legal Regulation of Policing', *Journal of Law and Society* 17, 3, pp. 345–62.

[40] According to Blackstone, arrest is 'the apprehending or restraining of one's person in order to be forthcoming to answer an alleged or suspected crime'. Quoted in

division of powers is quite clear and explicit, although as in many other areas, inadequate knowledge of the law and inaccurate interpretation may lead to ambiguity.

Entry and search of premises

Prior to PACE, it was widely recognised that police officers often relied on 'consent' in order to gain entry to, and search, premises. In many cases, however, it was clear that what 'consent' meant was questionable because it was often obtained by bluff or as a result of the property owner's ignorance.[41] Police constables have the power to enter and search premises without a search warrant in a variety of circumstances, although with the exception of the power of entry to save life or limb (or prevent damage to property), the conditions of entry are somewhat limited. Section 17 of PACE preserves the common law powers of a constable to enter property to deal with or prevent a breach of the peace. PACE also gives constables the power to enter and search the premises of any person detained for an arrestable offence. There are no similar powers available to private individuals either to enter premises or to apply for warrants to search premises. Indeed, the search of premises is resistant to legal regulation because of its fluid nature, the police often relying 'on a potent combination of three factors—householders' ignorance of the law; their unquestioning belief in the power of the police; and their implied guilt if they refuse access'.[42] In this sense, the real powers available to the police officer wishing to enter and search premises are often much greater than the legal powers would suggest. This kind of ambiguity does not only apply to members of Home Department police forces. Some other enforcement bodies, such as television license inspectors, routinely gain access to private property by 'consent', although the householder would in most cases be legally entitled to refuse entry.

With respect to entry and search of *commercial* premises, members of some other policing bodies arguably have greater powers than those of police constables. For example, HSE investigators have a significant range of powers deriving from the Health and Safety at Work Act 1974, section 20.[43] HSE inspectors may enter premises

Bevan, V. and Lidstone, K. (1991) *The Investigation of Crime: A guide to police powers*, London: Butterworths, p. 215.

[41] See Dixon *et al.* (1990).   [42] Ibid, p. 356.

[43] For certain categories of premises, local authority EHOs undertake the Health and Safety inspection functions; for more details, see Hutter, B. M. (1988) *The*

without a warrant at any reasonable time, or any time if they believe a situation to be dangerous. If inspectors expect to be refused entry, or fear physical assault, they will usually ask a police constable to accompany them. HSE inspectors also have a range of powers to carry out examinations and investigations, and to take measurements and photographs. They can seize goods or samples—either to make a dangerous substance safe, or to enable further tests to take place. One recent example involved a fire on a train, resulting in the 'seizure' of the entire train by HSE inspectors in order to subject it to forensic tests. In addition, the HSE can insist that people leave equipment and so on undisturbed subject to their investigation. HSE inspectors have significant access to records and files during an investigation. They may request information and take statements, if necessary under caution, and all investigators are trained in the PACE regulations.

There is not sufficient space to detail the various statutory powers of the other regulatory and investigatory bodies covered by this study. However, the examples above serve to highlight that statutory law enforcement powers are held by a number of bodies. These bodies are distinguished from Home Department police forces by the fact that what are often quite significant legal powers are limited to particular circumstances and functions. A senior manager at one large commercial warehouse in Wandsworth pointed out that the 'policing' powers of EHOs regarding health and safety were far more relevant to his working life than the powers of the Metropolitan Police, reporting that the local EHO could 'shut us down tomorrow'.

Stop and search of persons

This is an important policing power which has been the focus of much controversy in the past, mainly because of the evidence which suggests that the use of stop and search powers was closely related to deteriorating relations between police and certain sections of the public, in particular young black men. Under PACE, a police constable has the power to stop and search a person for various articles provided that (s)he has reasonable grounds for suspicion. The PACE codes of practice require the police constable to complete a record which provides details of the searching officer, the suspect, and the grounds for the stop and search. Although PACE attempted to

Reasonable Arm of the Law: The law enforcement procedures of environmental health officers, Oxford: Clarendon Press.

regulate the use of such powers more tightly, research has suggested that the changes had little effect on the way that police officers used their powers of stop and search. Dixon and colleagues again highlighted the use of 'consent' by police officers to obtain compliance for a voluntary search, such compliance often relying on the legal ignorance or even fear of the suspect.[44] Similarly, Sanders came to the conclusion that PACE provided a series of 'presentational' rules which changed the way officers accounted for the use of their discretion in stop and search, rather than changed the way in which the discretion was actually used[45].

Dixon *et al.* distinguished mass searches of supporters entering football grounds from those undertaken under PACE. These searches are usually justified as being voluntary, and undertaken as part of a condition of entry. In this sense they are more similar to routine searches of people by private security employees as a condition of entry onto private property. A property owner may delegate any power (s)he possesses to someone else. Thus, a private security guard working on private property may, at the request of the owner, ask persons to submit to a voluntary search as a condition of entry, but they have no power to conduct a search without consent. There were a number of examples of private security personnel carrying out such voluntary searches. For example, entry to any of the nightclubs in the Borough is conditional on a body search by door supervisors checking for drugs and weapons. The college security guards reported that on occasion they ask students to turn out their pockets, and have also searched cars leaving the car-parks. However, these searches are again voluntary, and should the student refuse to co-operate, they are not forcibly searched, but are reported to the college management. Although we did not find any specific examples in Wandsworth, some companies make compliance with searches of the person a condition of the employment contract. In this case, private security personnel working in offices would be able to search people on entry and exit.

Use of force

There is no clear distinction between the legal power of police constables and other citizens in using physical force. As long as the

[44] Dixon *et al.* (1990).
[45] Sanders, A. (1993) 'Controlling the discretion of the individual officer', in Reiner, R. and Spencer, S. (eds.) *Accountable Policing*, London: Institute for Public Policy Research.

person concerned is justified in making a lawful arrest, or is acting in self-defence, then the law provides that 'reasonable force' may be used. What actually constitutes 'reasonable force' is a matter for the courts and is determined in light of the circumstances of each individual case. Leigh noted a number of cases, backed up by Home Office guidance, which say that handcuffing is only justifiable when necessary to prevent an escape, or to terminate a violent breach of peace by the prisoner.[46] When a person is handcuffed in cases when it is not necessary to do so, even if the arrest is lawful, the handcuffing is unjustified and will constitute trespass.

In practice, of all the policing bodies it was the Metropolitan Police which had the greatest potential for recourse to the use of force. At one extreme, the Metropolitan Police had the possibility of using lethal force, and all officers were armed with the new 'side-handled baton' during the course of the study. In addition, officers had the traditional handcuffs with which to restrain prisoners. Although the Parks Police are not armed with truncheons, they do carry handcuffs for the restraint of prisoners, and have received training in their use. In addition, the security guards at one of the shopping malls in the borough had access to a pair of handcuffs in the control room. Their use was extremely rare, but they had been employed to restrain a violent prisoner. A POID representative reported that the mailbag robbery squad (the nature of whose work makes it relatively likely for them to undertake citizen's arrests) may use handcuffs to restrain a prisoner.

In most cases, private security personnel were encouraged to use minimum physical force. For example, store detectives are told that if a suspect will not be detained voluntarily and becomes threatening, they should make their own safety paramount. We have already referred to the fact that guards in the shopping malls were required not to chase people outside the shopping centre itself. However, the implicit threat of the use of force was often an important part of the effectiveness of some personnel. In particular, the security guards at one college were mostly large, well-built ex-servicemen. There was an air of physical superiority about them which appeared to be extremely effective in inducing respect, and perhaps nervousness, among the students. Thus, without having to resort to actual physical force, the employment of large ex-service people was deliberately

---

[46] Leigh (1985).

intended to imply that this might occur. A similar development was visible in one shopping mall, where security guards were mainly large, tough-looking men, who patrolled in military-style pullovers and looked intimidating. This was clearly a deliberate, and in the circumstances understandable, policy on the part of the centre management. They were pleased with the apparent effectiveness of this approach.

Uniforms

Under section 52(1) of the Police Act 1964, it is an offence for any person to impersonate a member of a police force with intent to deceive, or to make any statement or do anything to suggest that (s)he is such a member or constable. This makes unlawful the wearing by private individuals of uniforms or badges which might mislead the public into believing that they are, or have the authority of, police officers. The Parks Police uniform is not dissimilar to that of the Metropolitan Police; a policy which clearly gives the officers added credibility.[47] This clearly causes confusion in the minds of members of the public. One senior council official interviewed during the study described how, after a break-in at the council offices, the police were called, and a uniformed Parks officer arrived, and interviewed people about the incident. It was only later that she realised this was one of the 'council police' and was not a 'proper police officer' (her words). The Parks Police are very clear that when they make an arrest outside the parks, they are using citizens powers. However, it is possible that the fact that they are wearing a police-type uniform on these occasions will give the arrestee the impression that they are acting with the full powers of a constable. As we outlined earlier, this is not usually important in practice, for nearly all arrests by the Parks Police are accepted and processed by Metropolitan Police custody officers. However, the potential for legal problems in this regard has not gone unnoticed by senior Metropolitan Police officers, both in the local divisions and at New Scotland Yard. The same problem applies to BTP officers when acting outside of their jurisdiction.

Legal boundaries—an overview

There are clearly significant and important distinctions between the legal powers of different policing bodies. Nevertheless, it is important

---

[47] The Parks Police are not alone in this regard of course. Others such as the BTP also have very similar uniforms.

to remember that there are particular bodies involved in 'policing' functions whose staff have powers which are comparable to, or sometimes greater than, those held by police constables. To highlight the crucial distinction between such bodies and the 'public police' (in this case, the Metropolitan Police), we should turn to Egon Bittner. Bittner was quite clear that there are a range of important bodies outside of the police which have important law enforcement powers and functions. However, unlike the police, 'there is no mystery about the proper business of such law enforcement agents, and citizens are generally quite able to hold them to their limits'.[48] The police, in contrast, have a much more general legal mandate and, because of their symbolic role, a much wider functional mandate. Thus society accepts, and sometimes justifies, police acting beyond their specific powers in a way which would not be accepted if it were done by a member of another 'policing' body. An important illustration of this was provided by an HSE inspector, who referred to a case in which he had been accompanied by a police constable on a visit to some premises. It was the HSE inspector, not the police constable, who had the statutory power of entry. However, the police constable was taken along to give the HSE inspector added authority, as well as to prevent a possible breach of the peace should the property owner forcibly resist access.

Although, in the main, the law as framed is clear, it remains the case that there is a good deal of ambiguity in the way that it is operationalised. In practice, although uniformed BTP and Parks Police officers sometimes undertake arrests outside their jurisdiction, this is rarely challenged by the arrestee. In this sense, members of these non-Home Department policing bodies are being required to rely on ignorance of the law, or forced acquiescence, in the same way as Metropolitan Police officers who undertake searches 'by consent'. The practical power is related only indirectly to the legal power. This indirect relationship is utilised by some policing bodies to provide them with a degree of flexibility in carrying out their task. As society becomes more litigious, we may see an increasing number of civil cases which will have the effect of reducing this practical ambiguity, and relating actions more directly to statutory powers.

[48] Bittner (1974) p. 20.

Functional Boundaries

We turn last to the function which is usually considered first in discussions about policing bodies—namely, the functional dimension—and examine what exactly it is that the various policing bodies do. As we suggested in Chapter One, Johnston has argued that functional definitions of policing are of little use, for it is the case that private security does everything that the public police do and much more besides.[49] We consider below whether this general statement applied in Wandsworth, and we also consider a number of more specific issues relating to the functions performed by different policing bodies.

Table 7.3 provides a simple, yet graphic illustration of one element of the policing division of labour. Across the top of the table are listed some of the main policing bodies operating in Wandsworth at the time of the study (the Metropolitan Police, the Parks Police, British Transport Police, Environmental Health Officers and Health and Safety Executive inspectors, Housing Patrol, Post Office Investigation Department, and private security). Down the left hand side of the Table are a selection of what we take to be the key functions performed by Home Office constabularies. Asterisks in the relevant boxes indicate that the function in question is carried out by the relevant policing body.

What conclusions can one draw from Table 7.3? Clearly, the table illustrates that within the complex patchwork which makes up the 'security quilt'[50], there is no clear overall functional division of labour between different agencies (although clearly some are more specialised than others). There is considerable overlap between the activities carried out by very different bodies. Moreover, the table ostensibly lends support to Johnston's contention that, in functional terms, there is little to separate the private security industry from the public police. This superficial functional similarity camouflages a number of rather important dissimilarities. First, it presents a very superficial view of the 'market' in policing services, in that, as outlined above, one of the distinguishing characteristics of the public police is the wide-ranging nature of their remit. They are a 'catch-all' service, called upon to do a variety of tasks, and meet an almost limitless range of demands which are growing in complexity. And all this must be done from within a single, bureaucratic organisation.

[49] Johnston (1992).   [50] Ericson (1994)

Table 7.3: Functional boundaries in policing

Function	Metropolitan Police	Parks Police	British Transport Police	Environmental Health Officers/ Health and Safety Executive Inspectors	Housing Patrol	Post Office Investigation Department	Private security
Respond to calls	*	*	*		*		*
Investigate crime	*	*	*	*		*	*
Arrest offenders	*	*	*			*	*
Maintain public order	*	*	*		*		*
Visible patrol	*	*	*		*		*
Traffic control	*	*	*				*
Parking enforcement	*	*	*		*		*
Accident investigation	*	*	*	*			*
Crime pattern analysis	*	*	*				*
Security surveys	*	*	*				*
Alarm response	*	*			*		*
Noise/harassment	*	*		*	*		*
Prisoner escort	*		*		*		*
CCTV monitoring	*	*	*				*

Indeed, for Bittner, of course, the boundless nature of their remit is a significant defining characteristic.

In contrast to this large, multi-functional organisation, the title 'private security industry' grossly simplifies the way in which private security services are provided. The Table gives the impression—and this is often the way the industry is talked about—that there is a homogenous entity called 'private security' carrying out a range of tasks. Of course, there is not. As we have shown in some detail, the private security industry consists of a large number of organisations of varying sizes, many of which are highly localised and even more highly specialised. This highlights one of the crucial differences between public and private policing bodies. In the main it is the case that public policing bodies have extremely wide functional remits. Indeed, as Bittner argues, it is hard to imagine anything which could not under some circumstances become the business of the police.[51] By contrast, the vast majority of private policing bodies are functionally specialised. Indeed, even those with broad mandates exhibit a greater degree of functional specialisation than the police. This quite clearly needs to be borne in mind when making comparisons between the activities and performances of public and private policing bodies. Just as the police may be stretched because of their spatial and geographical breadth (they have wide geographical remits and regional, national, and even international responsibilities), so their functional responsibilities may make competing with organisations whose remit and focus are much narrower extremely problematic. Some of the difficulties associated with this position have been neatly summarised by Bottoms and Wiles:

. . . the new forms of segmentation and fragmentation in the late modern city have produced very different social control needs and these, like any differentiated market, can often be most effectively responded to by dedicated, targeted services. The public police, by attempting to remain a generalist service, inevitably incur much higher costs than these specialised providers.[52]

A second important qualification of the picture presented by Table 7.3 is that it presents an overly-narrow view of the Metropolitan Police function due to its focus on local divisions. The Table does not include some important functions that remain the exclusive remit of the 'public' police, although they are not carried out within the local divisions of the Metropolitan Police; these include prisoner escort for

---

[51] Bittner (1974).   [52] Bottoms and Wiles (1994) pp. 38–9.

category A prisoners, 'national security' functions, Special Branch operations, and royalty and diplomatic protection functions.[53] Despite the increasing degree of functional overlap then, it remains true that some specific functions remain firmly outside the remit of private security and other 'policing' bodies.

Table 7.3 is also valuable for its illustration of the importance of analysing policing bodies across a number of dimensions. For example, it is a central distinguishing feature of public constabularies that they are functionally far less specialised than many of the firms offering services for profit. Within a limited set of functions, private security can provide a very effective service. As we have seen in our analyses of the other dimensions, the distinguishing feature of the police is that they are generalist across all the dimensions considered.

Conclusions

The primary aim in this chapter was to explore the contemporary policing division of labour in one London Borough, and to consider how the boundaries of different policing organisations might best be conceptualised. Building on a considerable body of work on the sociology of the police, together with more recent writings on the 'rebirth' of private policing, we suggested that there exist five dimensions—the sectoral, spatial, legal, functional, and geographical—which it is necessary to consider in order to draw a fully-rounded picture of the activities, powers, and remit of contemporary policing bodies.

In relation to the sectoral dimension, it is our contention that it is not possible to demarcate in a consistent fashion between 'public' and 'hybrid' policing bodies. Indeed, the term 'hybrid' seems to us to be a problematic conceptual tool. Because of this, we suggest that, at least in relation to the sectoral dimension of policing if not to the spatial, the traditional public–private divide retains quite a strong utility. Having said this, we were nevertheless able to detect a growing degree of sectoral complexity amongst the policing bodies in Wandsworth. Such complexity is visible in the operation and organisation of the Metropolitan Police, and other public bodies, in at least

---

[53] This is not to say, of course, that Metropolitan Police officers carrying out such functions have no connection with the local level. Local intelligence officers will have ongoing liaison with central squads at New Scotland Yard, and the operations of specialist squads will from time to time bring them into the Borough of Wandsworth.

as significant a respect as the private bodies in the Borough. The most fundamental distinctions between the policing bodies on the ground were not to be found along the sectoral dimension, however, but along other boundaries identified by the research. In this sense, there remained an important distinction between those bodies largely funded from taxation, and staffed by state officials (either national or local), and those bodies selling 'policing' services in the free market, and whose income primarily came from private consumers.

Spatially, the situation is rather different. Despite a degree of spatial overlap, a number of quite strong patterns were visible. First, and predictably, public constabularies tend to work primarily in public space, though for non-Home Office forces the public space in which they operate is generally significantly and, occasionally, problematically circumscribed. Similarly, the private security sector operates primarily in private space. However, this predictable divide hides a significant degree of complexity and overlap, which places major limitations on the utility of the public–private dichotomy. Consequently, at this point we reintroduce the term 'hybrid'—rejected as unhelpful in relation to sectoral boundaries—to refer to a series of spaces which in some sense are neither unambiguously public nor unambiguously private. For example, colleges of higher and further education were once unambiguously publicly-controlled and funded by the Inner London Education Authority (ILEA). Responsibility transferred to the local authority when the ILEA was abolished during the 1980s. The next stage was to make these bodies independent of local government, and set them up as independent entities. Government liberalisation policy has thus led to institutions of further and higher education increasingly being encouraged to act independently, as quasi-private organisations, despite the fact that the majority of funding still comes, albeit indirectly, from the public purse. A similar situation pertains to Trust-status hospitals. Nevertheless, the colleges and hospitals are increasingly policed by private security. But this is not quite the 'corporate policing' of Shearing and Stenning's analysis. Furthermore, it is difficult to represent this as a straightforward displacement of the public police by private security. Although college campuses and hospitals are increasingly reliant upon contracted-in security guards, prior to their arrival these premises were not routinely patrolled by the public police. Arguably, such mass property was never part of the 'natural domain' of the public police. Although it is the case that, the more private spaces become, the more likely they are to be policed by private bodies (or a combination of public and private bodies), it nevertheless remains the case that, the relationship between the sectoral status of the policing provider and the spatial context of the policing is mediated by a number of other factors, including the legal powers and functional remit of the bodies involved.

There is also a degree of ambiguity in relation to legal boundaries of policing, though in the main this stems from the way in which the law is operationalised rather than framed. Thus, in a number of areas, there is a degree of ambiguity on the ground about the legal limitations on the activities of different policing bodies, even though the legislative position with regard to their powers may be relatively clear. This apparent ambiguity is frequently exploited by policing bodies in order to allow them a degree of functional and spatial flexibility.

Finally, we detect what appears to be a large (and perhaps growing) degree of functional overlap between public and non-public policing organisations. The Metropolitan Police have accepted this to a degree, but have become more defensive when certain boundaries are threatened, particularly where these are perceived to threaten their 'symbolic power'.[54] For example, the strong opposition to the extension of Parks Police patrols to housing estates illustrates this. The problem for the public police is that they are a large, multifunctional organisation, with high overheads and labour costs, and an extremely unpredictable workload. Although in limited ways they are increasingly expected to compete with the private sector, this will always be an uneven contest given their extremely broad functional (and spatial) remit. Because of this it is perhaps not surprising that smaller, specialist firms can take on one or two functions of the public police, and provide them more effectively, and at lower cost.

This chapter has worked towards a conceptual framework which is able to capture in an adequate manner the fragmentation and complexity which is visible in contemporary policing, and yet which allows us to consider the distinctive contribution of the public police to the local security patchwork. In general, it appears that although the boundaries between the public police and other bodies are blurred, they are still quite detectable. The defining characteristic in the case of each boundary appears to be the wide-ranging nature of the police mandate. Sectorally, it is reasonable to argue that 'market

[54] Loader, I. (1997*a*) 'Policing and the social: Questions of symbolic power', *British Journal of Sociology*, 48, 1, 1–18.

pressures' on public policing are impinging more significantly on the police organisation, than 'public service' pressures are impinging on the private security industry. Spatially, the police are far more generalist than any of the other bodies under consideration.[55] Legally, the mandate of the public police is wider than that of other policing bodies. Even where such bodies have greater legal powers than police constables, the symbolic role and the wide functional remit of the public police means that they are required to 'underwrite' the actions of these more specialist bodies. Finally, as we have seen, the public police are required to carry out a much wider range of functions than any other policing body. As outlined above, this leads to particular difficulties when the public police are expected to 'compete' in a local 'market' for policing services. If market decisions are based on pure economic rationality, this is a competition in which, in the long run, the public police have little chance of winning.

[55] This 'generalist' aspect also applies to the fifth dimension under consideration, what we have called the geographical dimension. This concerns the level of organisation of policing services on a central–local scale. For example, a guard working for a private security firm guarding one of the colleges outlined that, for example, they do not have to worry about staff being withdrawn to deal with a public order problem on another site. They also do not have to worry about the problem of displacement, as was graphically illustrated by the guard's clear indication that whatever went on outside the college gates, even if it was directly in front of them and involved students from the college, was not their business.

8

Making Sense of the Policing Division of Labour

In this concluding chapter we return to a number of the central debates in the sociology of policing (and the sociology of the police) and reflect on the direction of some of the most significant changes that appear to be taking place in contemporary policing. More particularly, we reconsider what is meant by 'policing' and whether it is possible to develop some form of conceptual definition of policing that doesn't separate out those activities undertaken by the (public) police. In addition, and by contrast, we consider whether, and on what basis, one can distinguish the 'role' of the public police from those of other policing bodies. Not only do we ponder the meaning of the term 'policing', we also consider how useful the public–private dichotomy is in the context of policing and, by implication, what part the notion of 'hybridity' should play in this context. This discussion leads directly to an issue that has been central to our work, namely how are we to understand and conceptualise the boundaries of 'public' and 'private' policing? Finally, having considered what is happening to contemporary policing and how it is to be understood, we offer some reflections on the future of policing.

What is meant by 'policing'?

As we have said repeatedly, it is only relatively recently that sociologists and criminologists have started to pay attention to private policing. There are basically two reasons for the re-emergence of private policing within criminology. First, it has happened as a consequence of the generally heightened visibility of the industry as it has expanded both in size and scope. Second, academic attention has been attracted by the actual, proposed, or anticipated acts of

248 Private Security and Public Policing

privatisation that have occurred not only in policing, but in criminal justice more broadly (including, for example, the privatisation of prisons, prisoner escort, and, within policing, initiatives like the Core and Ancillary Tasks Review). Together these have undermined the general tendency to talk of policing and the police as if they were one and the same. As attention has been drawn to 'other' policing organisations, so questions have arisen about the relationship between these bodies and the police. In one form or another the focus of this book has been on these matters; what has been referred to as the increasingly complex 'policing division of labour' and the nature of its component parts.

Although what we are attempting to do in this book therefore involves something of a departure from much of the early sociology of policing, nonetheless it also shares a number of attributes with that body of work. One of our central concerns is a desire not only to consider policing in a broader sense, but also to explore the possibility of locating and identifying the key attributes of 'the police'. In part this depends upon moving beyond early sociological treatments, such as those by Banton, Cain and others, which focused down on the 'function' of the police. As a consequence of that focus, for some time academic and professional debates about policing centred on the relative importance of such functions as law enforcement, 'social service', and order maintenance or peacekeeping to the task of the police and to the daily lives of frontline police officers. Although there was disagreement about the weight that should be given to each, few demurred from the idea that together these constituted what was considered to be 'policing'.

Beginning in the 1970s, a challenging and alternative approach to such questions was offered by the American sociologist, Egon Bittner. He redirected attention towards the qualities that police officers bring to their functions, and prioritised the 'means' of policing over the content. In doing so, he was able to highlight what he took to be the characteristics which distinguished public policework from other forms of policing. The distinctiveness of public policing for Bittner rested on two characteristics. First, that their mandate was so broad that it was all but impossible to imagine a human problem which could not be their proper business. Secondly, not only is their potential mandate incomparably broad, but the way in which the problems they confront are dealt with is unique. It is unique because the police have a distinctive capacity which enables them to deal with any eventuality—the capacity to use coercive force on behalf of the state. Now clearly, in most cases such coercive force is not used but, Bittner argued, it is the fact that it could be, that it is symbolically present, which allows the police officer to settle disputes and problems in a way that is different from other officials involved in policing.

Bittner's conceptual approach has been adopted by many leading writers on the police. Reiner, for example, in his criticism of those who reduce policing to a simple dichotomisation of law enforcement and 'social service', argued that the bulk of policework is best described as order maintenance: 'the settlement of conflicts by means other than formal law enforcement'.[1] Though there is much support for this position, it has itself been subject to criticism. Thus, for example, Johnston has suggested that the difficulty with this view of what is supposedly distinctive about policework is that it quickly breaks down if one begins to think about the broader policing division of labour. Thus, he argues, if one includes the functions performed by, and the legal capacities of, non-public policing bodies, the explanatory capacity of an approach which emphasises order maintenance and access to the legitimate use of force diminishes quickly. In terms of functions, as Johnston has put it: 'private security does anything that the public police (or other state officials with special powers) do, and rather more besides'. Furthermore, in relation to the legitimate use of force there are things that the police do without the authority of the state—police corruption, police vigilantism. Moreover, the coercive acts carried out by non-state employees are little different in character from those things police officers do without the authority of the state. As a consequence, he contends, explanations which seek to reduce policing to essential functions or a fundamental legal capacity skate over the complexities that are visible in the policing division of labour.

Ironically, a degree of 'essentialism' has also characterised much writing on private security. Thus, for example, although Shearing and Stenning—probably the leading writers in this field—are careful to observe that the private security industry is broad in terms of the functions it performs, they suggest that its 'role' is primarily determined by its clients. They argue that private security is essentially preventative in character, and that what it aims to prevent is *loss*. Moreover, not only do they specify the function or role of private

---

[1] Reiner (1992*b*) p. 142.

policing very particularly, but they also identify what they take to be the primary means private policing uses to secure this end: *surveillance*. The main shortcoming of such a conceptualisation of the role of private security is that it prioritises guarding in particular, and staffed services in general, over the other elements of the industry. Thus, although there is evidence that CCTV and electronic security manufacture and installation are the major growth areas of private security, when discussing the distinction between public and private policing sectors, authors such as Shearing and Stenning tend to talk of private security as if its essence consisted of 'manned guarding'. Whilst for the sake of comparison it obviously makes sense to consider the work of 'personnel'—and thus security guards and frontline police officers are an obvious comparison—this rather undersells the complex nature of both public and private policing bodies. A more realistic comparison must involve the range of activities undertaken by both sets of organisations and, as a consequence, is likely to be more complex.

Their focus on personnel leads Shearing and Stenning to argue that what is fundamentally public about the role of the police officer is not to be found either in functions or legal powers, but is to be found in the nature of the 'contract' underpinning the work:

What principally distinguishes private security from the public police . . . is that private security personnel are generally not under any legally defined public duty to perform their duties in the public interest, as public police personnel (by virtue of their oath of office) generally are.[2]

The implication is that private security guards do what they do because they are specifically contracted and paid to do so, and that what in general determines their courses of action will be the contents of that contract in general, and the requirements of the purchaser in particular. Though there are other factors to consider, according to Shearing and Stenning it is this that distinguishes them from their public police colleagues who have a broader mandate to fulfil. Whilst at an abstract level this appears a convincing distinction between public and private policing, one might echo Johnston's point here that there are activities which the police undertake which, legal duty or not, would be hard to defend in terms of some form of wide 'public interest'. Moreover, as public police forces increasingly contract with outside bodies to provide specific, highly defined services,

[2] Shearing and Stenning (1981) p. 210.

it is questionable whether the distinction is as clear as it might at first seem.

In addition to questioning the extent to which such a public duty is perceived and acted upon by all police officers all the time, we might ask whether such a public duty serves as the basis on which users distinguish between public and private police services. In one sense clearly it does. Thus, it is undeniable that many purchasers of private policing services have relatively specific requirements, and that Shearing and Stenning's observation that 'the role of private security may be characterised by its emphasis on a preventative approach to the protection of assets and the maximisation of profits' consequently has some force. However, when we move between public and private space with the consequent changes in the nature of the policing that we might experience, do we necessarily change our assumptions about the way in which we expect to be policed in those places? Of course this is difficult territory. What one expects from a nightclub bouncer no doubt differs markedly from what one expects from a police officer. However, what one expects from a bouncer no doubt also differs markedly from what one expects from a blazered security official in the foyer of a City of London insurance company. The point is that expectations are most likely finely-graded rather than fundamentally divided. We do not, necessarily, make crude distinctions between public and private officials; at least, not simply in terms of some idea of public duty. There is, as yet, no evidence that those asked to distinguish between different policing services prioritise the idea of 'public duty' and its consequences. Although research in this area is generally lacking, preference for police officers over security guards (for example, in relation to patrol, where it is expressed) lies primarily in their perceived greater competence as a result of better training, greater experience, and better pay.[3]

Senior police officers tend to link issues of pay and training with the wider question of *accountability* when distinguishing public policing from private security. On this view, the police service is subject to a range of accountability mechanisms, including review of policing policy by national and local government, the existence of established complaints mechanisms, and financial audit of their use of

---

[3] Mawby, R., Bunt, P. and Redshaw, J. (1995) 'Police performance: the consumer view', Paper presented at the British Criminology Conference, Loughborough, 18–21 July 1995.

public funds.[4] In contrast, they argue, the private security sector is largely unregulated, and subject only to the crude accountability of the marketplace. Such arguments should be qualified in a number of ways. First, there is a large body of literature which has questioned the effectiveness of accountability mechanisms for the public police in Britain. Although, as a whole, the police service is clearly subject to greater formal accountability than the private security industry, it is not always the case that such mechanisms are effective. On the contrary, it is possible to think of examples in which the contractual accountability of the marketplace would be far more immediate and effective than political forms of accountability. The shopping mall security firm whose staff are threatening or abusive to customers will more than likely be removed and replaced with another 'professional' firm.

We would not wish to deny that, at least in theory, the nature of the 'contracts' underpinning the work of public and private officials in policing are distinguishable from each other, in that some form of wider public duty may well be largely absent from the private sector. However, we remain unconvinced that this provides the essence of the distinction between different forms of provision. In practice at least, the private security industry is so varied—in the functions it performs and for whom it performs them—that general statements about the nature of the activity involved appear rather rudimentary. In this case, such a view leads Shearing and Stenning to offer other general statements about private security. Of these, two are key: first, that whereas the form of preventative work undertaken by the police is *crime prevention*, private security is primarily involved in *loss prevention*; and, second, not only do they specify the function or role of private policing very particularly, but they also identify what they take to be the primary means private policing uses to secure this end, namely surveillance.

How are we to respond to their view that 'the role of private security may be characterised by its emphasis on a preventative approach to the protection of assets and the maximisation of profits' and that 'the feature uniting the diverse activities undertaken by private security under the heading of prevention is surveillance'?[5] In order to

    [4] See Newburn, T., and Jones, T. (1996) 'Police Accountability', in Saulsbury, W., Mott, J., and Newburn, T. *Themes in Contemporary Policing*, London: Policy Studies Institute/Police Foundation.
    [5] Shearing and Stenning (1981), p. 209.

consider these questions it is worth revisiting briefly what we have been able to determine on the basis of empirical research about the nature of the private security industry in the UK.

Private Security: What is it and what does it do?

Before looking at the nature and activities of the private security industry, once again we need to clarify the terminology were are using. Quite clearly, in order to discuss the nature and activities of private security we have to make a decision about what to include under this rubric and what to exclude. This requires us to be clear about what we mean by 'public' and 'private'. In Chapter Two we suggested that the public–private dichotomy could not be used systematically to sort institutions or practices into neat, hermetically-sealed categories but that, despite this, it remains a useful, didactic tool. We outlined a number of ways in which the public–private divide has been understood, and suggested that two of these were key to making sense of the role and distinctiveness of private security. The first, and perhaps the commonest use of the dichotomy, distinguishes the provision of services through the free market with those available via state-organised provision. This, following Johnston, we referred to as the 'sectoral dimension' of policing. The second use of the dichotomy revolves around ideas of accessibility and openness rather than the nature of ownership and control, and is more appropriate to a discussion of what we have termed the 'spatial dimension' of policing.

Most commonly, when the terms public and private are used in relation to policing, what is being referred to is the 'sectoral' status of the bodies involved. Crudely, this allows a distinction to be drawn between state officials and those working for profit-making organisations. In his thorough examination of policing bodies Johnston argues that the public–private dichotomy is insufficiently sophisticated to deal with the sectoral complexity that is visible in contemporary policing. Whilst in some senses we agree with his position, we have argued in this book that the insertion of a category of 'hybrid policing' to describe those bodies whose sectoral status is not unproblematically public or private is largely unhelpful. Although, as we found in Wandsworth, there is a high degree of sectoral complexity in contemporary policing, the bulk of policing bodies that would in Johnston's terms be categorised as hybrid are, in an important sense, public. Thus, although there are distinctions to be drawn between Home Department forces, other bodies of constables, and other public bodies, they are all distinguishable sectorally from *private security*. What draws together 'public' bodies is that they are predominantly publicly funded, are staffed in the main by public officials, and do not depend for their survival on the selling of services for profit. Consequently, private policing bodies can be considered to be those in which the majority of funding does not come directly from the state (be that national or local state), whose employees are not public officials, and who are financially dependent on the sale of services in the market.

In the event we included five categories of organisation under the rubric of private security: staffed services; electronic security equipment (CCTV, alarms, etc.) manufacture and installation; investigatory services; bailiffing and debt collection; and physical security equipment (locks, safes, etc.) manufacture and installation. The range of functions is therefore very broad. Staffed services—guarding—is what usually springs to mind when private security is mentioned and, indeed, this remains an important segment of the industry, accounting for several hundred million pounds worth of business every year. Extrapolating from the data collected from our national survey it may be that this sector of the industry could include over 950 firms, employing up to 47,000 people. However, we should reiterate at this point that the industry is extremely diverse and overlaps considerably with the other major sectors. As we have argued, it is the electronic security equipment market that appears to be growing most quickly. The manufacture, installation and maintenance of alarms remains the largest part of this sector, though CCTV has been expanding rapidly over the past decade or so. Our survey suggested that as many as 2,500 firms may now be operating in this sector of the industry, employing, we estimate, over 100,000 people. The other three main sectors of the industry, bailiffing and debt collection, locks, bolts and safes, and investigation services, are significantly smaller but still important. The list of functions undertaken by this sector of the industry is a graphic illustration of the heterogeneity of private security. The functions undertaken by private investigators include: tracing missing persons; accident investigation; asset tracing; collection of forensic evidence; industrial counter-espionage; trademark protection and matrimonial/maintenance inquiries among many others.

Such heterogeneity should make us wary of reducing explanations of the function of private security to loss prevention (though this function is clearly very significant), or reducing the means by which private security performs its functions to surveillance. Whilst identifiable functional and procedural differences may exist between important parts of the private policing sector and its public counterpart, it is overstretching the argument to then promote such differences to the role of defining differences between the sectors. Unfortunately, for the result is a much more complicated explanatory model, we have to adopt a more finely-graded means of distinguishing policing bodies from each other.

The boundaries of private security and public policing

One of the dominant themes in recent writing about the contemporary policing division of labour has been the fragmentation that, it is argued, is now visible in policing provision.[6] The boundaries between different policing organisations are becoming increasingly 'blurred', it is suggested. This is a position with which we not only agree, but for which we are able to provide evidence. However, where our analysis differs from many others is that we have sought to define the boundaries which may, or may not, be being blurred. Following, but revising, the work undertaken by Johnston, we have sought to argue that there are at least five dimensions or sets of boundaries that have to be considered in a fully developed analysis of policing. These dimensions we called the sectoral, spatial, legal, functional, and geographical.

It is, as we have suggested above, the sectoral dimension that gives rise to the terms public and private policing. Though the use of the dichotomy is by no means unproblematic, we have argued that it retains sufficient utility in relation to this particular dimension that the inclusion of the idea of hybridity—a middle-ground category which contains those policing organisations which display both public and private elements—is unhelpful. It is in relation to the spatial dimension of policing—where policing takes place—that the idea of hybridity is useful. This is the case because there exist a variety of forms of space—mass private property being one example—where the nature of the ownership and access to the property make their 'status' ambiguous. Consequently, in describing and analysing the

---

[6] See Reiner, (1992a); Johnston (1993); Leishman *et al.* (1996).

spatial dimension of policing, we have referred not only to public and private, but also to 'hybrid space'. Whilst our research led us to qualify Shearing and Stenning's mass private property thesis in some important respects, the increasing importance of hybrid space and its effects on policing provision parallels their argument in some ways. Whilst in Wandsworth there was a clear association between public space and public policing, and private space and private policing—though they were by no means fully coterminous—the fragmentation of space is closely associated with the fragmentation of policing.

The sectoral and spatial dimensions of policing are closely associated then, but they are also mediated by a number of other factors. Two of these concern the elements of policing that have dominated so much of the sociological discussion of the nature of policing: function and powers. Functionally, there is clearly significant overlap between the public and private sectors and, consequently, it is not possible to identify a clear division of labour between policing bodies. Indeed, it is the apparently increasing degree of overlap in this regard which worries so many commentators. However, this crude picture of the functional division of labour hides a number of complexities. First, the police have a much wider functional mandate than do other bodies of constables or those organisations that go to make up the private security industry. Bittner's suggestion that it is hard to imagine a human problem that might not become the business of the police largely holds true. That it does not hold for most other policing bodies is also, for our purposes here, of great importance. Although the private security industry does much of what the police do (along with a number of functions that they do not), there is no single body within the industry that could lay claim to such a description. In functional terms, most are quite circumscribed, relative to the police. It is only the conglomeration of private security bodies that is able to match the police in breadth of function. This remains the case despite the transfer of a number of functions from the police to other bodies. Importantly, despite the official transfer of functions such as prisoner escort, and the policing of noisy parties, the public police must retain a residual capacity to undertake such functions. For example, the police continue to undertake prisoner escort duties for prisoners considered to be particularly dangerous. Furthermore, when officials of other bodies are threatened, attacked, or otherwise unlawfully prevented from carrying out functions, it is to the symbolic power of the public police that they turn. Bodies that have a functional mandate that comes close in breadth to the police are few and are invariably public organisations—the British Transport Police being perhaps the best example. However, their functional breadth is not matched by a similarly broad spatial mandate. Bodies such as the BTP have significant limitations placed upon the exercise of their powers. In the main, these limitations are jurisdictional or spatial, rather than legal. There are, then, two linked senses in which legal boundaries need to be considered in relation to the policing division of labour. The first and most obvious 'boundary' concerns the differing degrees and range of powers available to different policing organisations. The second we have just referred to: that is, where these powers can be exercised.

As far as available powers are concerned the police generally have a broader legal mandate than members of other security organisations—except where they are specifically empowered, such as the Wandsworth Parks Police and those guards involved in functions such as prisoner escort. Most other members of private security organisations have no specific powers over and above those of the ordinary citizen. A greater range of powers are held by members of other public policing bodies. They range from the broad legal, but functionally specific, powers available to environmental health officers and health and safety inspectors, to the broad legal, but spatially circumscribed, powers available to the officers of British Transport Police, Ministry of Defence Police, and the UK Atomic Energy Authority Constabulary. In general terms public bodies with special legal powers have a well-defined legal mandate which delineates their functions. By contrast Home Office forces have a broad, but equally importantly, a *permissive* legal mandate. Rather than constraining or limiting them functionally, this permissive legal mandate provides the basis for their almost unlimited functional remit. Not only do members of Home Office forces appear to have broad powers and a sweeping functional remit when compared with most others involved in policing but, as we have seen, their spatial remit is also significantly broader than those of other officials involved in policing.

There is one final point we need to make in relation to powers. This returns us to the question of whether we can distinguish the police from other bodies involved in policing. The traditional means of doing this has been to invoke Bittner's argument that it is the police that are the carriers of the state's monopoly of the legitimate use of force. This position, as we have seen, has been subjected to

quite strong criticism in recent times. Johnston ends his critique of
the extant sociology of policing in the following way: '. . . policing
consists of a complex of connections between formal and substantive
powers, and between private and public activities . . . policing can be
defined neither in terms of some essential legal capacity, nor in terms
of some essential set of functions'.[7] This is a statement with which it
would be hard to disagree. However, accepting this does not involve
rejecting Bittner's position. Clearly, 'policing' cannot be reduced
either to a set of functions—we have seen how variable the functional
remits of policing bodies can be—or to the possession of the legitimate use of force—the majority of policing bodies have no such
capacity. 'Policing' is something much broader. It involves law or rule
enforcement, order maintenance, peacekeeping, the investigation and
prevention of crime as well as other forms of investigation. It may
involve a conscious exercise of coercive power, though it need not
and, rather than including all forms of organised social control, policing, we argue, is best understood as including the above activities
when they are undertaken by individuals or organisations that view
these activities as a central or key defining part of their work.

Within this, what the police do, can also be distinguished. It is *the
police* (for our purposes here the police are defined as 'Home Office
forces'), and only the police, who may bring to bear coercive force
on behalf of the state across the range of policing functions, and
across a wide geographical and spatial remit. Indeed, a definition
which allows us to make sense of the special position of the police
has been available for some time, and it is one that uses functions
and powers in combination. Here we would repeat part of a quote
from Bittner that we first used in Chapter One: 'the police are
empowered and required to impose or, as the case may be, coerce a
provisional solution upon emergent problems without having to
brook or defer to opposition of any kind, and that further, their competence to intervene extends to every kind of emergency, without any
exceptions whatever. This and this alone is what the existence of the
police uniquely provides'.[8] In our view, sociologists have not improved upon this definition in the past twenty-five years.

---

[7] Johnston (1992) p. 190.   [8] Bittner (1971) p. 18.

The recent history and the immediate future of policing

In order to consider the near future of policing, we have to consider the immediate past. It is only by considering how we have reached this current stage in the history of policing that we can speculate about what the future holds. Here we are talking about policing generally: how is it that the policing division of labour has reached its present form? In distilling the reasons for the changes that have taken place in recent decades what assumptions can we make about how the policing division of labour is likely to change in years to come?

Earlier in the book we outlined the two major approaches that have been adopted in attempting to explain the growth of the private security industry and, by implication, the changing policing division of labour. We suggested that each, taken on its own, is inadequate: that the changing face of 'policing' in Britain could not be explained solely by reference to the level of funding devoted to public constabularies, or to the rise of mass private property. Nonetheless, we also suggested that both approaches contain much that it is useful to hold on to. Thus, funding or, more particularly, the level of demand in relation to public funding, has undoubtedly been an important factor in stimulating growth in the private sector. In recent years such growth has been aided by a government that is ideologically committed to increasing competition between public and private sectors. In addition, the 'new' mass public spaces highlighted by Shearing and Stenning have potentially quite profound implications for how we are policed. There are dangers, however, in translating too directly from the North American experience—we are still some distance from the 'enclavisation' and privately patrolled domestic fortresses of Mike Davis's Los Angeles.[9]

Furthermore, we have argued that although the expansion of private security has been significant, the limited data that are available to measure change over time do not suggest an explosive growth over more recent times. In fact, as was outlined in Chapter Four, Census data suggest that the rate of growth of employment in security and related occupations over the last thirty years or so has been similar to the growth in numbers of police officers. This suggests that the growing focus on private security results not only from rising employment, but also from increasing visibility. This is related both to the existence of 'mass private property' patrolled by private

[9] Davis (1988).

security guards, and to the increasing tendency for firms to contract out security services to specialist guarding firms. The local study suggested that it was not so much the police, but agents such as caretakers, park-keepers, and bus-conductors whose roles are now increasingly the province of uniformed security guards.

In any case, there is much more happening to policing in the late twentieth century than can be captured by either fiscal crisis or mass private property theories. This has been implied by Johnston with his invocation of a third line of explanation—what he referred to as 'late modern social change'. This way forward was first signposted by Robert Reiner who argued:

[T]the deeper social changes of postmodernity are transforming the role of the police institution within the whole array of policing processes. The rise of *the* police—a single professional organisation for handling the policing function of regulation and surveillance, with the state's monopoly of legitimate force as its ultimate resource—was itself a paradigm of the modern. It was predicated upon the project of organising society around a central, cohesive notion of order . . . The role of the police, especially in Britain, was always more important for its dramaturgical function, symbolising social order, than for any instrumental effects in successfully controlling crime. The changes in social structure and culture which have been labelled postmodernisation render this conception of policing increasingly anachronistic. There can be no effective symbol of a unitary order in a pluralistic and fragmented culture. . . . In short, policing now reflects the processes of pluralism, disaggregation and fragmentation which have been seen as the hallmark of the postmodern.[10]

The social order being policed is, Reiner argues, in essence 'postmodern' and by implication so is policing. It has been subject to what he calls 'organisational bifurcation' and what Johnston refers to as 'spatial polarisation': in which nationally and internationally policing is dominated by an ever-decreasing number of centralised agencies, whereas locally the accent is on decentralisation and fragmentation. As we suggested in Chapter Four, however, whilst on the surface this is an attractive approach, and one we concur with in part, it nevertheless leaves much unexplained. More concretely, whilst we have been able to show in some detail how 'fragmented' the contemporary policing division of labour is, and there is evidence to suggest that much of the wider society is similarly fragmented, the

[10] Reiner (1992*a*) pp. 779–80.

connections between the two remain somewhat unclear. In fact, the link is rarely fully explained.

What we would like to argue is that whilst there is much to be said for such an approach, the foundation of the changes we seek to explain may well lie in the decades immediately following the Second World War. To take an important example, many of the regulatory functions gathered by public constabularies during the course of the nineteenth century were gradually transferred to specialist agencies as the British welfare state was established from the 1920s, reaching its heyday in the post-war corporatist bargain. The major expansion in private security would appear to have begun in the 1960s. Two points arise from this. First, the factors lying behind the growth of so-called 'hybrid policing' and those stimulating the rebirth of private security may not overlap completely. Second, given that we need to go back to the 1950s and 1960s to trace both sets of factors, caution must be exercised in considering the chronology of 'postmodernisation'.

When thinking about changes in the policing division of labour there is much to be said, we would argue, for looking at what in certain respects are arguably the building blocks of theories of postmodernity—'post-industrialism', or more particularly the 'information society', and 'post-Fordism'. One of the difficulties with such an explanation lies in its complexity. Within it there lie a number of interlinked processes—changes in the nature of the nation-state, the rise and commodification of new technologies, changes in the organisation of production and consumption, the fragmentation of the city, the changing nature of risk and trust—each of which is the subject of a considerable literature.[11]

We begin with the nation-state. As is well-known, the establishment of the 'New Police' in 1829 was the beginning of the 'modern' period in British policing history. As we outlined in Chapter One, before this date policing had been provided in a range of ways, some of which were 'private' and less formal, and others, for example the institution of frankpledge, which although not directly provided by the state were quintessentially public.

The emergence and legitimation of a professional state police force

---

[11] Good introductions can be found in Harvey, D. (1989) *The Condition of Postmodernity*, Cambridge: Polity Press; and, Kumar, K. (1995) *From Post-industrial to Post-modern Society*, Oxford: Basil Blackwell.

was the culmination of a process that began well over a century earlier and in which the work of the Fieldings in the mid-eighteenth century was key. As Rawlings argues: 'In contrast to the eighteenth century paradigm in which individuals and communities were centrally involved in policing, the implication of the Fieldings' work was to restrict, or even to exclude, the people from such involvement by redefining policing as the work of a state bureaucracy.'[12] Indeed, he rightly goes on to argue that the effects of this are visible in present day police work and, further, in the 'broader move away from popular involvement in the criminal justice system to a situation in which control over investigation, trial and punishment is, supposedly, in the hands of professionals and in which intervention is tightly controlled by laws of evidence and procedure'.[13]

Policing, as we said at the beginning of this book, has overwhelmingly come to be associated with the police. The re-emergence of private policing, which has been the central focus of this book, exposed the 'mythological nature of the project of crime control and order maintenance by a state bureaucracy'.[14] Not only this, however, but it has arguably also exposed significant changes which have been taking place in the nature of the state and in the role of 'the community' in criminal justice more generally.[15] Indeed, Shearing has argued that we have entered a post-Keynesian era of governance in which the 'steering' and 'rowing' of policing are once again being uncoupled and new responsibilities established.[16] The balance of policing responsibilities is changing, he argues, and the networks of public and private institutions through which it takes place are becoming increasingly complex. What lies behind this?

The argument, central to theories of postmodernisation, is that the nation state—'the classic political embodiment of modernity'[17]—has been progressively undermined by a combination of globalising and localising forces. In part this reflects the changing nature of capital and business, which as they have been internationalised, or as Bottoms and Wiles put it 'transnationalised', have become increasingly outside the control of individual nation states. Although such

---

[12] Rawlings, P. (1995) p. 143.   [13] Ibid.   [14] Ibid, p. 144.

[15] Lacey, N. and Zedner, L. (1995) 'Discourses of community in criminal justice', *Journal of Law and Society*, 22, 3, pp. 301–25.

[16] Shearing, C. D. (1996) 'Public and private policing', in Saulsbury, W., Mott, J. and Newburn, T. (eds.) *Themes in Contemporary Policing*, London: Police Foundation/Policy Studies Institute.

[17] Kumar (1995) p. 152.

'globalisation' is a key feature of late modern society, it does not undermine the importance of locality. This linkage has perhaps best been captured by Harvey who suggests that: 'the free flow of capital across the surface of the globe . . . places strong emphasis upon the particular qualities of the spaces to which that capital might be attracted. The shrinkage of space that brings diverse communities across the globe into competition with each other implies localised competitive strategies and a heightened sense of awareness of what makes a place special and gives it a competitive advantage'.[18] Both processes—globalisation and localisation—contain tendencies, the argument goes, which lessen the power and influence of the nation-state; it is 'hollowed-out' from both directions.

Another of the features of modernity is that surveillance is itself increasingly globalised. The new technologies of communication extend surveillance far beyond the borders of the nation-state. As was first identified by Bell[19], and later developed by Giddens[20], one of the consequences of the development of new technologies has been the foreshortening of time. This, together with the eclipsing of distance offered by both new forms of communication and improved means of transport, has meant that 'space has been enlarged to the entire globe, and is tied together, almost, in "real time"'.[21] The mass global production of information has, according to Bell, gradually replaced the more traditional mass production industries.

Bell generally hesitates to go further than the 'techno-economic structure' in theorising the changes resulting from the development of what he called an 'information society'. Nevertheless, the suggestion that we are presently living through something of a qualitative shift in the nature of modern social relations—and that this involves changes in the role of information and surveillance—remains extremely plausible. One of the developments we can identify which appears to distinguish contemporary uses of information and contemporary surveillance from previous forms is the process of 'commodification'. One of the distinguishing features of contemporary societies is the fact that much of the information that is accumulated is collected for commercial reasons and, even when the reason for its collection is non-commercial, there often remains a considerable and

[18] Harvey (1989), p. 271.
[19] Bell, D. (1973) *The Coming of Post-Industrial Society*, New York: Basic Books.
[20] Giddens, A. (1990) *The Consequences of Modernity*, Cambridge: Polity Press.
[21] Bell, quoted in Kumar (1995) p. 11.

profitable market for it; one of the most rapidly expanding markets being in surveillance and control. According to Bottoms and Wiles, late modernity has affected social control in the city in a number of ways. One of the most visible is the use of new technologies such as CCTV, entry and exit devices, PIN number access systems, entry phones and so on.[22] This, as we have sought to argue, represents perhaps the major growth area within the private security industry in the past thirty years.

Theories of the 'information society' are, in some respects, quite closely linked to another school of post-industrialism known as 'post-Fordism'. Crudely, if Fordism was characterised by mass production and hierarchical organisations, 'post-Fordism' is characterised by 'flexible specialisation' and the decentring and dispersal of production. Where Fordism mass-produced standardised goods cheaply, the new post-Fordist industries grew up as markets fragmented and demand for goods changed unpredictably and constantly. The result has been a move away from mass-production and large-scale hierarchical organisations, towards highly specialised and much smaller units of production—often organised as satellites around a central core—in which 'delayered' organisations have highly skilled staff using sophisticated new technologies. As mass production industries have progressively been replaced with 'niche industries' targeting specific and highly defined consumers, so it has become increasingly necessary—or, put another way, the commercial imperative has increased—to guide, to stimulate, to channel, and to monitor consumption. Whilst the rhetoric talks of choice, variety, and opportunity, the reality of modern consumer society also includes surveillance and social control. Baumann has argued persuasively for the placing of consumerism as a key aspect of post-modern social arrangements and, if we accept this as having some force, then it is surely also reasonable to assume that the consumer should be one of the key targets of any new or emergent social control arrangements.[23]

For our purposes, the other key set of changes are linked to what we have identified in previous chapters as the fragmentation of space, and what we might refer to here as the progressive commodification of space. One of the most significant trends associated with urbanism

---

[22] Bottoms and Wiles (1994).
[23] Baumann, Z. (1992) *Intimations of Postmodernity*, London: Routledge.

is the increasing extent to which life is lived in what are almost exclusively settings which are manufactured. The extent to which these settings can be considered 'public' or 'private'—and the process of fragmentation giving rise to the increasing visibility of what we have termed 'hybrid space'—form the backdrop to the key arguments about the nature of the contemporary city and the changing nature of the policing of urban environments. The new technologies have resulted in radical changes in spatial organisation. The requirements of industrial capitalism are becoming decreasingly important in dictating the shape of urban communities. Post-Fordist flexible specialisation has had a spectacular impact. The economic decline and deindustrialization of once prosperous industrial regions has been accompanied by the industrialisation and economic development of previously poor regions, leading to a form of role reversal or recycling in which regions are restructured in relation to each other.

Similar processes have been at work in contemporary cities. The continuing decline of manufacturing has led to the deindustrialization of certain urban sectors, and selective reindustrialisation has occurred in other sectors associated with low wage tertiary employment. This, together with the changes taking place in local labour markets, with their increasing emphasis on skilled workers at the 'top' and part-time workers at the 'bottom', with those in the middle being squeezed, are producing a more fragmented and kaleidoscopic landscape than has hitherto existed. Central to this, obviously enough, are significant changes in the distribution and uses of 'space'. However, until relatively recently much social theory has paid relatively little attention to the idea of, and importance of, space. As Giddens put it: 'At first sight, nothing seems more banal and uninstructive than to assert that social activity occurs in time and in space. But neither time nor space have been incorporated into the centre of social theory; rather, they are ordinarily treated more as 'environments' in which social conduct is enacted'.[24]

In his theory of structuration, Giddens begins to redress this position by arguing that the actions of classes or groups of people must in part be understood in terms of their position in space and time. Indeed, he conceptualises the problem of social order as the binding together of social systems in time and space. Space, he argues, is of

[24] Giddens, A. (1979) *Central Problems in Social Theory*, Basingstoke: Macmillan, p. 202.

relevance both at the level of social integration and system integration. Social integration—'reciprocity between actors in contexts of co-presence'[25]—is facilitated by the development of familiar 'regions' of life in which individuals engage in familiar routines and interact with others with their own routines and regions. This familiarity and routinisation forms the basis of what Giddens refers to as 'ontological security'—that state which expresses 'an autonomy of *bodily control* within *predictable routines*'.[26] Crucially, it is the very predictability of routine and the formation of trust relationships that underpin this general sense of ontological security.

In Giddens' view, however, the move from pre-modern to modern societies has affected the basis of ontological security and has, in fact, heightened, feelings of insecurity. Centrally, Giddens argues that we have witnessed the decreasing importance of 'place' in modern societies as a result, on the one hand, of what he calls 'time-space distanciation' (the progressive stretching of social systems across time and space as human mastery over nature and social organisation increases) and, on the other, of 'disembedding mechanisms' (whereby social activities are 'lifted out' from localised contexts, with the result that social relations are reorganised across large time-space distances.)[27] The combination of the fragmentation of space, of knowledge, and of culture, together with the perception (and possibly reality) that contemporary life is increasingly risky, heighten feelings of insecurity.

Addressing such insecurity is now big business. 'Security' itself has become a commodity to be bought and sold in the marketplace. Those factors which underpinned the process of the increasing legitimation of public policing during the nineteenth and early twentieth centuries—their ever-expanding functional and geographical remit for example—now stretch the police in a way that threatens to undermine them. 'As a generalisation', Bottoms and Wiles argue, 'at present [the previously existing dominant form of policing] is fragmenting into forms designed to deal with the problems of *policing different places* or to provide *policing of different functions*'.[28] In part the fragmentation of 'social control needs' in late modern society has undermined the ability of an all-purpose public service to work efficiently and effectively—general providers inevitably being more expensive than specialist providers. The fragmentation of needs

[25] Giddens, A. (1985) *The Nation State and Violence,* Cambridge: Polity Press, p. 28.
[26] Ibid, p. 50.   [27] Giddens (1990).   [28] Giddens (1994) p. 38.

has been matched by the increasing diversity of providers in the marketplace. Simultaneously, public services generally have been under attack from successive political administrations favouring a privatised and individualised social world. In part this reflects a broader structural transformation in which 'scientific' certainty has gradually been replaced by a new era characterised by uncertainty and danger or, in Beck's terms, risk.[29] One of the consequences of this 'new modernity' is, according to Bottoms and Wiles, that the social world is increasingly 'perceived as a series of private realms which must take responsibility for their own problems, and where the public good is simply the market outcome of those processes. In such a framework, private interests will expect their control needs to be met on their own terms—something a public police is least equipped to do, and indeed, was partly developed to prevent'.[30] Put another way, 'risk society' is characterised by a diminution in the power of collective social identities, the progressive individualisation of 'risk'—at least on a subjective level—and a declining faith in collective responses to such risks. In such a world a quasi-monopolistic public service appears to be increasingly anachronistic.

Whilst there is certainly room for disagreement about the theoretical analysis of the consequences of 'late modern social change', there is little to suggest that the general thrust of these changes will be altered in years to come. The fiscal constraints on the public service are, give or take minor alterations, set to remain. Changes in property relations and the fragmentation of space, particularly within the contemporary city, are certainly unlikely to be reversed. The new technologies of surveillance and social control have an, as yet, uncharted capacity. The pressure on the police to explore new means of sponsorship and funding not only increasingly complicates their status, but lends further legitimacy to the idea of purchasing policing (or its more ephemeral counterpart, security) in the marketplace. The policing division of labour can only become more complicated.

As Brogden and Shearing have put it in relation to South Africa—though it is increasingly apposite in the UK—'the state police are seen as one player among many in the business of policing—and as the player who is very often the least important'.[31] Looking at the

---

[29] Beck, U. (1992) *The Risk Society: Towards a new modernity*, London: Sage.
[30] Bottoms and Wiles (1996) p. 25.
[31] Brogden, M. and Shearing, C. D. (1993) *Policing for a New South Africa*, London: Routledge.

implications of this they draw the conclusion that not only are police practices forced to undergo a fundamental revision—moving progressively from 'bandit-catching' to 'problem-solving'—but, more fundamentally, 'instead of the police using communities as a resource to tackle problems, it is 'communities'—be they territorially based or deterritorialized—who, on occasion, use the police to assist them to supplement their civil policing'.[32] This raises two centrally important questions for the future of the police. First, what is the value of the police, for example, within these emergent complex policing or security 'networks'? Or, put another way, why, within an increasingly fragmented world which houses an ever-more fragmented policing division of labour, does it remain important to retain a public police force? Secondly, how are the police to be distinguished from the other providers of policing?

The answer to the first question, though complex, is largely reducible to issues of legitimacy and political authority. As Loader argues, security is an indivisible social good: 'something that refers not only to the inevitability of collective consumption and the ensuing difficulties of free-riding, but also to the ways in which public safety is inexorably connected with the quality of our association with others'.[33] Related to this is the symbolic authority of the public police. Through their association with the state they are invested with authority which retains particular resonance with most citizens. For example, in circumstances where officials such as health and safety officers have greater legal powers than the police, they may still require the symbolic authority of the police constable in order to exercise those powers. This symbolic authority depends fundamentally on public legitimacy. Thus, the term 'policing by consent' is not some idle assumption about the desirability of public support, but rather a recognition that it is only through the achievement of a certain level of general trust that the public police can hope to operate effectively. Where such legitimacy is missing, it is not only the efficacy of the police organisation that is challenged but also the wider institutions of civil society. This is not to dismiss the growing pervasiveness of private and other forms of policing at the local level, but rather to recognise the differences between public and private providers and the limits to which 'security' can be purchased in the marketplace.

[32] Ibid, p. 174.
[33] Loader, I. (1997b) 'Thinking normatively about private security', *Journal of Law and Society*, 24, 3, p. 28.

Ironically, one of the consequences of the advent of a 'risk society' may be the growing assumption that individualised solutions to the problems of security hold the greatest promise. As others have argued, however, the expansion and increasing visibility of private security personnel and hardware may make people feel less rather than more 'secure'.[34] Moreover, not only may they feel less secure, but the inevitably unequal distribution of private security will almost certainly result in some people actually becoming less secure as others hide themselves behind ever higher barriers and stronger bars. If private security and other forms of policing provision are to play an increasing role in the provision of public safety (i.e. in the policing of public spaces), without compounding the inequities that already exist, then they will have to be made subject to some form of democratic governance. This is something more than a contractual relationship between purchaser and provider, or even an economic or legal form of regulation. It concerns what are essentially a set of political decisions about the common good and the balancing of conflicting interests.

The answer to the second question—how are public and other providers of policing to be distinguished—is similarly complex, and has formed the core matter of this book. As we have shown there are a variety of ways in which policing bodies can be distinguished. Previous work has tended to focus on either functional or legal distinctions, though the work of Johnston has highlighted the importance of other dimensions. We have argued that any fully developed analysis of the policing division of labour must recognise and consider the sectoral, spatial, legal, functional, and geographical boundaries of policing. It is in the wide-ranging nature of the public police mandate on each of these dimensions that we find their defining characteristic. It is this general mandate which is also the source of the burgeoning demands on the public police, and which gives more specialised providers their potential advantage in the 'marketplace'.

The consequence of this is that public policing is being 'stretched'. As yet there appear to be no obvious solutions to what is perhaps the fundamental dilemma now facing the public police: that they must respond to developing regional, national, and international demands to broaden their functional capacities, and to take on ever-greater

---

[34] See Spitzer, S. (1987) 'Security and control in capitalist societies: the fetishism of security and the security thereof', in Lowman *et al. Transcarceration: Essays in the Sociology of Social Control*, Aldershot: Gower; and Loader (1997*b*).

legal responsibilities whilst simultaneously being forced to compete with providers whose remit is geographically, functionally, and legally limited. If these trends continue, we face the prospect of an ever-more distant and beleaguered public police struggling alongside an increasing array of for-profit providers meeting the demands of those who can pay. The provision of public safety can be undertaken by a diverse network of providers, but if the worst excesses of the market are to be avoided, then such networks need to be located within the sphere of local democratic decision-making. Consequently, it is the public police organisation, with its historical and continuing links with the institutions of democracy, which needs to play a key role in the future in ensuring that the provision of policing is consistent with the public good.

Bibliography

Advisory Commission on Intergovernmental Relations (1989) *Residential Community Associations: Private Governments in the Intergovernmental System?* ACIR: Washington DC.

Appleby, P. (1995) *A Force on the Move*, Malvern: Images Publishing.

Ascher, K. (1987) *The Politics of Privatisation*, London, Macmillan.

Audit Commission (1989) *Improving Vehicle Fleet Management in the Police Service*, London: HMSO.

—— (1989) *The Management of Police Training*, London: HMSO.

—— (1990) *Taking Care of the Coppers: Income generation by provincial police forces*, London: HMSO.

—— (1990) *Effective Policing—Performance review in police forces*, London: HMSO.

—— (1991) *Reviewing the Organisation of Provincial Police Forces*, London: HMSO.

Banton, M. (1964) *The Policeman in the Community*, London: Tavistock.

Baumann, Z. (1992) *Intimations of Postmodernity*, London: Routledge.

Bayley, D. (1983) 'Knowledge of the police', in M. Punch (ed.) *Control in the Police Organisation*, Cambridge, Mass.: MIT Press.

—— (1987) 'Foreword', in Shearing, C. D. and Stenning, P. C. (1987) *Private Policing*, Newbury Park, Cal.: Sage.

—— (1994) *Police for the Future*, New York: Oxford University Press.

Beck, A. and Willis, A. (1995) *Crime and Security: Managing the Risk to Safe Shopping*, Leicester: Perpetuity Press.

Beck, U. (1992) *The Risk Society: Towards a new modernity*, London: Sage.

Becker, T. (1974) 'The place of private police in society: an area of research for the social sciences', *Social Problems* 21, 3, pp. 438–53.

Bell, D. (1973) *The Coming of Post-Industrial Society*, New York: Basic Books.

Benn, S. and Gaus, G. (eds.) (1983) *Public and Private in Social Life*, London: Croom Helm.

Benson, B. L. (1990) *The Enterprise of the Law: Justice without the state*, San Francisco: Pacific Research Institute for Public Policy.

Bevan, V. and Lidstone, K. (1991) *The Investigation of Crime: A guide to police powers*, London: Butterworths.

Bittner, E. (1974) 'Florence Nightingale in pursuit of Willie Sutton: A theory of the police', in H. Jacob, (ed.) *The Potential for Reform of Criminal Justice*, Newbury Park, CA: Sage.

Bittner, E. (1980) *The Function of the Police in Modern Society*, Cambridge, Mass.: Oelgeschlager, Gunn and Hain.

Bobbio, N. (1989) *Democracy and Dictatorship*, Minneapolis: University of Minnesota Press.

Boleat, M. and Taylor, B. (1993) *Housing in Britain*, London: The Building Societies Association.

Bottoms, A. E. and Wiles, P. (1994*a*) 'Crime and insecurity in the city', Paper presented at the International Course organised by the International Society of Chriminology, Leuven, Belguim, May, 1994.

—— (1994*b*) 'Understanding crime prevention in late modern societies', Paper presented to the 22nd Cropwood Round Table Conference: Preventing Crime and Disorder: Targeting Strategies and Community Responsibilities, Cambridge: Institute of Criminology.

Bozeman, B. (1987) *All Organisations are Public*, San Francisco.

British Security Industry Association (1987) *The British Security Industry Association*, London: BSIA.

—— (1994), Evidence to the House of Commons Home Affairs Select Committee, October 1994.

Brogden, M. and Shearing, C. D. (1993) *Policing for a New South Africa*, London: Routledge.

Bunyan, T. (1977) *The Political Police in Britain*, London: Quartet.

Business Round Table (1994) *The Growing Demand for Security: Opportunities for UK Suppliers*, London: Business Round Table Ltd.

Caddle, D. (1995) *A survey of the prisoner escort and custody service provided by Group 4 and by Securicor Custodial Services*, Research and Planning Unit Paper 93, London: Home Office.

Cain, M. (1979) 'Trends in the sociology of police work', *International Journal of the Sociology of Law*, 7, 2.

Cameron, A. (1997) 'In Search of the Voluntary Sector', *Journal of Social Policy* 26, 1, pp. 79–88.

Cohen, S. (1979) 'The punitive city: Notes on the dispersal of social control', *Contemporary Crisis*, 3, 4, pp. 339–64.

—— (1985) *Visions of Social Control*, Cambridge: Polity Press.

Coleman, A. (1985) *Utopia on Trial*, London: Hilary Shipman.

Colquhoun, P. (1796) *Treatise on the Police in the Metropolis explaining the various Crimes and Misdemeanours which are at present felt as a pressure upon the Community, and suggesting Remedies for their Prevention, by a Magistrate,* Second Edition (originally published, 1795) London: H. Fry for C. Dilly.

Community Associations Institute (1993) *Community Associations Factbook*, Alexandria, Va.: CAI.

Critchley, T. A. (1978) *A History of Police in England and Wales*, London: Constable.

Crook, S., Pakulski, J. and Walters, M. (1993) *Postmodernization: Change in Advanced Societies*, London: Sage.

Cunningham, W. C. and Taylor, T. (1985) *Private Security and Police in America* (The 'Hallcrest' Report), Portland: Chancellor Press.

Daly, M. and McCann, A. (1992) 'How many small firms?' *Employment Gazette*, Feb. 1992.

Davis, M. (1990) *City of Quartz*, London: Vintage.

Department of Trade and Industry (1995) *Small and Medium Sized Enterprise Statistics for the UK, 1993*, Small Firms Statistics Unit, DTI, June.

de Waard, J. (1993) 'The private security sector in fifteen European countries: size, rules and regulation', *Security Journal*, 4, pp. 58–63.

den Boer, M. and Walker, K. (1992) 'European Policing After 1992' *Journal of Common Market Studies*, 31, 1, pp. 3–28.

Dixon, B. and Stanko, E. A. (1993) *Serving the People: Sector policing and public accountability*, London: Islington Council.

Dixon, D., Coleman, C. and Bottomley, K. (1990) 'Consent and the Legal Regulation of Policing', *Journal of Law and Society* 17, 3, pp. 345–62.

Donzelot, J. (1979) *The Policing of Families*, London: Hutchinson.

Draper, H. (1978) *Private Police*, Sussex: Harvester Press.

Dunlop, R. (1995) *Public Art and the Contemporary Urban Environment*, Unpublished Ph.D. thesis, University of Westminster.

Emsley, C. (1983) *Policing and its Context 1750–1870*, London: Macmillan.

—— (1991) *The English Police: A political and social history*, Hemel Hempstead: Harvester Wheatsheaf.

Ericson, R. (1994) 'The division of expert knowledge in policing and security', *British Journal of Sociology*, 45, 2, pp. 149–75.

Fielding, N. (1988) *Joining Forces: Police training, socialisation and occupational competence*, London: Routledge.

—— (1993) 'Policing and the role of the police', in, Dingwall, R. and Shapland, J. (eds.) *Reforming British Policing: Missions and Structures*, Sheffield: University of Sheffield.

Fijnaut, C. (1991) 'Police cooperation within Western Europe', in Heidensohn, F. and Farrell, M. (eds.) *Crime in Europe*, London: Routledge.

Finn, P. (1983) 'Public function–private action: A common law dilemma', In S. Benn and G. Gauss (eds.) *Public and Private in Social Life*, London: Croom Helm.

Flavel, W. (1973) 'Research into security organisations', Paper presented to Second Bristol Seminar on the Sociology of the Police (unpublished).

Foucault, M. (1977) *Discipline and Punish*, Harmondsworth: Penguin.

Fyfe, N. R. (1991) 'The police, space and society: the geography of policing', *Progress in Human Geography* 15, 3, pp. 249–67.

Garland, D. (1996) 'The Limits of the Sovereign State', *The British Journal of Criminology* 34, 4, pp. 445–71.

George, B. and Button, M. (1994) 'The need for regulation of the private security industry', A submission to the House of Commons Home Affairs Select Committee, Nov. 1994.

—— and Watson, T. (1992) 'Regulation of the Private Secuirty Industry', *Public Money and Management*, 12, 1.

Giddens, A. (1979) *Central Problems in Social Theory*, Basingstoke: Macmillan.

—— (1985) *The Nation State and Violence*, Cambridge: Polity Press.

—— (1990) *The Consequences of Modernity*, Cambridge: Polity Press.

Gorz, A. (1989) *Critique of Economic Reason*, London: Verso.

Hanmer, J., Radford, J. and Stanko, E. A. (eds.) (1989) *Women, Policing and Male Violence*, London: Routledge.

Harvey, D. (1989) *The Condition of Postmodernity*, Cambridge: Polity Press.

Hauber, A., Hofstra, B., Toornvliet, L. and Zandbergen, A. (1996) 'Some new forms of functional social control in the Netherlands and their effects', *British Journal of Criminology*, 36, 2, pp. 199–219.

Henry, S. (1983) *Private Justice: Towards integrated theorising in the sociology of law*, London: Routledge and Kegan Paul.

—— (1987) 'Private justice and the policing of labor: the dialectics of industrial discipline', in Shearing C. D. and Stenning P. C. (eds.) *Private Policing*, Newbury Park, Cal.: Sage.

Hobbes, T. (1651) [1968] *Leviathan*, Harmondsworth: Penguin.

Hobbs, D. *Doing the Business: Entrepreneurship, detectives and the working class in the East End of London*, Oxford: Clarendon.

Hobsbawm, E. (1962) *The Age of Revolution 1798–1848*, London: Weidenfeld and Nicholson.

Holdaway, S. (1979) *The British Police*, London: Edward Arnold.

—— (1983) *Inside the British Police*, Oxford: Basil Blackwell.

Home Office (1979) *The Private Security Industry: A discussion paper*, London: HMSO.

—— (1995) *Review of Core and Ancillary Tasks*, London: HMSO.

Hoogenboom, A. B. (1989) 'The privatization of social control', in R. Hood (ed.) *Crime and Criminal Policy in Europe: Proceedings of a European Colloquium*, Oxford: Oxford Centre for Criminology Research, pp. 121–4.

—— (1991) 'Grey policing: a theoretical framework', *Policing and Society*, 2(1).

Horton, C. and Smith, D. J. (1988) *Evaluating Police Work*, London: Policy Studies Institute.

House of Commons Home Affairs Select Committee (1995) *The Private Security Industry*, First Report, Session 1994–1995, London: HMSO.

Hunter, A. (1995) 'Private, parochial and public social orders: The problem of crime and incivility in urban communities', in Kasinitz, P. (ed.) *Metropolis: Centre and Symbol of our Times*, Basingstoke: Macmillan.

Hutter, B. (1988) *The Reasonable Arm of the Law*, Oxford: Clarendon Press.

Jacobs, J. (1961) *The Death and Life of Great American Cities*, New York: Random House.

Johnston, L. (1992) *The Rebirth of Private Policing*, London: Routledge.

—— (1993) 'Privatisation and protection: spatial and sectoral ideologies in British policing and crime prevention', *Modern Law Review*, 56, 6, pp. 771–92.

—— 'Privatisation: Threat or Opportunity', *Policing*, 10(1), Spring, pp. 14–22.

—— (1996a) 'Policing diversity: the impact of the public–private complex in policing', in Leishman, F., Loveday, B. and Savage, S. (eds.) *Core Issues in Policing*, Harlow: Longman.

—— (1996b) 'What is vigilantism?', *British Journal of Criminology*, 36, 2, pp. 220–36.

Jones, T. (1995) *Policing and Democracy in the Netherlands*, London: PSI.

—— and Newburn, T. (1995) 'How Big is the Private Security Sector?', *Policing and Society*, 5, pp. 221–32.

—— and Newburn (1997) *Policing After the Act*, London: Policy Studies Institute.

—— —— and Smith, D. J. (1994) *Democracy and Policing*, London: PSI.

Jordan and Sons Ltd. (1987) *Britain's Security Industry*, London: Jordan and Sons Ltd.

—— (1989) *Britain's Security Industry*, London: Jordan and Sons Ltd.

—— (1993) *Britain's Security Industry*, London: Jordan and Sons Ltd.

Joslin, P. (1994) 'Traffic and crime go together', *Police*, Feb. 1994.

Kakalik, J. S. and Wildhorn, S. (1972) *Private Police in the United States* (the Rand Report) (4 vols.) National Institute of Law Enforcement and Criminal Justice, Washington: US Department of Justice.

Kasinitz, P. (ed.) (1995) *Metropolis: Centre and Symbol of our Times*, Basingstoke: Macmillan.

Kinsey, R., Lea, J. and Young, J. (1986) *Losing the Fight Against Crime*, Oxford: Blackwell.

Kumar, K. (1995) *From Post-industrial to Post-modern Society*, Oxford: Basil Blackwell.

Lacey, N. and Zedner, L. (1995) 'Discourses of community in criminal justice', *Journal of Law and Society*, 22, 3, pp. 301–25.

Lavery, K. (1995) 'Privatisation by the Back Door: The Rise of Private Government in the USA', *Public Money and Management* 15, 4, Oct.–Dec. 1995.

Leigh, L. (1985) *Police Powers in England and Wales*, London: Butterworths.

Leishman, F., Cope, S. and Starie, P. (1996) 'Reinventing and restructuring:

towards a "new policing order"', in Leishman, F., Loveday, B. and Savage, S. (eds.) *Core Issues in Policing*, Harlow: Longman.

Lipietz, A. (1992) *Towards a New Order: Postfordism, Ecology and Democracy*, Cambridge: Polity Press.

Loader, I. (1996) *Youth, Policing and Democracy*, Basingstoke: Macmillan.

—— (1997*a*) 'Policing and the social: Questions of symbolic power), *British Journal of Sociology*, 48, 1, pp. 1–18.

—— (1997*b*) 'Thinking normatively about private security', *Journal of Law and Society*, 24, 3, pp. 1–31.

—— (1997*c*) 'Private Security and the demand for protection in contemporary Britain', *Policing and Society* 7, pp. 143–62.

Loveland, I. (1989) 'Policing welfare: local authority responses to claimant fraud in the Housing Benefit Scheme', *Journal of Law and Society*, 16, 2, pp. 187–209.

Lyon, D. (1994) *The Electronic Eye*, Cambridge: Polity Press.

McClintock, F. H. and Wiles, P. (eds.) (1972) *The Security Industry in the UK: Papers presented to the Cropwood Round-Table Conference*, July 1971: Cambridge Institute of Criminology: Cambridge.

McLaughlin, E. and Muncie, J. (1994) 'Managing the criminal justice system', in Clarke, J., Cochrane, A. and McLaughlin, Ed. (eds.) *Managing Social Policy*, London: Sage.

Manning, P. (1977) *Police Work*, Cambridge, Mass.: MIT Press.

Marx, G. T. (1987) 'The interweaving of public and private police in undercover work', in Shearing, C. D. and Stenning, P. C. (eds.) (1987).

—— (1988) *Undercover: Police surveillance in America*, Berkeley: University of California Press.

Mason, D. (1991) *Private and Public Policing: Improving the service to the public through cooperation*, Brookfield Papers No. 6.

Matthews, R. (1989) 'Privatization in perspective', in Mathews, R. (ed.) *Privatizing Criminal Justice*, London: Sage.

MATSA (1983) *Report on the private security industry*, Esher.

Mawby, R., Bunt, P. and Redshaw, J. (1995) 'Police performance: the consumer view', Paper presented at the British Criminology Conference, Loughborough, 18–21 July 1995.

Miller, J. P. and Luke, D. E. (1977) *Law Enforcement by Public Officials and Special Police Forces*, London: Home Office.

Morgan, R. and Smith, D. J. (1989) 'Opening the Debate', in Morgan, R. and Smith, D. J. (eds.) *Coming to Terms with Policing,* London: Routledge.

National Economic Development Office (1988) *Security Equipment: A growth market for British Industry*, London: NEDO.

Newburn, T., and Jones, T. (1996) 'Police Accountability', in Saulsbury, W., Mott, J. and Newburn, T. *Themes in Contemporary Policing*, London: Policy Studies Institute/Police Foundation.

Office for Population Census and Surveys (OPCS) (1994) *Social Trends 1995*, London: HMSO.

Olsen, M. (1971) *The Logic of Collective Action*, Cambridge, Mass.: Harvard University Press.

Pitkin, H. (1984) *Fortune is a Woman*, Berkeley: University of California Press.

Police Foundation/Policy Studies Institute (1996) Independent Committee of Inquiry into the Role and Responsibilities of the Police, *Final Report*, London: Police Foundation/Policy Studies Institute.

Poole, R. (1991) *Safe shopping: The identification of opportunities for crime and disorder in covered shopping centres*, Birmingham: West Midlands Constabulary.

Popper, K. R. *The Logic of Scientific Discovery*, New York: Harper and Row.

Pospisil, L. (1971) *Anthropology of Law*, New York: Harper and Row.

Punch, M. (1979) 'The secret social service', in Holdaway, S. (ed.) *The British Police*, London: Edward Arnold.

Radford, J. and Stanko, E. A. (1996) 'Violence against women and children: the contradictions of crime control under patriarchy', in Hester, M., Kelly, L. and Radford, J. (eds.) *Women, Violence and Male Power*, Milton Keynes: Open University Press.

Randall, P. and Hamilton, P. (1972) 'The security industry in the United Kingdom', in McClintock, F. H. and Wiles, P. (eds.) (1972) *The Security Industry in the UK: Papers presented to the Cropwood Round-Table Conference*, July 1971: Cambridge Institute of Criminology: Cambridge.

Rawlings, P. (1995) 'The idea of policing: a history', *Policing and Society*, 5, pp. 129–49.

Reichman, N. (1987) 'The widening webs of surveillance: Private police unravelling deceptive claims', in Shearing, C. D. and Stenning, P. C. (eds.) *Private Policing*, Newbury Park, Cal.: Sage.

Reiner, R. (1978) *The Bluecoated Worker*, Cambridge: Cambridge University Press.

—— (1991) *Chief Constables*, Oxford: Oxford University Press.

—— (1992a) 'Policing a postmodern society', *Modern Law Review*, 55, 6, pp. 761–81.

—— (1992b) *The Politics of the Police*, Hemel Hempstead: Harvester.

—— (1992c) 'Police Research in the United Kingdom' In M. Torsy and N. Morris (eds.) *Modern Policing: Crime and Justice: A Review of the Research*, Chicago: University of Chicago Press.

—— (1993) 'Police accountability: principles, patterns and practices', in Reiner, R. and Spencer, S. (eds.) *Accountable Policing: Effectiveness, empowerment and equity*, London: IPPR.

Reiss, A. J. (1971) *The Police and the Public*, New Haven: Yale University Press.

Reiss, A. J. (1987) 'The legitimacy of intrusion into private space', in Shearing, C. D. and Stenning, P. C. (1987) *Private Policing*, Newbury Park, Cal.: Sage.
—— (1988) *Private Employment of Public Police*, Washington: US Dept. of Justice, Government Printing Office.

Rosenthal, U. and Hoogenboom, B. (1988) 'Some fundamental questions on privatisation and commericalisation of crime control, with special reference to developments in the Netherlands', Paper presented to the eighteenth criminological research conference on the privatisation of crime control, Council of Europe, Strasbourg, 21–5 Nov. 1988.

Rowlingson, K., Whyley, C., Newburn, T. and Berthoud, R. (1997) *Social Security Fraud: The role of penalties*, London: Stationery Office.

Sanders, A. (1993) 'Controlling the discretion of the individual officer', in Reiner, R. and Spencer, S. (eds.) *Accountable Policing*, London: Institute for Public Policy Research.

Savas, E. S. (1982) *Privatising the Public Sector*, Chatham, New Jersey: Chatham House Publishers.

Schmitter, P. (1974) 'Still the century of corporatism?' *Review of Politics*, 36, pp. 85–131.

Scottish Office Central Research Unit (1995) 'Does closed circuit television prevent crime? An evaluation of the use of CCTV surveillance cameras in Airdrie town centre', *Crime and Criminal Justice Research Findings No. 8*, Edinburgh: Scottish Office Central Research Unit.

Shapland, J. (1989) 'Views on crime: public and private problems', Paper presented at the British Criminology Conference, Bristol Polytechnic, July 1989.
—— and Vagg, J. (1987) 'Policing by the public and policing by the police', in Willmott, P. (ed.) *Policing and the Community*, London: Policy Studies Institute.

Shearing, C. D. (1992) 'The Relation between Public and Private Policing', in Tonry M. and Morris N. (eds.) *Modern Policing: Crime and Justice: A Review of the Research*, Vol. 15, pp. 399–434. Chicago: University of Chicago Press.
—— (1994) 'Reinventing Policing: Policing as Governance'. Paper presented at a conference on 'Privatisation: Retreat or Proliferation of State Control', Bielefeld, Germany, 24–6 Mar. 1994.
—— (1996) 'Public and private policing', in Saulsbury, W., Mott, J. and Newburn, T. (eds.) *Themes in Contemporary Policing*, London: Police Foundation/Policy Studies Institute.
—— Farnell, M. and Stenning, P. C. (1980) *Contract Security*, Toronto: Centre of Criminology, University of Toronto.
—— and Stenning, P. C. (1981) 'Modern private security: Its growth and implications', in Tonry, M. and Morris, N. (eds.) *Crime and Justice: An Annual Review of Research*, Chicago: University of Chicago Press.

—— and —— (1983) 'Private Security—implications for social control', *Social Problems* 30, 5, p. 496.

—— and ——(eds.) (1987) *Private Policing*, Newbury Park, Cal.: Sage.

—— and —— (1987) 'Say "Cheese"!: The Disney order that is not so Mickey Mouse', in Shearing, C. D. and Stenning, P. C. (eds.) *Private Policing*, Newbury Park, Cal.: Sage.

Sherman, L. W. (1992) *Policing Domestic Violence: Experiments and dilemmas*, New York: Free Press.

Skogan, W. (1990) *The Police and Public in England and Wales: A British Crime Survey Report*, Home Office Research Study No. 117, London: HMSO.

Smith, A. [1776] (1981) *The Wealth of Nations*, Harmondsworth: Penguin.

Smith, D. J. (1983) *Police and People in London III: A survey of police officers*, London: Policy Studies Institute.

—— (1987) 'The Police and the Idea of Community', in Willmott, P. (ed.) *Policing and the Community*, London: Policy Studies Institute.

—— and Gray T. (1983) *Police and People in London IV: The Police in Action*, London: Policy Studies Institute.

South, N. (1988) *Policing for Profit*, London: Sage.

Spitzer, S. (1987) 'Security and control in capitalist societies: the fetishism of security and the secret thereof', in Lowman, J., Menzies, R. J. and Palys, T. S. (eds.) *Transcarceration: Essays in the sociology of social control*, Aldershot: Gower.

—— and Scull, A. (1977) 'Privatisation and capitalist development: the case of private police', *Social Problems* 25, 1, pp. 18–29.

Stanko, E. A. (1988) 'Hidden violence against women', in Maguire, M. and Pointing, J. (eds.) *Victims of Crime: A New Deal?*, Milton Keynes: Open University Press.

Steedman, C. (1984) *Policing the Victorian Community: The formation of English provincial police forces 1856–80*, London: Routledge and Kegan Paul.

Stenning, P. C. and Shearing, C. D. (1980) 'The quiet revolution: the nature, development and general legal implications of private security in Canada', *Criminal Law Quarterly*, 22.

Waddington, P. A. J. (1993) *Calling the Police*, Aldershot: Avebury.

Walker, N. (1993) 'The international dimension', in Reiner, R. and Spencer, S. (eds.) *Accountable Policing: Effectiveness, Empowerment and Equity*, London: Institute for Public Policy Research.

Walzer, M. (1995) 'Pleasures and costs of urbanity' in Kasinitz, P. (ed.) *Metropolis: Centre and Symbol of Our Times*, Basingstoke: Macmillan.

Wandsworth Borough Council (1995) *Report by the Director of Leisure and Amenity Services on the Wandsworth Parks Constabulary*, Paper 95/39, January 1995.

Weatheritt, M. (1986) *Innovations in Policing*, London: Croom Helm.

Weatheritt, M. (1993) 'Measuring police performance: Accounting or accountability?', in Reiner, R. and Spencer, S. (eds.) *Accountable Policing: Effectiveness, Empowerment and Equity*, London: Institute for Public Policy Research.

Weintraub, J. (1995) 'Varieties and Vicissitudes of Public Space', in Kasinitz, P. (ed.) *Metropolis: Centre and symbol of our times*, Basingstoke: Macmillan.

Weiss, R. P. (1987) 'From "slugging detectives" to "labour relations": policing labour at Ford, 1930–1947', in Shearing, C. D. and Stenning, P. C. (eds.) *Private Policing*, Newbury Park, Cal.: Sage.

Williams, D., George, B. and MacLennan, E. (1984) *Guarding Against Low Pay*, Low Pay Unit.

Wilson, J. Q. and Kelly, G. (1982) 'Broken Windows' *Atlantic Monthly*, March, pp. 29–38.

Wilson, S. (1966) *New Challenges for Work and Society: Can the Social Economy Provide An Answer?* Report of a Seminar of the Franco-British Council, 5–6 Dec. 1995. London: Franco-British Council.

Younger, K. (1972) *Report of the Committee on Privacy*, London: HMSO.

Index